Film and Politics in America

D0062844

In *Film and Politics in America: A Social Tradition*, Brian Neve presents a study of the social and political nature of American film by concentrating on a generation of film-makers whose formative experiences were those of New York politics and theatre in the 1930s, and who began careers as directors or writer-directors in the Hollywood of the 1940s. Neve discusses the work of this group with reference to the wider industrial, political and social context of American film from the late 1930s to the 1960s.

Among the film-makers discussed are Orson Welles, Elia Kazan, Abraham Polonsky, Robert Rossen, Joseph Losey and Jules Dassin, but Neve also examines debates about the social significance of Frank Capra's middle period films, and of *film noir*.

The book provides readings of key films and uses archival and secondary sources to examine the changing production process, with particular reference to the decade of industrial change and ideological conflict following the Second World War. Neve places his case study of 'social' film-making within a wider assessment of the impact on film of Hollywood radicalism and liberalism, and the later effects of the Congressional investigations and the blacklist.

Brian Neve is a lecturer in Politics at the University of Bath.

Studies in film, television
and the media
General Editor: Dr Anthony Aldgate
The Open University

Film and Politics in America

A Social Tradition

Brian Neve

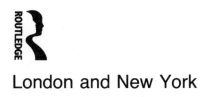

London and New York

First Published 1992
by Routledge
11 New Fetter Lane, London EC4P 4EE

Simultaneously published in the USA and Canada
by Routledge
a division of Routledge, Chapman and Hall, Inc.
29 West 35th Street, New York, NY 10001

© Brian Neve
Typeset in 10/12pt Baskerville by
J&L Composition Ltd, Filey, North Yorkshire
Printed in Great Britain by T.J. Press (Padstow) Ltd, Padstow,
Cornwall.

British Library Cataloguing in Publication Data
Neve, Brian
    Film and politics in America: a social tradition
    I. Title
    791.43

Library of Congress Cataloging-in-Publication Data
Neve, Brian
        Film and politics in America: a social tradition/Brian Neve.
        p.   cm. —(Studies in film, television, and the media)
        Includes bibliographical references and indexes.
    1. Motion pictures—Social aspects—United States.   2. Motion
pictures—Political aspects—United States.   3. Motion picture
industry—United States—History.   I. Title.   II. Series.
    PN1995.9.S6N46   1992
302.23'43'0973—dc20   92–5196

ISBN 0–415–02619–9
    0–415–02620–2 (pbk)

Contents

Illustrations

Preface

This study developed from an interest both in the politics of the American film industry – documented in the last decade by such writers as Schwartz, Navasky, and Ceplair and Englund – and in a generation of broadly social filmmakers whose formative experiences were arguably those of the thirties, and who began working in Hollywood as directors in the forties.[1] The object was to produce an empirically based book on the work of this group, discussing the films in broad historical context, and in particular with reference to the changing nature of the industrial and commercial process of filmmaking.

What follows is a modest and by no means comprehensive attempt to discuss issues relating to the social and political content of American film – issues that, as Ceplair and Englund point out, have yet to receive systematic study, at least for the period prior to the sixties. While there are clearly dangers in making the individual filmmaker the focus, rather than the production system itself, and the broader codes and ideologies of film and their relationship to economic and political power, there are, it is hoped, also some advantages of such an approach. The notion of a particular group, however arbitrary – in the sense that there would be no precise agreement on who to include – provides a sample of films at the centre of the study that could then be examined in terms of what Jim Cook and Alan Lovell, in their dossier *Coming to Terms with Hollywood*, see as the process in which this generation of artists 'negotiated' their relationships with the film industry.[2]

The questions asked here overlap with a broader question – that of the effect on American film of the politicisation of Hollywood discussed in Ceplair and Englund and elsewhere.

While the general constraints on writers under the studio system are well documented, along with the particular demand for left-wing writers during the war years, it is often empirically difficult to assess the contribution of particular screenwriters. Various drafts and source novels need to be compared, where they are available. But it is hoped that some partial answers emerge from the study of radicals such as Robert Rossen and Abraham Polonsky, who moved from writing to directing in the immediate post-war period. Arguably Rossen had some effect – for example in contributing to the tone of *Marked Woman* (Warner Bros, 1937) – by specialising in 'social' subjects at a studio where such films were seen as an important part of its public image. In the post-war period of flux, cases can also be found of either cooperation between director and writer, or unusual control by a writer – Polonsky and *Body and Soul* – over the production process.

The group of directors and writer-directors given particular emphasis in the book, with particular reference to the post-war decade, is as follows (with date of birth): Elia Kazan (1909), Joseph Losey (1909), Abraham Polonsky (1910), Nicholas Ray (1911), Robert Rossen (1908), Orson Welles (1915), John Berry (1917), Cy Endfield (1914), Martin Ritt (1914), Edward Dmytryk (1908), John Huston (1906) and Jules Dassin (1911). No single set of common experiences covers this group, and the political and artistic differences were considerable. They were, of course, all male. Welles and Huston were liberal activists, while many or most of the others were in the Communist Party or close to it for some time during the period from the mid-thirties to the late forties and beyond. Again, it is arguable that the most critical distinction can be made between radicals and liberals. For some a period in the Communist Party was a rite of passage, reflecting the alienation of young would-be artists in the Depression years, while for others it reflected something close to a lifelong social-ist commitment. Reading backward from conduct during the second wave of House Committee investigations of the early fifties, some would draw political inferences from whether individuals 'named names' or not. Yet this is difficult to do; although politics was clearly crucial to Polonsky's life and art, it was not central to Kazan's – at least as judged by his autobiography. Yet the shock caused by Kazan's decision to cooperate with the committee in 1952 tends to indicate that he was often regarded as part of a broad movement – to use

Margaret Thatcher's phrase he was seen as broadly 'one of us' – by those with similar thirties experiences.[3]

The directors are not given equal attention, and I give particular space to the work of Kazan and Polonsky. It could be argued that the two directors, who have never met, represent opposite poles of the 'social' outlook discussed in this book. Kazan's formative experiences were in the Group Theatre, and in a number of his better-known films of the fifties he used the approach to acting developed there and in the Actors Studio to capture the energies and social feelings of his actors. (Kazan once expressed his goal in casting in terms of looking for someone who can experience the experience of the character.)[4] In *On the Waterfront* Marlon Brando brings something of his own feelings into the film, undercutting both the documentary basis of the story and the intention of Kazan and Schulberg to make a point about testifying. In *The Visitors* (1972) any general point about the effects of the war back home is diluted by the director's tendency to see everyone's point of view. The blacklist allowed Polonsky only three films as director, but in *Body and Soul*, on which he had particular influence, and in *Force of Evil* and *Tell Them Willie Boy is Here*, there are precise attempts to convey political meaning. Kazan's emphasis on personal feeling – including his own, particularly in his autobiographically based work – brought social meanings into his films; Polonsky's work reflects the influence of the tradition of radical politics, philosophy and art that is central to the author's life. The fierce debate between Rossen and Polonsky over the ending of *Body and Soul* – discussed in Chapter 5 – seems indicative of broader differences between those whose main concern was to bring a pessimistic realism into film, and those, like Polonsky, who played with the space between the social determination of his characters' lives and the possibility of individual choice and growth.

It is hoped that the following study sheds some light on questions concerning politics and American film, particularly in the years just after the war, and on the question of the effect of the blacklist on film. The 'group' is a loose, organising device, and it is quite likely that early experiences – for example the very different family backgrounds of Losey and Kazan – had as much or more influence than politics or thirties theatre. My efforts in some directions were hindered by my inability to view certain films, in particular *The Lawless* and *He Ran All the Way*. Indeed I was unable to see enough of his films to attempt any adequate assessment of John Berry. Nor have I followed the careers of directors abroad – where some, notably Losey, found their métier in the European art film, while also – in Losey's case – still dealing with issues of class and change. What most of the individuals did have in common was a tendency to define their artistic aspirations in social terms, something that reflected the importance of the Depression and the Second World War (and fascism) as formative experiences. As well as the fortunes of blacklisted writers and directors abroad, another area that might repay further study is the effect of radio – in which Polonsky was involved as well as Welles and Ray – on the 'social' tradition of filmmaking that I discussed. The balance between dialogue and visuals in defining the meaning that critics and audiences 'saw' in the films of this period is also open to wider debate.

The first three chapters of the book deal primarily, but not exclusively, with aspects of popular culture that related to the Popular Front cultures of the later thirties and of the war years. The discussion of the work of Frank Capra transcends this period, and raises broader questions about the meanings that can be attached to the director's middle period films. On the war chapter I am particularly indebted to those historians who have documented the relationship between film and government. The second part of the book, encompassing chapters 4–6, deals with the period 1945–51, including a chapter assessing efforts – running against the critical tide – to see social meanings in the films known collectively as *film noir*. In approaching what Polonsky called the 'interesting ideas' of this period I was also influenced by the work of Dorothy Jones, and of Thomas Cripps, who provocatively wrote of the possibility that the post-war congressional investigations were in part a reflection of the fears of right-wingers in the industry that liberals and radicals were threatening to exert a new influence over the mass entertainment industry. The final two chapters deal with aspects of the film of the fifties and with – in particular – the work of Rossen, Kazan, Dassin and Polonsky in the sixties.

A different approach to this might have discussed the wider economic and political parameters of American filmmaking, relating films to other forms of elite opinion in newspapers, politics and radio. A broad study of the political relationship between Hollywood and society would also demand a systematic examination of the way the Production Code was enforced, and the way strict enforcement began to decline after the war. Others would feel that American film of this period, and particularly of the forties and fifties, would be best addressed by examining recurring myths and narrative structures. Rightly or wrongly, this study implies that mass culture does at times show up the interplay between dominant and oppositional ideologies, and that production histories shed light on such meanings. (While I have used some archive sources I have also tried to bring together a large secondary literature on the filmmaking process.) How individuals viewed films is another matter, although this study leans to the assumption that meanings available to me were in most cases also available to 'entertainment' audiences at the time.

As well as my intellectual debts – particularly to those referred to above – I need to thank a number of people for practical help during the long period of preparation of this book. First, I am very grateful to Joan Cohen (of the writers' research service *Legwork*) for her hospitality in Hollywood in the summer of 1988, and for her help subsequently. Secondly, I am indebted to a number of archivists and librarians for their help. In particular I would like to mention Leith Adams of the Warners collection, Archives of Performing Arts, USC, whose assistance by cor- respondence and in person covered a long period, and was much appreciated. My thanks are also due to Ned Comstock of the Archives of the Performing Arts, USC; Samuel Gill of the Margaret Herrick Library, Academy of Motion Picture Arts and Sciences; Brigitte Kueppers of the Theater Arts Library at UCLA, Michael T. Meier of the National Archives (Washington, DC), Charles Silver at the Film Studies Center of the Museum of Modern Art, and staff at the Louis B. Mayer Library (American Film Institute), the Wisconsin Centre for Film and Theatre Research, the UCLA Film Archive, and the Lincoln Center for the Performing Arts. In addition I am grateful to Professor John O'Connor for permission to use some material that appeared first in two articles, in 1984 and 1987, in *Film & History*.[5]

My thanks are also due to the staff of the British Film Institute library, for their help over the years. I would also like to thank

Richard Taylor, Roger Eatwell and Laurence Jarvik for their generous and helpful comments on particular draft chapters, and David Caute for inviting me to a National Film Archive viewing of *The Big Night*. I am also very grateful to Dr Tony Aldgate, academic editor of this Routledge series, for his general support, and in particular for his valuable encouragement at around the middle of the journey. Thanks also to Jackie Morris of the National Film Archive, at the British Film Institute. I'm grateful to a number of friends for their support over some difficult years, and most of all I owe much to my parents, Jean and George Neve, for their steadfast encouragement. In particular my father contributed a good deal to whatever merits the book might have by his painstaking notes on English and style. The faults, of course, are mine.

Chapter 1

Out of the thirties

To Lary May the steady rise in cinema attendances during the thirties, accompanied after 1932 by the opening of newly designed 'moderne' theatres, contributed to the emergence of the country's first national mass culture. Cinemas increasingly symbolised not European decadence but the American way of life and the aspiration to middle-class status, and for the growing immigrant audience the cinema was a powerful influence on their dawning American identities. How audiences interpreted the films that they viewed in new theatres and old is more difficult to ascertain. The Lynds reported in their 'Middletown' survey that exhibitors detected a public desire for pictures 'on the happy side' during the Depression years, but if consumers were unable to check their anxieties at the door they may have supplied their own ambiguity to even the most – perhaps especially the most – anodyne of Louis B. Mayer's 'confections'. As Levine suggests, substantial numbers of viewers may have been aware of the ambiguities of the films that they were viewing, despite or because of their optimistic conclusions.[1]

While audiences increasingly sat in modern cinemas they often watched films that harkened back to more settled times. The success of the thirties Capra films is often attributed to a middle-class nostalgia for pre-Depression values, while the popularity of late thirties films that recreated the past, and of the MGM Andy Hardy cycle, might similarly be interpreted in terms of a desire by both producers and consumers to reaffirm traditional values. More specialist audiences may have interpreted what they saw through the prism of their own perspectives and prejudices, even to the point of cognitive dissonance. While many critics saw *Blockade* (1938) as indicative of Hollywood's

extreme reluctance to commit itself politically, the critic for the
New Masses found in the film a 'vigorous plea for the loyalist
cause'. While passive escape was undoubtedly there to be found,
there are plenty of testaments to the formative impact of
particular films. John Cellon Holmes remembers the effect on
him of his first exposure, at the age of thirteen, to 'the anchor-
less, half-bitter, half lyrical, unkempt, rebellious figure, of John
Garfield' in *Four Daughters* (1938).[2]

It is generally suggested that in the second half of the thirties
few important films had much social or political relevance. The
campaign by the Catholic Legion of Decency in 1934, and the
establishment in the same year of the Production Code Administration, had led to the strict enforcement of a code which was
designed both to restrict the portrayal of sex and violence, and,
as Black argues, to 'use popular entertainment films to reinforce
conservative moral and political values'. From 1934 the Production Code was a powerful influence on what the public could see
on the screen; Black cites the required changes that led MGM
to withdraw from a plan to film Sinclair Lewis' *It Can't Happen
Here*, and Breen's insistence that *Fury* (MGM, 1936) not deal
with racial prejudice or criticise Southern authority.[3] (Lang's
film remained disturbing, despite its tacked-on ending, precisely
because of the lack of any real explanation for the collective evil
which the townspeople discover within them.) This cooperative
censorship, preferred by the studios to the federal controls that
were threatened in the early thirties, underscored the emphasis
in Hollywood film on individualism, the very notion that, for
more politicised Americans, the Depression had called into
question. Levine argues that 'popular culture throughout the
Depression decade remained a central vehicle for the dissemina-
tion and perpetuation of those traditional values that emphasised
personal responsibility for one's position in the world'.[4]

Yet this conservative influence, this very selective reflection of
the social and political reality of the Depression era, went side
by side with a powerful cultural impact. By presenting the
primarily WASP Hollywood stars as role models and generally
downplaying ethnicity in the social rituals and practices portrayed on the screen, the cinema arguably played a key role in
promoting and even defining a new national culture, at a time,
in the late thirties, when more young 'ethnics', low income and
rural Americans were joining the urban middle classes in the

cinemas. The promotion and merchandising of stars was a powerful and much-needed spur to the economy, and the metropolitan culture was powerfully disseminated, with an often liberating effect. The impact, of course, was not limited to the United States, with 35 to 40 per cent of studio revenues coming from abroad. While this represented a powerful cultural imperialism, American films were sometimes welcomed, as in Britain, for their relative 'classlessness', in comparison to the local product.[5]

In surveys of politics as a theme in films of this decade reference is made to the fearful, fickle nature of the mass public. Like the later 'mass society' theory, Hollywood seemed uncertain of the strength of democracy, conscious of the threat of fascism. Bergman sees a distrust of the populace tempered by the assumption, in the later thirties, of federal benevolence. Levine writes of a 'conversation' between Hollywood and its audiences, rather than seeing the films as either determined by dominant economic forces, or by the conscious or unconscious concerns of the populace. For black Americans the ideological limits were still clear; Bogle sums up the thirties as the age of the Negro servant, while Cripps points out that the cycle of lynching films 'missed the point that Negroes were the historic victims of lynching'. In terms of the portrayal of women Andrea S. Walsh sees Ma Joad (Jane Darwell) as a representative heroine of the late thirties – strong but 'safely maternal'. But the social comedies of the later thirties, and in particular the films that Stanley Cavell calls the 'genre of remarriage', seem to provide evidence, in their depiction of independent women – albeit within the realm of romance – that feminist consciousness in the thirties was not as dormant as has been suggested.

The general distaste for politics did not prevent the making of a small number of films in the mid-thirties that satirised radicals. In *Red Salute* (1935), a film that was picketed by some groups on the left, Barbara Stanwyck plays Red, a young woman who – the daughter of a general – is determined to marry a radical, a foreign student. The bulk of the film shows her reluctant involvement – in a form borrowed from *It Happened One Night* – with a soldier who she calls Uncle Sam. At the climax of the film the student makes an anti-militarist speech to a student meeting, and then Uncle Sam seeks to demonstrate that the students are patriotic Americans, properly respectful of the flag. After a fight breaks out the radical is conveniently deported leaving Red, looking rather sullen, to begin a tour in a motor-drawn caravan with Uncle Sam. But, with the politicisation of the Hollywood community in the later thirties, and the arrival of Jewish émigrés from Nazi-occupied Europe, it was the Popular Front agenda that occasionally broke surface in the Hollywood film. Of the 1,500 film professionals to leave Germany after 1933 and Austria after 1938, over half settled in Hollywood. To Billy Wilder, who arrived in the United States, like Fritz Lang, in 1934, the immigration helped to internationalise American tastes, via the film industry, in such areas as horror and sophisticated comedy.[6]

Some reports of two low-budget Republic films, *The President's Mystery* (1936) and *It Could Happen to You* (1937), written by Nathanael West with Lester Cole and Samuel Ornitz respectively, indicate that both showed an unusual political awareness. The first film was seen in 1940 as 'outright propaganda for President Roosevelt's re-election' and as 'an undisguised sermon against the American Liberty League'. While writers themselves had little bargaining power, despite the central importance of scripts for the whole production process, at times their role was strengthened either because of the nature of the material, or when they were able to make alliances with other creative personnel. Candace Mirza discusses the degree of autonomy that Donald Ogden Stewart, George Cukor and Katharine Hepburn were able to enjoy in their work on *Holiday* (1938), for Columbia Pictures. At the age of 41, in 1935, Stewart had discovered the 'oppressed, the unemployed, the hungry, the sharecropper, the Jew under Hitler, the Negro', and his changes to Philip Barry's play contributed towards its transformation into what Mirza sees as 'a more radical critique of patriarchal capitalism'.[7]

Left-wing writers like Howard Koch and John Wexley were in demand as anti-fascism belatedly reached the Hollywood agenda, and Wexley played an active role in promoting *Confessions of a Nazi Spy* (1939) both within Warners, and with the Breen Office. In the area of domestic politics there was also a slow opening towards a more critical agenda, albeit one in which problems were generally solved by New Deal figures of authority. The left-wing documentary filmmaker Sidney Meyers, who reviewed films under the name of Robert Stebbins, felt that it was important to maintain a balance between 'the quality of criticism we apply and an appropriate sense of wonder and gratitude that films of even half-statement reach the screen'. The critic Philip Sterling cited a number of films of the late thirties that he felt broadened 'the channels of democratic thought on the screen'. The list included *Dead End* (1937), *The Life of Emile Zola* (1937), *Juarez* (1939), *A Man to Remember* (1938), *Mr Smith Goes to Washington* (1939) and *Boy Slaves* (1939). The last film named broadly fits into the social problem film formula defined by Roffman and Purdy as an 'indictment of personal villainy which the films' social agencies do away with in the final reel'. In *Boy Slaves* (RKO) a kindly policeman and an even more saintly judge resolve the problem of the exploitation and ill-treatment of boys by a turpentine-producing company. (The judge has this final remark for the villain: 'And while in jail you might study the works of Abraham Lincoln.') Yet remembering Levine's point about endings, it may be that the social impact of such films has been underestimated. Margaret Farrand Thorp, in her survey of the film industry in the thirties, refers to this film – based on a story by 'the frankly radical writer', Alfred Bein – as 'outspoken as few movies have been in the realism of its backgrounds of poverty and its types of Southern officers of the law'.[8]

NEW YORK, THEATRE AND POLITICS

Warren Susman has seen the thirties decade in terms of a crisis of faith in the traditional American belief in individualism, and in the emergence of new forms of group activity which provided meaning and a sense of belonging. Among the groups that arose to meet this need in the Depression years were a number of new theatre companies which broke away from the predominantly apolitical traditions of the twenties. The social and radical theatres of New York in the thirties provided, at the same time, a means of political commitment and protest and – for some second-generation immigrants – a step towards assimilation and the American mainstream. Many of the writers and playwrights who came to Hollywood, particularly in the second half of the thirties, were 'shaped by the decade's political hopes', and were 'steeped in the thirties combativeness, ethnic origins, and the sense of the tough city'. While the studios hired novelists, publicists, newspapermen and others from all over America, the mix of ethnicity, politics and theatrical innovation in New York seemed in particular to be a formative experience for a group of individuals who found themselves directing in Hollywood for the first time in the forties.[9]

Of the social and radical theatre groups that emerged in the thirties the best known, spanning the whole of the decade, was the Group Theatre. The leaders for much of the decade, Harold Clurman, Cheryl Crawford and Lee Strasberg, had all worked in the Theatre Guild, and they built a company that was socially conscious rather than politically committed, and which was concerned to 'find truth on the stage'. Clurman remembered the aspiration to be 'a creative and truly representative theatre', while Arthur Miller remembered the brilliance of the ensemble acting and the impact on audiences who were 'moved not only in their bellies but in their thoughts'. Lacking money, and going against the grain of the commercial theatre with which it competed, the Group was also divided for a time between its paternalistic leaders and teachers and a younger and more radical group of actors and apprentices. Yet the theatre survived until 1941, championing playwrights from John Howard Lawson to Clifford Odets, and bequeathing to Broadway and Hollywood, and to the Actors Studio, a theatrical tradition based on a naturalistic style and the acting techniques associated with Stanislavsky. While there were competing traditions of Stanislavsky's work on acting and the theatre, the emphasis in the Group was on improvisation, and on the emotional honesty of the actors, a perspective that contrasted to notions of drama that favoured dispassionate acting, stylisation and an emphasis on political instruction. The ideas of German exiles Bertolt Brecht and Erwin Piscator remained at the edges of the new theatre movement of the thirties, where naturalism was the dominant form.[10]

Overlapping with the Group, in the first half of the thirties, were the numerous workers' theatres, including the Workers Laboratory Theatre (called the Theatre of Action from 1934). In 1932 the Communist Party established a League of Workers Theatres (later the New Theatre League) to coordinate the new, mainly amateur theatres and supply them with suitable plays. The early emphasis was on agitprop plays, designed to inspire the unemployed to political action, but the party later encouraged a shift towards more realistic plays on proletarian themes.

Younger Group actors were involved in the Theatre of Action in the mid-thirties, as well as in the Theatre Union, a professional group that presented eight plays during its four year existence. Albert Maltz – who had been a friend of Kazan at Yale Drama School – and George Sklar were regular playwrights at the Theatre Union, which was committed to professional productions from a broadly left perspective. Created in 1933, the Theatre Union introduced American audiences to a version of Brecht's notion of 'epic theatre' – although not a version acceptable to Brecht – with its unsuccessful production of *Mother* in 1936.[11]

In the later thirties the energy of the social theatre movement moved from the workers' theatres and the Group towards the Federal Theatre, established in 1935 as part of the Works Progress Administration's work relief programme. While there was a movement from the short skits and didactic theatre of the early thirties to more realistic drama, the Living Newspaper provided some of the most radical and theatrically innovative work on the New York stage during its early years.

Out of the Jewish community in New York came the tradition of Yiddish theatre, which helped to introduce the practice of Stanislavsky's theories of acting and the stage. Another workers' theatre of the time was the Yiddish Artef (Arbeter Theatre Farband, or Workers Theatre Organisation), which had been founded in 1925 as an agitprop theatre, reflecting the Soviet practice of the time. The style of the theatre has been described as eclectic, reflecting the influence of Vakhtangov, but also of 'a touch of Brecht, agitprop, and undistilled Stanislavsky'. Jules Dassin, who was born in Middletown, Connecticut in 1911, of Russian immigrant parents, drifted into the theatre in New York as an actor in 1933, and soon after began directing for Artef, while also working at Jewish camps and hotels in the Adirondacks. Out of the so-called 'Borscht' circuit came many later graduates to Hollywood, including Sidney Lumet (who worked as a child actor, and later appeared in the Broadway production of Sidney Kingsley's *Dead End*), Martin Ritt, John Berry and Dore Schary. Dassin worked briefly with Elia Kazan on a Federal Theatre production of a Marxist children's play, *The Revolt of the Beavers*, which was closed down after three weeks by the New York police commissioner. He is said to have joined the Communist Party in the late thirties and to have left in 1939, the year he first worked in Hollywood, as an apprentice at RKO. In 1940 he directed a play in New York, *Medicine Show*, that was a plea for a national health plan, performed in the manner of the Federal Theatre's Living Newspaper Project, and it was not until 1942 that he directed his first film, at MGM. Dassin also taught at the Actors Lab, which was established in Los Angeles in 1940, and where a number of east coast actors and directors worked, particularly those with experience in the Group Theatre.[12]

Related to the obvious suffering of the period, particularly in the early thirties, was the rise in interest in radical political ideas. In the early years of the Depression the Communist Party had maintained a policy that was hostile to intellectuals and writers who were sympathetic to its stance but were not prepared to accept the ideology and discipline implied by membership. Particularly attracted to the party, either as members or as sympathisers, were the children of first-generation immigrants, individuals who, as they came of age amid the traumas of the Depression, were often alienated both from the culture of their parents and from that of mainstream America. With the shift to a Popular Front policy in the late thirties the party retreated from revolutionary ideas and played a role in organising and encouraging a broad coalition of progressive forces in America; by 1937 'Communism is Twentieth Century Americanism' had become a party rallying cry.

For some the religious affiliation brought with it a legacy of old country socialism. Abraham Polonsky, born in 1910, was untypical by virtue of his academic and legal rather than theatrical interests in the thirties, and in his union involvement in New York; in 1939, at the same time as he gave up law for radio writing, he began his union work for the Communist Party. He was brought up in a 'socialist Jewish milieu', and he recalls that 'the idea of utopian socialism was always present as a solution to all the world's economic problems'. In addition Polonsky attended the City College of New York during the height of the Depression, in the early thirties, when so many were searching for solutions to what was seen as a world disaster. Robert Rossen, who was born in New York in 1908, lived in a number of different neighbourhoods in the city, after his early childhood on the Lower East Side. After school he 'worked occasionally for his father, passed time in poolrooms, did some fighting, and kept reading'. He later remembered watching hoboes gathering on the steps of the 42nd Street library in winter to keep out of the cold. The grandson of a rabbi, Rossen was descended on his mother's side from the Russian-Jewish intelligentsia, and he later said 'I guess a bit of that rubbed off on me'. After working his way through New York University Rossen began writing for the theatre in the early thirties.

The New York theatre groups reached out to new audiences and explored European, and particularly Russian, thinking about drama and society. Paths frequently cross in the various theatres of this period, and a variety of dramatic styles, from agitprop to expressionism and from various forms of naturalism to epic theatre and documentary, were explored and developed. But the social theatre had a weak commercial base and was sustained in part by the Depression culture of the thirties; throughout, on the opposite coast, there was the flashing green light of Hollywood. While those in the Group viewed Hollywood with some disdain, seeing it as a diversion from their most important and satisfying work, the movie capital represented both a constant temptation and a valuable source of funds.[13]

John Howard Lawson, who was born in 1894, had achieved his first major success with the play *Processional* in 1925; using the subtitle 'A Jazz Symphony of American Life', Lawson drew on vaudeville and burlesque to reflect the atmosphere of a West Virginia coal town. His plays for the Group, in the early thirties, helped to define the theme of that company; Clurman saw the essence of *Success Story* as an 'account of what happens to an idealistic force when it finds no effective social form to contain it'. Lawson collaborated on a much weakened Hollywood version, with all reference to Jewishness deleted, in 1934. The play influenced Clifford Odets, although Lawson was later to object to what he saw as the psychological trend of the younger playwright's work for the Group; to Lawson the function of revolutionary drama was to 'circumvent a Freudian escape from truths people wish to avoid'.

After the failure of his second play for the Group, in 1934, Lawson joined the Communist Party, confessed the faults of his work, and became more committed to a rigorous analysis of the social scene. Lawson felt that the artist was now forced to take sides, and in a 1936 book he criticised contemporary plays for their pessimism and lack of development. In his later writing Lawson wrote of Hollywood as a 'sea of banality', but praised *The Story of Louis Pasteur*, *Fury* and *Modern Times* because their protagonists, although buffeted and torn, did not accept defeat. Lawson's proletarian play *Marching Song* (1937), was the last production of the Theatre Union, and has been seen as an example of 'socialist realism', reflecting the form officially favoured in the Soviet Union. Thereafter he devoted himself primarily to screenwriting.[14]

Elia Kazan, who was born in Constantinople, is best seen as a second-generation immigrant as he was only four years old when his father brought him to New York, in 1913. At Williams College, Kazan's experience was of 'antagonism to privilege, to good looks, to Americans, to Wasps', while from 1934 he was for two years an active member of the Communist Party cell within the Group Theatre – at a time when the party predominantly consisted of first- or second-generation immigrants, particularly in New York. Kazan, an apprentice with the Group in the early thirties, began writing and directing for the workers' theatres, and notably the Theatre of Action. In 1934 he wrote, with fellow Group actor Art Smith, the agitprop drama *Dimitroff*, for a New Theatre League benefit, and the same year he co-directed *The Young Go First*, a play which attacked the Civilian Conservation Corps, for the Theatre of Action. Kazan the actor was at his most powerful as the strike-leading taxi-driver in the 1935 Group run of *Waiting for Lefty*, and in 1936 he directed his friend Nicholas Ray, as well as a young Martin Ritt, in Michael Blankfort's *The Crime*.

Kazan claims to have been politicised by the effect of the economic collapse on his father's business and health. He was a Communist Party member during this period, joining in 1934 and resigning in 1936, having been called to account for failing sufficiently to press the concerns of the party cell in the Group. Kazan's experience in the party later returned to haunt him, and he was later to point to the experience of his wife, Molly Day Thatcher, who was assistant editor of *New Theatre and Film*, when criticism by the party, and in particular by John Howard Lawson, led to its closing. But at the time these frictions between the party and those in the workers' theatres seemed less important than their shared attitudes, and their artistic and political admiration for the Soviet Union. Kazan remained devoted to the Group, and he did much to continue and develop its traditions, notably in the Actors Studio that he helped found in 1947.

During the mid-thirties Kazan also gained his first experience in filmmaking, acting in *Pie in the Sky* in 1934, and later assisting Ralph Steiner in the direction of *People of the Cumberlands* (1937). The first, short film was a satire on the failure of the church and welfare authorities to cope with the hunger and poverty of the day; it consisted of a series of improvisations that came out of the street theatre skits of the Theatre of Action. *People of the Cumberlands* reflects the emerging tradition of documentary in the thirties, and some of Steiner's photography recalls that of Dorothea Lange and Walker Evans. In his days in the party Kazan travelled to the South with his Theatre of Action friend Nicholas Ray, who remembered playing 'every strike, every picket line, political campaigns, the backs of trucks'. Ray, born in 1911, had moved to New York from Wisconsin in the early thirties; like Kazan, Ray earned his living as an actor but aspired to direct, and – like Kazan and Odets – he was for a short time a Communist Party member. Kazan has written of the influence on him of the Stanislavsky method, as taught by Clurman and Strasberg, and of Stanislavsky's follower Vakhtangov. Ray has testified to learning much of what he knew about acting from Kazan, although he also worked with Joseph Losey in the Federal Theatre on non-realistic productions; Ray acted in and was stage manager of *Injunction Granted* for director Losey. Kazan, Losey and Ray tried unsuccessfully to start a theatre in New York, the Social Circus, based on Meyerhold's approach to theatre. Ray also ran a folk music programme for CBS radio and had helped to bring Woody Guthrie, Burl Ives, Pete Seeger and others to national attention.[15]

It was during this climax of the period of agitprop drama that Clifford Odets suddenly became *the* playwright of the left theatre. Odets had written *Waiting for Lefty* while a party member, following a request by the New Theatre League to the communist cell of the Group for a suitable play for a benefit night. Following the impact of *Waiting for Lefty* and the success of *Awake and Sing*, written in 1933 but performed in 1935, Odets became the playwright most identified with the Group's concerns. Looking back, Alfred Kazin writes of the passion shared by actors and audience at the Group productions of Odets' plays, contrasting this excitement and conviction with what he remembers as the 'declamatory heroics' at the Theatre Union and the 'gloomy editorials' of the Federal Theatre Project. Also writing later, Harold Clurman saw his friend as a 'headlong romantic' who had a 'bursting love for the beauty immanent in people', and was influenced in the language and feeling of *Awake and Sing* by Lawson's *Success Story*. To Clurman the two plays shared a mixture of 'lofty moral feeling, anger and the feverish argot of the big city'.[16]

Odets later argued that he had been radicalised not by the Communist Party but because his mother 'worked in a stocking factory in Philadelphia at the age of eleven and died a broken woman . . . at the age of forty-eight'. Odets claimed to have been in the Communist Party for at most eight months, and that he was frustrated by the hostility shown by the party's cultural critics towards his later plays, beginning with the Group's *Awake and Sing*, in early 1935. (Brecht admired Odets' *Waiting for Lefty*, but he found the playwright's sympathy for all the characters in *Paradise Lost* 'misplaced', and generally decried, like Lawson, the psychological and naturalistic concerns and forms of his later plays.) The plays were romantic treatments of what the stage and later screen designer Mordecai Gorelik saw as the familiar formula of Group plays: 'For what is a man profited, if he shall gain the whole world, and lose his own soul?' The idea is also suggested by the Odets line that life should not be printed on dollar bills. Odets returned from a trip to Hollywood in 1937 with *Golden Boy*, a play which captured the desire for success and the belief that such success would be at the expense of the finer feelings, the true self. Boxing was the metaphor for a system of capitalist competition that divided men from others and from themselves. This play seemed to influence a number of key social realist–humanist films of the post-war decade, often involving artists who played a part in the New York theatre in the thirties. Odets wrote in his diary in 1940: 'I want to be a poor poet and a powerful businessman, a sensational young man and a modest artist with a secret life.'[17]

Others who were involved in the New York theatre of the thirties were John Wexley, Martin Ritt and John Berry. Wexley, a proletarian novelist, wrote an early play dealing with the Scottsboro case which, to his surprise, was bought and performed by the Theatre Guild. A reviewer of the production praised its dramatisation of the 'social attitudes and terrorism by which the Southern white ruling class seeks to keep the Negro down'. Martin Ritt appeared in a number of Group productions, and he met Kazan while working with the Theatre of Action. He joined the Communist Party in 1936 but left at the time of the Nazi–Soviet pact. Ritt later identified himself as part of the 'great liberal surge' of the thirties, and returned to the humanism of that period in seeking material for his films. John Berry's experience in the late thirties was as an actor and stage manager with the Mercury Theatre company that Welles and John Houseman had established in 1937.[18]

Joseph Losey and Orson Welles were involved in the late thirties with two innovative units of the Federal Theatre Project, itself part of the Works Progress Administration, established by the Roosevelt administration in 1935. Losey was involved with the Living Newspaper Unit during its most radical early phase, before resigning when the run of *Injunction Granted*, his second production for the unit as director, was halted in 1936 because of political pressures on the head of the Federal Theatre. Welles also left the Federal Theatre, and his Project 891, in June 1937. Both *The Cradle Will Rock* and *Injunction Granted* 'offered up radical interpretations of unionisation'. The departure of both directors amid political controversy prefigured the eventual demise of the Federal Theatre Project in 1939, when funds were cut off following criticisms by the newly formed House Committee on Un-American Activities.

Injunction Granted, which played for three months on Broadway to packed houses, traced the history of American labour, and ended by advocating union solidarity behind the newly formed CIO. In 1935 Losey had spent eight months in Moscow, where he had directed an English-language production of Odets' *Waiting for Lefty*, and where he had been particularly interested in the work of Nikolai Okhlopkov, a protégé of Meyerhold, in presenting theatre in the round. Losey met Brecht in Moscow, and again the next year, when the playwright was visiting New York. To Losey the Living Newspaper was a 'form of agitational-propaganda', and this radicalism embarrassed the Director of the Federal Theatre Project, Hallie Flanagan, with the result that Losey left the unit. Flanagan felt that the production was 'bad journalism and hysterical theatre', and that it fell back on 'the old cliché of calling labour to unite in the approved agitprop manner'. Later productions of the unit, including the enormously successful *One Third of a Nation*, were more influenced by documentary, and were more in tune with the New Deal.[19]

Orson Welles, born in 1915, came of age in the late thirties, when the New Deal, and the attendant feeling of optimism, had replaced the despair of the early thirties. In this period Welles became nationally known through radio, and his earnings of $3,000 a week from that source enabled him to decline an offer from David Selznick, and to finance the Mercury Theatre. Welles organised his series of radio adaptations in the late thirties, using writers such as Howard Koch and, in 1939, Abraham Polonsky. Elia Kazan also played his familiar stage gangster role in the popular mystery series in which Welles played 'The Shadow'. On stage Welles' reputation was based on a production of *Julius Caesar* that stressed parallels with contemporary European fascism, his all-black *Macbeth*, and his collaboration with Marc Blitstein on *The Cradle Will Rock*. While Welles welcomed the politically uncompromising theme of *The Cradle Will Rock*, other productions caused controversy with the left, notably *Danton's Death* and *Macbeth*, which was picketed for its 'white chauvinism'. As well as his Mercury players, who he was to take to Hollywood in 1939 as part of his unprecedented contract with RKO, Canada Lee, Will Geer and Howard da Silva also worked for Welles, and later went to Hollywood. Welles was to pay tribute to the Stanislavsky-trained actors of that era, while also stressing that he always aimed to bring home to audiences that they were in a theatre.[20]

THE CASE OF ROBERT ROSSEN AND WARNER BROS

Robert Rossen had grown up with a variety of ethnic groups and had learnt something about 'the impact of environment on character and vice versa'. He was involved in the New York theatre of the first half of the thirties, directing two plays in 1932 – *Steel*, by John Wexley, and *The Tree*, a play by Richard Maibaum about lynching. The next year Rossen and Irving Barrett staged Maibaum's play *Birthright*, one of several anti-Nazi dramas produced in the year of Hitler's accession to power. The themes of Rossen's unproduced play of 1936, 'Corner Pocket', prefigure the plots and motifs of many of his films. The play dealt with the lives of a group of unemployed young men who hang out in a poolroom learning about life. There is talk of petty crime, of women, of gambling, and of soap box socialist politics. Among the general tone of despair, of being pushed around, there are some individuals who still have dreams for the future. Another Rossen play, *The Body Beautiful*, lasted for only four performances on Broadway in 1935, but it led directly to his writer's contract at Warner Bros. Mervyn LeRoy, a Warners director since 1928, admired the play and brought the 28-year-old writer to the studio under personal contract in 1936.[21]

By the mid-thirties Warners had established itself as the Hollywood studio most interested in contemporary social and political events, and in the lives and problems of working people. Its policy of basing a proportion of films on contemporary newspaper headlines dated from 1930, and in the early thirties, before the Production Code was more strictly enforced, films more frankly reflected the despair and cynicism of the time. In *Little Caesar* (1931) and *The Public Enemy* (1931) the studio had produced two of the three definitive gangster films of the early thirties, and had created the association of the studio with the genre. As Nick Roddick argues in his study of Warners in the thirties, whereas the films of the early thirties imply the breakdown in the 'normal mechanisms of American society', those in the second half of the decade show these mechanisms to be largely restored, and deal with organisations which provide only a passing threat to society. The new cycle of social and gangster films that began production in the mid-thirties was less critical, reflecting a more optimistic feeling that the New Deal could defeat the manifest injustices of American life. After the enforcement of the Code an 'amoral world view', and anti-social protagonists, were no longer possible.[22]

Richard Griffith argues that it was Warners that led the way in the thirties in accustoming audiences to the notion that 'the screen could legitimately take its place beside the printing press as a channel for the discussion of public ideas'. Jack and Harry Warner remained intimates of President Roosevelt, and Jack campaigned for him in 1932, but by 1936 they had reverted to the norm of regular support by the studio moguls for the Republicans. In terms of finance Buscombe suggests that Warners, like Columbia, was less tied to the banks in the thirties, and was therefore less sensitive to their interests in choosing subject matter. If superstructural factors explain the distinctive product of the studio, two interrelated factors may have been the personality of Jack Warner and the social characteristics of the studio's stars during this time. Gabler argues that the Warner brothers saw themselves as outsiders, and that their ambivalence towards traditional American values surfaces in the films. To Gabler the Warners' vision was the least assimilative of the Jewish visions of the thirties studios.[23]

The Warners machine that Rossen joined in 1936 was tightly organised with the object of producing films that were economical and which made maximum and disciplined use of their contracted personnel. Hal Wallis, production chief in the period 1933–42, kept a tight rein on the production process, liaising with directors and associate producers, and critically watching dailies. Associate producers had usually to look over their shoulders at Wallis, and sometimes Jack Warner. To the Screen Directors Guild in 1938 this industry structure was 'an involved, complicated and expensive system of supervision which separates the director and writer from the responsible executive producers'. Wallis reminded everyone involved of the formulas that seemed the best predictor of box office success, and of the concern for economy that underlay the recovery of the studio from the near financial ruin of the early thirties. He often reminded directors, or did so through line producers, that they were shooting too many takes; the director was expected to take orders, and some directors with individual aspirations, such as William Dieterle, blamed Wallis for the sameness of much of Warners' product. Yet Wallis's commitment to quality, and to the degree of individuality and distinctiveness necessary for the success of even a genre product, was extraordinary, given the scale of production at the time.

In a discussion of Raoul Walsh's first three films at Warners – *The Roaring Twenties* (1939), *They Drive By Night* (1940) and *High Sierra* (1941) – it has been argued that the feeling for 'crime, working class life and radical politics' found in these films owed much to the New York experiences of the writers involved – Robert Rossen, Mark Hellinger and Jerry Wald. John Bright had co-written *The Public Enemy*, and Edward Chodorov had written the script of *The World Changes* (1933), but there were few radical writers at work at Warners in the thirties, and it was only with the rise in importance of anti-fascism as a theme that the studio hired a number of politically conscious writers, including Howard Koch, John Wexley and Albert Maltz.[24]

In terms of radical politics the leading role was played after 1936 by the Hollywood branch of the Commmunist Party. In that year V.J. Jerome came west to found the Hollywood party, and the late thirties saw the politicisation of Hollywood in terms of party membership, support for anti-fascist and progressive fronts and organisations, and battles over recognition for the Screen Writers Guild. The attractiveness of the Party to liberals and radicals alike had been enhanced by its adoption of a Popular Front policy in 1935; the CPUSA was increasingly to identify itself as part of a broad coalition supporting the New Deal and fighting fascism both at home and abroad. Rossen joined the Communist Party in 1937, remaining a member for at least ten years. He later argued that he had been looking for new horizons and 'a new kind of society': 'there weren't any values, and the Communist Party seemed to be a place that had the values'. Lester Cole has written of the late thirties as 'the time of the progressive, the anti-fascist, anti-racist, which we felt best described us'. The Communist Party's practical involvement with the Scottsboro trials and with the movement towards unionisation gave it a status as being at the forefront of progressive protest and politics.[25]

In his 1941 survey of the Hollywood community, Leo Rosten found that of all the groups involved in the production process, writers were most frustrated by the system – particularly by the 'constricting demands of producers, the public and censorship'. Yet in the tightly controlled system at Warners, the writer, constrained as he was, was often seen as setting the tone of the films: Richard Griffith saw 'writing construction' as central to the social problem films of the second half of the thirties. In addition, Warners was popular with writers, who felt that they had the respect of the studio, and of Hal Wallis in particular. Rossen endorsed this view:

> The subjects were not just shoved under your nose. Within reasonable limits you were able to choose from what went through the story department. Hal Wallis, the production chief, respected the writers and did not force them to accept assignments they didn't agree with. Within the necessary limits of a certain discipline, I was remarkably free.

Despite this recollection, however, archive material suggests that the writer was often frustrated by the demands of the system, and in particular by the interference of both the supervising producer and Hal Wallis, who in turn dealt with Jack Warner and the Production Code Administration. Yet Rossen was well rewarded for his work, and quickly became one of the best paid writers at the studio. He began working under personal contract to Mervyn LeRoy for $200 per week, rising to $450; by 1941 his salary was $1,000 per week. In 1938 41 per cent of employed writers at Warners, Twentieth Century-Fox and Columbia earned less than $250 per week, and only 20 per cent earned over $750.[26]

Rossen's first assignment at the studio, for producer Lou Edelman, concerned a script to be based on the trial of Charley Lucania (Lucky Luciano). A high-living gangster with interests in narcotics and gambling, Luciano had been convicted by the State Supreme Court in New York, in June 1936, of 'compulsory prostitution'. The conviction of Luciano – Johnny Vanning in the film – had been a personal triumph for Thomas E. Dewey, who had been appointed as New York special prosecutor in July 1935 with a mandate to wage war against the city's under-world corruption. The three-week trial produced sensational newspaper coverage nationwide, and attracted the attention of Warner Bros, who were particularly interested in the role of the prostitutes who Dewey had persuaded to testify about the New York 'industry' that Luciano headed and which employed around 1,000 girls in houses throughout the city. As raw material the screenwriters had not only accounts of the trial but 'confessions' from two of the prostitute witnesses, as they appeared in *Liberty* magazine.

Changing perceptions of the project were reflected in changes in the title. The first outline, of August 1936, was called 'The Men Behind' and emphasised the shyster lawyers and crooked politicians who hampered the efforts of the prosecutor – named Dewey at this stage – to break the case. A second outline in October, written by Rossen and Abem Finkel, was titled 'Five Women'; it built up the roles of the five women who had been key witnesses at the trial, portraying them as caught between a system that degraded and exploited them – but which, as one of them says, is 'better than the gutter' – and the risks of co-operation with an ambitious city prosecutor. By November,

Bette Davis, returning to the studio after a period of dispute, had been assigned to the project to play the most prominent of the women, Mary Dwight, and this triggered further re-writing, and the changing of the title to 'Marked Woman'.

The Production Code prohibited any depiction of the 'business of prostitution', and so the five girls, who share an apartment, become hostesses and singers. Final screenplay and film suggest that the women feel that 'the law isn't for people like us', and that they fear the consequences of testifying and are cynical of the benefits of convicting Johnny Vanning. After the trial Mary tells David Graham (the prosecutor) that they live in different worlds, and the ending of the film suggests this visually. (Hal Wallis interested himself in the details of shooting and lighting this scene.) When the trial is over, as Graham is hailed by reporters and photographers as a future governor, Mary rejoins the other women and the camera follows them, showing each of them in close-up, as they descend the steps together and walk off into the night and the fog. While the victorious prosecutor goes onward and upward, the women retain a quiet solidarity.

As Mary Beth Haralovich points out with reference to *Marked Woman*, there was often a contradiction between the effects of censorship, which deflected Hollywood from treatment of uncomfortable economic and political realities, and those of other aspects of the production process. While the Production Code Administration insisted that there be no reference to prostitution or vice, the narrative of the film made implicit reference to the economic and sexual basis of prostitution, and advertising and publicity for the film also promoted it on the grounds of the underlying reality of the events depicted. Given the need for narrative logic, even the Breen Office were reluctantly persuaded to accept a reference to the women's profession being 'unsavory and distasteful'. The depiction of Bette Davis as a star, and the usual Hollywood emphasis on female glamour, does not erase what Haralovich calls the 'intersection of economics and gender at the basis of *Marked Woman*'.

It is arguable whether Rossen's own politics – as a member of the Communist Party he would be aware both of general critiques of capitalism and of the 'woman question' – played some part, at least in making the writer more sensitive to underlying class relationships in the story. The *Daily Worker* pointed out that the ending recognised that 'as far as the girls are concerned theirs is a hopeless future'. In Polonsky's terms they accept that 'Everybody dies' and testify out of a residual dignity, while accepting that nothing will fundamentally change. (In reality the two key witnesses were forced to retract their evidence, although the original verdict stood.) The women in the film work the way they do because the alternative, as Mary says, is 'going hungry a couple of days a week so you can have some clothes to put on your back'. A class division is suggested, even if it is in no way explained or criticised, and in this sense the film departs from the social problem formula.[27]

Wallis had at first been unsure about Rossen's ability, but *Marked Woman* (1937) was a critical and commercial success; Jack Warner delighted in telling Bette Davis that it had a 'sock in every foot', and he told Wallis that 'everyone connected with the picture deserves tremendous commendation'. Rossen was quickly assigned to another project with a strong social content – the adaptation of *Death in the Deep South*, a novel by Ward Greene. The plot of the novel loosely follows the case of Leo Frank, a Jew who was accused in 1914 of murdering a 14-year-old girl, and who was lynched the next year after his death sentence had been commuted by the Governor of Georgia. The finished film, *They Won't Forget*, directed by LeRoy from a script by Rossen and Aben Kandel, opened in New York in July 1937, during a period of liberal concern at a renewed wave of lynching in the Deep South. An anti-lynching bill introduced by Congressman Joseph Gavagan of New York and sponsored by the NAACP had passed the House of Representatives in April, only to come to grief in the Senate as a result of Southern opposition.[28]

The script and film closely follow the narrative of the novel. The film concerns an investigation and a trial in a Southern small town following the murder of a girl student, Mary Clay (Lana Turner). The town's ambitious district attorney, Andrew Griffin (Claude Rains), conducts the investigation with an eye for 'something spectacular' on which to launch a campaign for the Governorship. The first suspect, a black janitor, does not meet that criterion, but he is brutally treated by the local police. Instead Griffin decides that his political impact will be greater if Robert Hale, a Northerner and Mary's college teacher, is indicted. While Mary Clay's brothers swear to avenge her death, local notables, including the press, arouse local feeling. Despite his Northern support at the trial Hale is found guilty and sentenced to death. The sentence is commuted by the Governor to life imprisonment, but Hale is removed from the train carrying him to prison and lynched by a mob.

Contemporary reviewers were quick to comment on the film's relevance to the Scottsboro case – rarely out of the headlines since 1931, when nine black men were first sentenced to death (for alleged rape of two white girls) in Alabama. The International Labor Defense, a communist New York-based organisation, had consistently supported the appeals of the Scottsboro defendants, and in a pamphlet published in 1934 it had argued that Thomas Knight Jr, the Alabama Attorney General, was the 'dapper song and dance leader for the Southern ruling class', and that he had no intention of allowing anything 'so trivial as indisputable evidence to stand in the way of his obtaining a lynch sentence'. *They Won't Forget* was first shown in New York in the same week in which one of the nine blacks involved was again sentenced to death in an Alabama court.[29]

Two visually striking scenes in the film are not in the novel, but are described in great detail in the screenplay. When Griffin is stuck on the case he discusses the possible suspects with his newspaper buddy, Brock; we see pictures of the suspects on the wall of Griffin's office, but a blank space is left unfilled. As they discuss the 'evidence' pointing to Hale's guilt Griffin looks at the blank space and there is a dissolve from the empty ellipse to Hale's reflection, as he adjusts his tie in front of an oval mirror. The noose figuratively tightens on Robert Hale's neck. The better known image comes at the end, when the lynching party hijack the train. As the mob carry off their victim we see another train, an express, snatching a mailbag strung up by the side of the track, vividly suggesting Hale's fate. The final script provides for a close shot of a railway arm which 'bears a sinister, macabre resemblance to a gallows'. Such detailed scripting indicates a cooperation between writer and director that was unusual at the studio, despite the gradual loosening of the production system at the end of the decade. (There are other signs of this, including the special treatment given to William Wyler, when he came to the studio to direct *Jezebel*.) Given that Rossen was originally under personal contract to LeRoy they would likely have consulted on the script on these and other 'effects' – the high angle shot of the interrogation of the janitor is another –

that distinguish the film visually from the average Warners product of the time.

The screenplay also strengthens the novel's depiction of the power structure of the town. In a scene that is not in the source book, Andrew Griffin is shown gauging local 'opinion' in a bar full of cronies; as he decides to prosecute Hale a voice is heard speculating on the attorney's chances of becoming governor. (The line, which the Breen Office objected to but which survives in the scene, recalls a similar one – again about a prosecutor's likely political elevation – in *Marked Woman*.) Another scene that reflects the sociology of the town is one in which Griffin discusses the case with a number of key townspeople; the scene is in the novel but is significantly expanded in the final screenplay. The novel describes a discussion between the DA and 'the merchants, the bankers, the landowners – the notables'. They remind Griffin of the 'powder keg' of unemployment and the dangers of exciting local opinion. In the final screenplay the men sitting in Griffin's office are introduced as 'typical representatives of the Southern upper class'. When a merchant asserts that he and his colleagues are only interested in the community, Griffin replies: 'You mean the property you own in the community.' He describes a leading banker as 'the man who moulds public opinion' and he concludes by telling his guests: 'You started it, my aristocratic friends, but I'll finish it.' The scene helps to extend the film's analysis a little beyond the 'shyster lawyer' figure so beloved of the traditional Hollywood social problem film.

The film was widely admired, and was promoted by Warners as a successor to *Little Caesar*, *The Public Enemy*, *I am a Fugitive from a Chain Gang*, *Bullets and Ballots* and *Marked Woman*. Although the film avoided confronting the racial motivation for Southern lynch law, and although the Breen Office apparently attempted to play down the criticism of Southern justice, it is still reported that the film 'could not be shown in theatres below Washington'. Otis Ferguson saw it as a picture of 'small change humanity in a small city, the individual characters demonstrating how the simplest of moral decencies may be brutalized into tragic and imbecile horrors by the workings of circumstance and inbred hostilities'. Frank Nugent in the *New York Times* saw it as a 'brilliant sociological drama and a trenchant film editorial against intolerance and hatred', finding it in many ways superior to *Fury* and *Black Legion*. Pare Lorentz linked the trial in the film with contemporary events in Decatur, Alabama, while in *New Masses* a reviewer felt that the film 'deserves our complete support' and remarked on the similarity of the scene in which the district attorney introduces the murdered girl's clothes as evidence, to an actual occurrence at the Scottsboro trial. A contemporary British critic found that the film 'offers no solution, calls for no action, presents no hopes'.[30]

Towards the end of 1937 Rossen began work with Leonardo Bercovici on another film to be based on the New York 'rackets' trials instituted by Thomas Dewey. Warners collected transcripts of a well-publicised trial – of March 1937 – dealing with extortion, bribery and murder in the trucking industry, and Rossen and Bercovici drew closely on the documents in writing an original story and a treatment called 'The Market'. The result, *Racket Busters* (1938) was a densely plotted, 71-minute B picture which, as with *Marked Woman*, emphasised the victims rather than the racketeers or the prosecutor. Alison (Walter Abel) is the Dewey-type character who is appointed by the Governor to clean up the rackets, while Martin (Humphrey Bogart) is the gangster who is attempting to extend his control into the city's trucking industry. Reflecting the script the film becomes involved in the lives of the truckers, principally Denny Jordan (George Brent) and Pop, the secretary of the truckers' association. Pop asserts the value of solidarity in the face of intimidation by the racketeers, while Denny is prepared to see the world in more individualistic terms – as a matter of 'every man for himself'.

While the film shows how co-operation with proper authority solves the problem, there is also a parallel debate between the principles of collective action and individualism. The 'problem' is personalised in the snarling gangster that Bogart played at this stage of his career, but there is some attempt to suggest the pressures on the independent truckers from business groups in league with Martin. The film endorses tough action by the state to fight the rackets, involving Alison charging unco-operative witnesses with contempt – something which Peter Biskind has seen as characteristic of Stalinists who would later identify with the state in the fifties. But at least as strong as the formulaic manipulation of the men by self-interested racket busters is a

Plate 1: Filming *Racket Busters* (Warner Bros, 1938). Reproduced courtesy of BFI Stills, Posters and Designs.

periodically powerful sense of democratic debate. Acting collectively is identified with co-operation with the prosecutor, and
by the end of the film Denny has renounced his individualism;
he tells his wife that he has learned one thing – that 'People like
us have only got one chance – to stick together.'

Racket Busters suffers from some unlikely plotting and characterisation, and in terms of production values and casting there
is no real comparison with Raoul Walsh's 1940 film about
trucking, *They Drive By Night*. *Racket Busters* contains nothing of
the analysis of the trucking industry that is found in the first
part of the later film. The *Daily Worker* criticised the failure of
Racket Busters to show the 'tie-up between the racketeers, big
business and Tammany politicians', although years later in the
same paper David Platt referred to the film as 'strongly "pro-
union"'. Howard Barnes found it to be a 'much better than
average melodrama with a message', while Bosley Crowther felt
that the use of actual court testimony gave the film a 'documentary authority which is both instructive and compelling'. In
contrast to *They Drive By Night*, which essentially pictures success
through individual effort and initiative, in *Racket Busters* the idea
of collective action is constantly referred to and is an element in
the resolution of the narrative in a way that arguably reflects
something of the political concerns of the writers.[31]

In June 1938 Warners had bought an unpublished novel by
Jerome Odlum, and this became the original source for the film
Dust Be My Destiny. The recession of 1937–8 had renewed
concern for the problems of unemployment and vagrancy
among young people, and Odlum's novel told the story of two
fugitives from justice who search for a place to live together, but
who find peace only in death. The novel ends melodramatically
with the male fugitive, Joe Bell, being shot dead in a courtroom
following the death of his wife Mabel. Evoking comparison with
the 1937 Fritz Lang film *You Only Live Once*, the novel closes with
Joe, dying in the courtroom, talking of imminent reunion with
his wife. Elsewhere the book details the involvement of Joe and
Mabel with criminal gangs and G-Men without – like Edward
Anderson's contemporary novel *Thieves Like Us* – suggesting any
wider criticism of American institutions.

There seems to have been some debate about how to exploit
Odlum's story. Rossen wrote a treatment that suggested the
social context of the central character's plight, seeing him as one

of droves of wandering men seeking work. Mark Hellinger advised Wallis to stress the love story, rather than the gangster elements. But Wallis's feeling, according to line producer Lou Edelman, was that we 'take out all of the migratory scenes and sociological references'. An outline produced in August 1938, in response to a request from Wallis, set out the new angle: 'This is the story of two people – not a group. It is an individual problem – not a national one.'

Rossen, along with Julius and Philip Epstein, helped to develop a social outcast role for John Garfield, who had already established himself at the studio playing 'nobodies' who are victims of a mixture of fate and social circumstance, as in *Four Daughters* (1938) and *They Made Me a Criminal* (1939). As Julius Garfinkel, Garfield had been born on the Lower East Side in 1913. Gaining a narrow hold on the acting profession in the depth of the Depression, Garfield met Clifford Odets, who eventually sponsored his membership of the emerging Group Theatre. Garfield's disappointment in not getting the lead role in the Group Theatre production of *Golden Boy* in 1937 led to his move to Hollywood, and after the success of *Four Daughters* he signed a seven-year contract with Warners, although it did allow him time to return to the New York stage. (In 1939 Garfield was earning $1,500 a week at Warners.)

At the beginning of final script and film the central protagonist, Joe Bell, is being released from prison after serving a sentence for a crime he did not commit. From this point Joe sees and expects the worst from everyone. A montage of signs reflects contemporary attitudes to those on the road: 'No Riders Allowed', 'Keep Moving', 'Vagrants Not Wanted', 'No Tramps Allowed' and 'Hoboes Not Welcome'. Armed men shoot at Joe, but when he enters a shop at midnight with a gun, intending to steal food, the serving woman offers to trust him for the money. Thus at Joe's eventual trial, which is the climax of the film, the subtheme of an often benign human nature is well established despite the indications that society has in other ways victimised and prejudged vagrants like Joe. Joe tells the court that the 'case isn't going to be decided on whether or not I committed this murder, but on who I am', but amid much sentiment the couple are judged to be innocent and, in accordance with the conventions of such films, what the defence counsel calls the 'whole system of American democracy' is reaffirmed and vindicated.

The tone of the film is inconsistent, with the grim reality of Joe and Mabel's life on the run at odds with comic and sentimental scenes, and with the editorialising of the final trial scene. James Wong Howe contributes a number of effective low-key lighting effects which enhance the darker elements of the film; we see, for example, the couple in a hotel room at night, where the shadows and flashing neon sign outside the window reflect their desperation and insecurity. At the time the *New York Times* described *Dust Be My Destiny* as the 'latest of the brothers' apparently interminable line of melodramas about fate dogged boys from the wrong side of the tracks'. The *Daily Worker* found Joe Bell's bitterness with society to be 'believable and real', but it found the film overall to be another example of a tired 'I'm a Fugitive and Nobody Cares for Me' formula. Compared with the unrelenting pessimism of the more individually crafted product, *You Only Live Once*, the Warners film strikes an affirmative note, endorsing not only the institutions of authority – and their ability to solve the problems of the Depression – but also the good will of the wider society.[32]

While Rossen's success rate was generally high, and he was generally happy at Warners, there were also frustrations implicit in a hierarchical system of film production in which the majority of writers had little status. For each project that reached production another was abandoned because of script or Production Code problems, or through difficulties with the availability of key stars. In the late thirties Rossen worked on a number of treatments on social themes which never reached script stage. (His last thirties credit – which he shared with the writing team of Jerry Wald and Richard Macaulay – was for *The Roaring Twenties* (1939), a film that had its origins in Mark Hellinger's exuberant treatment recalling the gangster era in New York.)[33] There were recurring creative tensions as Wallis, and occasionally Warner himself, second-guessed the efforts of associate producers, writers and directors. The status of writers increased only with the war years, and following the belated studio recognition of the Screen Writers Guild in 1941. But by specialising in social issues Rossen contributed to the relatively small strand in the studio's output that was important in moulding the studio's image. He worked within the conventions, but he helped to give them life. His political interests informed the dialogue, even if they had little impact on the structure, of the films on which he worked.

Chapter 2

Populism, romanticism and Frank Capra

POPULISM IN AMERICA

In the United States the weakness of socialism as an ideology has frequently been noted. Numerous reasons have been advanced, including the absence of feudalism, the influence of the frontier, the relative affluence of the American working class, federalism, and the extensive ethnic and racial diversity. Arguably the emphasis of American dominant ideology on political equality has also hampered efforts to organise Americans along class lines. Jerome Karabel has pointed to what he sees as the extraordinary power of the doctrine of 'popular sovereignty' in American political development, while others have stressed the importance of notions of political equality and democracy to American national identity. Leon Samson, writing in the mid-thirties, saw the 'pseudo-socialistic' idea of American democracy, and the belief in individual upward mobility, as overriding and concealing the reality of class in America, and he also cited Walt Whitman's poetic vision, his song of America, as representative of the culture's relative class unconsciousness.[1]

American political rhetoric has instead borrowed from the ideas and motifs of populism – both the particular tradition based on agrarian protest and the more amorphous cluster of ideas centred around the opposition of elites and 'the people'. More particularly, populism in the United States has historically been associated with the land, and with agricultural communities threatened by, and resisting, the processes of industrialisation and urbanisation. In a discussion of American populism, MacRae sees it as both reactionary, looking backward to the untamed virgin west and to the pastoral vision of Thomas

Jefferson, and also radical, in that it favours change away from the inequalities of bureaucracy towards a simpler, more fraternal life. The short-lived populist movement at the end of the nineteenth century pressed for government action, but had a moral rather than an ideological perspective on power in America, believing in the possibility of a rectification of elite corruption and expropriation without any fundamental change in the system. The populists were critical of urban interests, bankers, big business, machine politicians and intellectuals, and much of this demonology is also characteristic of Frank Capra's 'middle period' films.

Like the turn-of-the-century socialists, populists felt that the 'interests' had expropriated the wealth that rightly belonged to the producing classes. But while socialists favoured industrialisation, fundamental change and a coherent theory of history populists loathed the bureaucracy that they associated with industrial concentration, and talked of reform through the simple device of replacing corrupt and conspiratorial elites with representatives of the truer, agricultural America.[2]

Richard Hofstadter, in *The Age of Reform*, examined the reform period in the United States from the 1890s, and the era of Populism and Progressivism, until the New Deal of the 1930s. He saw the People's (or Populist) Party of the 1890s as only a 'heightened expression' of 'a kind of popular impulse that is endemic in American political culture', and stressed the impact on the national folklore of generations of Americans being brought up to revere rural life. Writing in the 1950s, Hofstadter saw Populist thinking as surviving as an 'undercurrent of provincial resentments, popular and "democratic" rebelliousness and suspiciousness, and nativism', and Progressivism as an attempt to restore 'a type of economic individualism and political democracy' that the corporations and corrupt political machines were seen to have destroyed. The two movements of the turn of the century were seen as reflecting a native response to the waves of immigration that fed the growth of urban political machines. The goal of revolt was not social democracy or social equality but 'greater opportunities'.

Hofstadter recognised the role of this 'liberal tradition in American politics', from Jeffersonian and Jacksonian democracy through to the New Deal, in humanising the working of the system, yet he was critical of the 'Populist–Progressive tradition' (of 1890 to 1917) for its moral certainty, and its tendency to blame conspiratorial forces for the evils of society. In addition he traced the origins of what he calls the 'cranky pseudo-conservatism' of the early fifties to the illiberal side of the earlier tradition, linking this development from reform to reaction to certain constant American tendencies, particularly in the Middle West and the South.

Hofstadter saw continuities in the American reform tradition, but he stressed those aspects of the New Deal that represented a sharp break with the past; with its concern with a new state role in relief and in the labour market, the new administration had a new 'social-democratic tinge'. He saw Franklin D. Roosevelt as uninterested in the Progressive issues of bossism and corruption; instead the early years of the New Deal were concerned with the National Recovery Administration scheme involving co-operation between business and government. The 1930s saw the triumph of the forces that populists had resisted, particularly big government and business, and the emergence of a strong role for intellectuals in Washington.[3]

Yet more recent scholarship on the Populist movement tends to stress its democratic basis and its concern with 'structural reform of the American economic system'. To Goodwyn the movement of farmers from West and South represented a challenge to the era of triumphant capitalism; rather than stressing the tendencies to conspiracy and anti-Semitism, this perspective sees the People's Party and the bodies that preceded it as an essentially forward-looking 'economic crusade'. Other writers have also drawn attention to populist themes as part of a progressive tradition in American history, and to the recurring notion that elites have usurped the power of the people. But such writers also admit that the tradition has been prone to reactionary bursts of nativism, despite the legacy of the 'gospel of cooperation' of the late nineteenth century. A student of the Dust Bowl migrants to California in the 1930s refers to the changing political colour of the populist perspective since the turn of the century; by the 1930s, he argues, many 'plain folk' remained sympathetic to 'appeals on behalf of the common man or against the "interests"', but 'they responded with equal vigour to symbols that recalled a white Protestant and intensely patriotic vision of Americanism'.[4]

Laclau found the notion of populism to be 'elusive', and one recent reviewer of the American debate remarks that 'populism is a slippery concept', and refers to 'the basic political ambivalence at the heart of the American populist tradition'. In historical terms the idea suggests a co-operative mass movement demanding economic reform, and the left in recent years has – in the absence of any wide class or ideological consciousness – used local issues to build community politics.[5] The imaginative world of Capra's films includes the demonology of populist rhetoric – the distrust of big business, finance and intellectuals – without offering any relevant alternative agenda. Good neighbourliness is not a serious answer either to depression or to corruption and lack of democracy. Co-operative action – central to the movement of the 1890s and even to Huey Long's campaigns in the 1930s – is not a narrative option in Capra's world, any more than it is in American cinema as a generality.

Yet Capra's heroes are men of the people in the symbolic if not the conventionally representative sense. What they really represent is a democratic ideal of America invoked throughout this century by those outside 'normal politics' who wish to call on the notion of 'the people' – with or without rural overtones – to attack the policies, if rarely the status, of powerful elites. The roots of populism in action in America are as a popular movement to redistribute power and resources, and in a country without an established language of socialism this remains a powerful mobilising ideology; but the language is available to all, and the right may find of particular use the myths and symbolism associated with a 'golden age' of given roles and structured relationships.

The case of Huey Long in the 1930s demonstrates the power of populism as a mobilising ideology related to issues of redistribution and powerlessness, although Long's demagoguery also illustrates the lack of real analysis in the populist critique of power. Populist leaders arrive in positions of power with a constituency, an enemy and a mandate, but without – certainly in Long's case – an analysis. Rising to power on the resentment of the rural poor against the ruling families of Louisiana, Long was unrestrained by any programme or ideology, and he seems to have represented, along with Father Charles Coughlin, the tendency of 1930s populist politics to degenerate into authoritarianism. Writing in the mid-1930s V.F. Calverton in *Modern Quarterly* warned of the rise of an American fascism controlled by industrialists and bankers but exploiting the fears and aspirations of the petit-bourgeoisie: 'Although the farmer opposed corporate capitalism and baited Wall Street, he never wished to abolish private property or the profit system.'[6]

Residues of populist sentiment recur in subsequent politics and culture. In the 1950s liberal anti-communist opinion saw the emergence of Senator Joseph McCarthy on to the national political scene as a reflection of a dangerously proto-fascist mass phenomenon.[7] They stressed links in McCarthy's support and rhetoric with the agrarian and mid-western 'left' populism of the 1890s, and saw the phenomenon as a threat to the party politics and civil liberties of 'normal' Schumpeterian competition between elites, and to pluralist politics. The 'radical right' was seen as threatening the liberal tradition that checked the powers of majorities. In fact, while McCarthy certainly drew on populist motifs in his speeches – notably in his condemnation of those 'born with a silver spoon in their mouths' as guilty of betrayal – his main theme was that of anti-communism, and his crucial political support came from business and political elites.[8]

Certainly the New Left counterculture of the 1960s and early 1970s was in part a protest against big, dehumanising corporations, and against universities which prepared students for them. Out of that period also came the revival of ecological and environmental ideas, of self-sufficiency and the commune. Hollywood discovered the new youth culture with the success of films that reflected a fantasised retreat from contemporary reality. In *Easy Rider* (1969) the protagonists pay homage to the idea of a purer, more communal America before they continue their mercenary journey, while *Alice's Restaurant* (1969) in particular captures an imperfect attempt to create a human scale maternal refuge from the wider society. On the right some analysts saw 1968 as the beginning of a fruitful alliance between conservative elites and a populist 'Middle American' reaction against a liberal establishment.[9] This revival of a conservative populist rhetoric, stretching from Richard Nixon to Ronald Reagan and beyond, was reflected in film with periodic success for vigilante themes, in which plebiscitary male leaders grapple with the results of liberal failure and betrayal.

The American democratic structure has arguably been less insulated from popular ideas, values and culture than traditionally more stratified countries where national identity is less clearly associated with democratic ideas. Precisely because of the broad ideological consensus that covers American elite politics, third party and non-party movements of right and left have often raided the same larder of ideas. Seeking to break through, they have validated their position by reference to the gap between elite values and attitudes and those of the particular 'community' or populace that such groups represent, or claim to represent. In doing so they have also made use of the poorly integrated cluster of categories and values associated with populism. Among such recurring motifs have been anti-intellectualism, the notion or myth of some lost 'golden age' in which life was purer and simpler, a reverence and nostalgia for the land and those who lived or live closest to it, and – perhaps most anachronistically in a society where private enterprise is as sanctified a notion as democracy itself – a distrust of money power. They also, in contradistinction to socialist ideology, put faith in notions of 'common sense', biblical morality, and leaders who can represent – or sometimes personify – these values.

While references to rural America in recent American politics have been largely symbolic – for example, Jimmy Carter's emphasis on both morality and his rural origins in opposition to the Washington of Watergate in 1976 – residues of populist politics remain. Rightist groups in the early eighties invoked the supposedly traditional values of the past, including 'the work ethic, the neighborhood, and patriarchal sex roles', while local left movements since the 1960s have also organised around issues of neigbourhood and community, rather than issues of class. Boggs sees the American New Left as more genuinely populist than the New Right, in the sense that its political campaigns more authentically reflect local and community concerns, rather than the interests of elites.[10]

AMERICAN FILM AND POPULISM

Garth Jowett calls his study of American cinema *The Democratic Art*, and certainly in the early years many films exhibited a sentimental affinity with the underdog, and even with the lower-middle-class man or woman lost in the crowd; Durgnat and Simmon refer to the mix of individualistic Christianity and agrarian myth in the early features of King Vidor, as well as to the more general identification with the lower classes in the work of D.W. Griffith and Chaplin. In terms of the rural myth, and the communitarian dream represented by the untamed territories of the frontier, it is the case that American film has tended to favour those who gain their living on the land, rather than in the city. From the city comes crime and corruption, and the 'gangster', while in the Western it is the settlers who – while rarely heroes – are depicted as carrying the values truest to the American dream.[11]

King Vidor's *Our Daily Bread* (1934) provides an example of the difficulty of classifying populist films of the thirties on a left–right spectrum. The film was criticised as left wing by the Hearst press, while *New Theatre* felt that it had tendencies towards fascism. A rural co-operative is shown as a response to the Depression, but the principles of private property and leadership are endorsed. MGM in the 1930s consciously provided reassurance by affirming traditional values, but in *The Good Earth* (1937), Irving Thalberg's last film, the studio came close to populist values, placing Dust Bowl images in the safe context of a literary classic set in China. Wang (Paul Muni) is most sympathetic when he and his wife are poor, and live close to the earth; as a rich man he attracts sympathy only during the fight to defend the wheat against the plague of locusts, and after the death of his wife. Warner Bros was the studio both closest to the New Deal in the 1930s, and which also – with its proletarian stars – most identified with what Roddick calls the 'model of the little man versus the world' in its crime and social problem genres. However, with few exceptions – possibly *Marked Woman* – this characteristic of the studio's product implied no lasting social contradictions.[12]

If populist cinema was one, belated reaction to the rise of industrial and urban America, another form that looked backward to the America of the late nineteeth century was the Western. The Western is often seen as part of the populist cultural tradition in America, favouring as it does the west over the east, and with its suspicion of large landowners, bankers and politicians. Some of the most successful Western films dramatise the conflict involved in the taming of the frontier, and the arrival from the east of 'civilisation' – and its discontents. The late 1930s is sometimes seen as the classical period of the genre, before social issues, and a self-consciousness about the genre by filmmakers, destroyed its 'innocence'. This notion can be debated, but this period has also been seen as the one in which John Ford produced his most populist work, including, in 1939, *Stagecoach*, *Young Mr Lincoln* and *Drums Along the Mohawk* and, the next year, *The Grapes of Wrath*.[13]

John Ford's vision was one of the Western and frontier values of family and community, and his films emphasise groups rather than individuals. Like Capra's work, Ford's films of the late 1930s were popular with the left, at a time when the left joined in the general affirmation of traditional American values. (In the 1930s Ford generally saw himself as a liberal or on the left.) It is in *Stagecoach* that Ford makes his first use of Monument Valley as a location, and against this setting – on the stagecoach journey to Lordsburg – a makeshift community of travellers is tried and tested. Ford – with his regular 1930s screenwriter, the liberal activist Dudley Nichols – favours the characters who are shunned by respectable society; it is the banker Gatewood who is throughout the least likeable character, while at the end of the film Doc Boone sends the prostitute Dallas (Claire Trevor) and the avenging outlaw the Ringo Kid (John Wayne) off on their own to an imagined rural paradise. They are, as Boone tells them, 'freed from the blessings of civilisation'. At the beginning of *Young Mr Lincoln* we are introduced to the young Abraham Lincoln before the events which made him into a mythic figure. Lincoln is shown receiving authority, in the form of law books, directly from the poor people – from a pioneer family – and he later uses the law to defend them. (Steve Neale points to the way the film also reflects some of the contradictions inherent in populist ideology: 'Lincoln, in incarnating the Law, is both *of* the "people" and *above* them'.) Ford's last film to be released in 1939, *Drums Along the Mohawk*, can also be interpreted in terms of a conspiracy between producers and consumers to reaffirm traditional American values.[14]

After Darryl F. Zanuck had purchased the rights to *The Grapes of Wrath*, the studio and the financing bank – the Chase National in New York – came under heavy pressure not to go ahead.[15] Joe Breen, in giving the judgement of the Production Code Administration, found the exposure of 'shocking' conditions to be balanced by 'good images' and, most important, by an 'uplifting ending', and this view – that the radical nature of the novel had been transformed in the film to something that was conservative – has also been offered by students of the film.[16] The politicisation of Tom Joad is retained in the film, but alongside this, as a response to Depression hardship and exploitation, are placed two other motifs: the New Deal, as represented by the government camp which offers safe haven to the Joads, and an emphasis on the persistence of the family. The film ends not with Tom Joad's departure – establishing Henry Fonda's liberal screen image – but with a scene in which the Joads are seen moving on again, and in which Ma Joad expresses the defiant, populist and ultimately conservative closing speech: 'Rich fellows come up. They die. Their kids ain't no good. They die out. But we keep a coming. We're the people that live. Can't lick us. We'll go on for ever, 'cause we're the people.' Yet, as with Capra's films, critics and censors may at times have given too much weight to endings which, for audiences, do not, or did not, suppress and resolve the 'problems' raised earlier. Gallagher, for example, argues that 'few films appear quite so seditious, bitter or daring' as *The Grapes of Wrath*. Pare Lorentz criticised the film's lack of a hard documentary sense of the 'miserable huts and busted windmills', but praised its faithful reproduction of 'the bloody violence' that accompanied economic upheaval.[17]

The decline of the Western may reflect not only the erosion of the relevance of its images and concerns, and the lack of a sense of tradition among the young, but also the extent to which, once the code of the Western was abandoned, there was little left. As the most central of American myths, the Western story was essentially naive and optimistic – a story of strong and simple men doing what they had to do, and thereby contributing to the righting of wrongs. In 1954 Robert Warshow saw the Western form as an American ritual, seeing George Stevens, in his direction of *Shane* (1953), as trying 'to freeze the Western myth once and for all in the immobility of Alan Ladd's countenance'. Increasingly the Western needed a greater social relevance to survive, and it travelled further and further from what some saw as its essentials. Will Wright has argued that the 'Professional Plot', which was increasingly associated with the Western of the 1960s and 1970s, reflected the inevitable intrusion of the contemporary world of monopoly capitalism into the world of the Western, finally destroying its code.[18]

In the gangster and *film noir* forms, both of which were to outlive the Western, images of the country play a small but significant role. They form a last, rural retreat for the criminal and misunderstood – in *High Sierra, You Only Live Once, Gun Crazy, The Prowler* and *The Asphalt Jungle.* John Harvey has demonstrated how the narrative of *Out of the Past* (1947) is based on a series of oppositions between the values of the country – the small town where Jeff Bailey (Robert Mitchum) is discovered at the beginning of the film – and those of the city, and of Bailey's past.[19] The values of the country are favoured, but they are no match for the power and energy of the forces that finally reach out for Bailey's soul – and life. It is as if small town values needed to be affirmed, but at the cost of cutting them off from real life.

PROBLEMS OF INTERPRETATION

While at the time, and in recent years, the celebratory and sentimental aspects of Frank Capra's work have been often invoked, a number of critics have drawn attention to pessimistic aspects of the director's vision which, they argue, become more and more insistent in his middle-period films.[20] Capra was born in Palermo and moved to Los Angeles in 1903, at the age of six. He began making films in 1921, and by 1934, when *It Happened One Night* scooped five Academy Awards, including best film and best direction, the director had played out the myth of the American dream, of upward mobility and success as a result of hard work. Reviewing the first forty years of his life in his autobiography, Capra remembers his own rededication to the task of making films about his adopted country and its people, as a way of saying 'Thanks, America'. Columbia Pictures was a close community that Capra had joined in 1928, when it was a poverty-row studio. Buscombe has argued that the fact that Columbia had no major theatre acquisitions to finance, and that the financial control of the studio was held by a small group including Harry and Jack Cohn and the banker A.H. Giannini, bolstered its independence, and the anti-establishment nature of some of its film product.[21]

Capra became a national celebrity in the later thirties, accepting further 'Best Director' Oscars for *Mr Deeds Goes to Town* in 1936 and *You Can't Take It with You* in 1938. After Pearl Harbor Capra was made a colonel, and appointed to head the US War

Department Documentary Film Unit, producing and at times directing a series of orientation and propaganda films to aid the war effort by explaining the causes of the war, the nature of the enemy and the values and beliefs for which America and its allies stood. After the war Capra returned to commercial film-making, at first in partnership with William Wyler and George Stevens in the independent production company Liberty Films. Yet none of the four feature films he made after the release of *State of the Union*, in 1948, until his retirement in the early sixties had anything like the impact of his earlier films. Capra seemed to lose his feel for his audience, the cinema and American concerns.

To Richard Griffith, the first critic to analyse the social significance of Capra's work, the 'blend of realistic problem and imaginary solution' found in the films 'epitomised the dilemma of the middle-class mind in the New Deal period'. Griffith links Capra's cycle of films not only with popular writers associated with the *Saturday Evening Post* but with all those members of the middle class whose 'sense of property had not been destroyed by the depression', and who expressed 'inchoate opposition to the experiments of the administration'.

Jeffrey Richards identifies these middle-class values articu-lated in Capra's films as those associated with the populist strain in the American political tradition, a strain going back to the Declaration of Independence via the Jeffersonian and Jacksonian movements, with their theme of 'the defence of individualism against the forces of Organisation'. In the thirties, Richards argues, quoting Griffith, the middle class 'stood for the preservation of values already lost'. Richards identifies populist values as self-help, equality of opportunity for each individual, good neighbourliness and leadership by decent men opposed to large-scale government and business, and to intellectuals.[22]

Given the new strength of corporate and government bur-eaucracy in the 1930s, such approaches associate Capra's work of the time, and in particular *Mr Deeds Goes to Town* (1936), with conservative opposition to the New Deal. Raymond Durgnat has seen Capra's position in this film as that of a moderate Republi-can, opposing what were seen as the federal excesses of the 'second New Deal'. Yet while Capra's work of the later 1930s may reflect the middle-class agenda of 'values already lost' – and Capra himself implied that he was a Republican voter

Plate 2: Longfellow Deeds (Gary Cooper) discovers the Depression in *Mr Deeds Goes to Town* (Columbia Pictures, 1936). Reproduced courtesy of BFI Stills, Posters and Designs.

– the films also seem to reflect elements of the broader and more progressive tradition of populism discussed earlier in this chapter.

There seems little evidence that Capra's films were any less popular with supporters of the New Deal, and it is at least possible that the consistent hostility to monopoly capital, and what Dickstein has seen as the 'recurring conspiracy of money and power against the common people', was significant in terms of what audiences 'constructed' from the various ideas on offer. The Roosevelt administration also used the language of the populist tradition, both in the rural iconography and practice of agencies such as the Farm Security Administration and the Rural Electrification Administration, and in the general emphasis both on the notion of 'the people' (taken up by Henry Wallace in the war years), and on the popular mandate of the President (for example against the Supreme Court).[23]

The reviewer for *New Masses* said about *Mr Deeds Goes to Town* that 'no other Hollywood film had an unemployed speak his mind with as much warmth and passion as does the farmer of this film'. Yet Deeds's closing speech – cited by Ronald Reagan in his 1980 campaign as the definitive expression of the notion of voluntarism – perfectly reflects the hero's rejection of the socialist goal of fundamental change.[24] The film dramatises more starkly than in any other Capra film an opposition between the values of small town and city, and favours the morality of the country and the small town. Yet the city's unstated virtue is excitement, both social and personal; Deeds pictures himself in Mandrake Falls talking to an imaginary girl, but in New York – the city of grand palaces without the noblemen – he has a real girl friend and comes to greater self-knowledge.

If *Mr Deeds Goes to Town* provides a strong case for the populist thesis with its sympathy for the masses and its advocacy of self-help, good neighbourliness and moral regeneration rather than structural change, then consideration of *Mr Smith Goes to Washington* (1939) requires assessment of the complicating involvement of the left-wing writer Sidney Buchman. (Buchman was uniquely close to Harry Cohn at Columbia Pictures from 1934 until the early 1950s, when he was blacklisted, following his refusal to provide the House Committee with names; in his 1951 testimony he admitted membership of the Communist Party from 1938 to 1945.)[25] Buchman provides a cynical portrayal of Congressional politics as the backdrop to Capra's, and James Stewart's, affirmative, and ultimately victorious, innocence and patriotic idealism. The analysis is more sophisticated, particularly concerning the power of media and business interests over politics in the Congress. In addition, the triumph of the small-town hero is in the later film only achieved by an unlikely plot device inside the last five minutes of the film.

Raymond Carney has produced what is by far the most detailed analysis of Capra's film work, and his perspective involves the rejection of populist interpretations, and sees the films as implicitly critical of 'all ideological and social structurings of experience'. Instead Carney sees an internal vision of individualism as crucial to the understanding of the key films of Capra's middle period (between 1936 and 1948); more than any particular social doctrine Carney sees the articulation of a personal attempt to resist the frustrations of social and institutional life and to defeat and overcome them by the public assertion of an internal vision. To Carney the content of this vision is less important than its existence. When Capra's heroes no longer fight back against the dominant bureaucratic engagements and ideological discourses of the time, the films themselves lose their originality and appeal.

Carney rejects sociological explanations for the themes in Capra's classic films; to him they are fictional explorations into the constraints that any society places on the individual imagination. The pessimistic vision of materialism in *It's a Wonderful Life* – and implicitly in other films – is seen as less central to Capra's art than the existential plight of the individual, trying to keep hold of a private vision while recognising society as it is. *It's a Wonderful Life* – although it was not seen as such at the time – has the pessimism of Arthur Miller's outlook of the same time, together with Capra's own affirmative vision. It is difficult to see how this vision can be separated from its social implications, however, and from Capra's perception of the constraints imposed on his hero by small-town capitalism on the one hand and his sense of social responsibility on the other.

It seems that there is less distance between sociological and transcendentalist interpretations than might be supposed. Carney sees Capra as an artist in the American romantic tradition – as well as in the Hollywood narrative tradition – who tells stories to express an internal imaginative vision, a vision which in part reflects the director's own battle for self-realisation and self-expression in the Hollywood culture industry. To James D. Hart the most profound and comprehensive ideal of romanticism is 'the vision of a greater personal freedom for the individual'. The two interpretations agree on much of the content of Capra's central films: the emphasis, for example, in *Mr Smith Goes to Washington*, *Meet John Doe* and *State of the Union* on the overwhelming forces of centralised control and manipulation bearing down on the individual. Capra's analysis – which Carney sees in terms of deconstruction – could equally well be described in the terminology of neo-Marxist theorists such as Marcuse or Althusser. In *State of the Union* the public world of organisation and manipulation extends to the individual's family and home.

Yet in terms of these films, and *Mr Deeds Goes to Town*, Carney makes no sociological connection – as Richards does – between the content of the hero's vision and social ideas and forces in American society. He seems either to deny the sociological meaning in films, or to downplay its importance compared to the meaning that relates to Capra's place in an American romantic pantheon beginning with William James and Emerson. Nor does Carney ignore the problems of individual authorship of industrial products such as motion pictures of that time. He admits that others may contribute meanings – for example in discussing the radicalising effect on Capra's work of the collaboration with Sidney Buchman in 1938. But Carney does not go far down this line of thinking, as it would lead him to notions of the social generation of meaning in feature films. He says nothing of the effect of box office, for example, and little of the constraints of studio production.[26]

In part this difference of reading reflects the specialism of contemporary professional criticism. Richards writes as a social historian, Carney is a student of literary meanings. Carney admits the public as an essential realm in Capra's films, but he sees it only as a foil to what really matters – the artist's own imaginative vision. If one accepts Carney's auteurial/ deconstructionist method, where does that leave other recurring themes in Capra's key films: in particular the dominance of materialism, and the economic control of politics. These meanings *were* seen at the time, and this is why Capra's films were so popular with the left. When is social meaning essentially background to an auteur's vision (itself a combination of conscious, unconscious and myriad notions and meanings related to the inevitably collective and industrial construction/production of such film) and when does it constitute social meaning independently of that vision? Is capitalism in *It's a Wonderful Life*, or politics in the other films under discussion, foreground or background?

The alternative tradition of interpretation does see Capra's films as having political significance. Some see the key films as populist, and link this ideology to the concerns and values of a particular section of American society at the time – namely the lower middle classes. There are two questions here: first, do the films reflect populist ideology, and what was and is the nature and status of this ideology in the United States at the time; and secondly, what function was played by the articulation of this ideology in popular film.

Richards' work on Capra has been as influential as it has been in part because it fits into several broad perspectives; he sees a coherent political philosophy where Carney sees only a fictional context for Capra's discussion of essentially existential problems of identity and expression. The perception of Capra as a populist director is convincing both to those who see an absence of class politics in America – so that particular strands of Jeffersonian democratic philosophy are invoked in order to criticise the actual practice of the American social system – and to those who see middle-class ideology as represented by the mass media, and who relate the meanings in Capra's films to the broad interests of capital. (Another example of the latter form of interpretation would be the *Cahiers du Cinéma* reading of John Ford's *Young Mr Lincoln*.)[27]

The individual vision in Capra's films is so often expressed in terms of a social and political context, and is so often seen to be inspired by key texts and symbols relating to particular political traditions in America, that it seems perverse not to embrace this aspect of their meaning. Whether this meaning is populist precisely, and whether it means much to label it as such, is another question. Capra's heroes are indeed from small-town America, and in *Deeds* and *Smith* their solutions are certainly populist in spirit, although the boys' camp plan in the later film seems more a plot device than an integral part of Smith's vision. Another aspect of populist rhetoric, the critique of money power, is certainly reflected in the films, but this might in part reflect a wider set of attitudes of the time (including that of Popular Front groups), and, in addition, the analysis of money is a good deal more ideologically sophisticated – with its emphasis on the relationships between corporate, media and political power – than the traditional populist critique of moral conspiracy.

Capra's key films do articulate a number of principles central to the democratic – rather than liberal – commitments of the early American polity. There is also the criticism of urban and corporate power, matching the perspective of Populists of the late nineteenth century. It is also true that these values were 'already lost' in the 1930s in the sense that the New Deal represented the beginning of big government, the recognition by government of the legitimacy of corporate and labour power, and the consultation of intellectual opinion. Against these forces the poetry of Capra's hero stands little chance, and in *Mr Smith Goes to Washington* Smith's 'lost cause' is saved only by an unlikely denouement. Only in fantasy – in *Lost Horizon* – is Capra's utopian vision, of a happy, co-operative community, made manifest.

If the two films of the 1930s combined personal/public vision and social critique within a variation of the 'comedy of reconciliation' form popular at the time, the films of the 1940s seem even less to privilege the co-operative vision over the dominant materialist forms and discourses. In *Meet John Doe* the analysis of economic power is really only balanced by the thoughts of a character already dead, and the emphasis, as in *Mr Smith*, is on the expropriation of public groups and institutions by unaccountable private interests. Radicals from Abraham Polonsky to Herbert Biberman recognise the social content in Capra's films of the period from the mid 1930s to the late 1940s.[28] Like Ford, Capra uses the Hollywood conventions and forms to suggest his own feelings about the individual in America; he accepts capitalism and materialism, but he shows how difficult these pervasive forces make it for the individual, privately and publicly. Carney sees the ending of *It's a Wonderful Life* not in terms of the happy ending that has contributed to the film's image as the epitome of Capra-corn but as an expression of George Bailey's 'moderate alienation' from American small-town life. Capra pays homage to an American icon, but he is too honest to suggest that in practice it is any utopia.

MR DEEDS AND MR SMITH

In *Mr Deeds Goes to Town* financial elites use the law in an attempt to prevent Deeds giving his fortune to farmers who are willing to help themselves. In *Mr Smith Goes to Washington*, Smith introduces his own bill, and writer Sidney Buchman also supplies Claude Rains with a brief speech in which he defends the shoddy compromises of politics as sometimes necessary to the other, beneficial aspects of his work as a senator. Politics is most often portrayed as either manipulated or corrupt; the notion of the politician is viewed sceptically, reflecting the plebiscitary element of the populist outlook.

Mr Deeds Goes to Town (1936) was the first of the series of Capra films dealing with social issues. In what has been called 'the most stridently populist of nations', Capra's post-1936 films echoed, if not the concerns and politics of the Populists of the end of the nineteenth century, the more general populist features of American culture.[29] The 1936 film raises the problem of unemployment, but this issue is not the subject of the film, nor is it integrated into the central opposition of the film's narrative, that between Longfellow Deeds, and the values he stands for, and the finance and culture of the city. There is no populist social movement in *Mr Deeds*, and if anything the final trial scene suggests the Hofstadter/Bell perspective of the illiberal tendencies exhibited by populist leaders and masses. Deeds's values are activated only when he encounters an unemployed farmer and is shocked into social responsibility. His response is to assert his right to practise good neighbourliness and encourage self-help by giving his fortune to several thousand unemployed farmers. In his speech to the sanity hearing – the speech quoted by Ronald Reagan in 1980 – Deeds comes nearest to a coherent social statement; accepting that there will always be inequality in society, he argues that those who are more successful should help those who are struggling – as long as the latter are genuinely trying to improve themselves. Deeds in no sense responds to collective action by farmers, only to the one farmer who is driven by his circumstances to threaten him with a gun; only when Deeds decides that the farmer is not a 'moocher' does he decide to help him, and those like him.

There is no pretence that Deeds' action 'solves' the Depression. While the private nature of Deeds' decision, together with Cedar's reference to the effects on the 'governmental system', have been interpreted as representing a moderate Republican, anti-New Deal position, this seems to put too much emphasis on what is really part of the film's plot mechanism rather than a central element of its meaning. The film in no sense endorses the Hoover principle that the acceptance of Federal money by the unemployed undermines their self-respect.[30] Opinion on the Works Progress Administration, which came into being in 1935, and which was also designed to help the unemployed by giving them work, was at the time divided, but it seems easier to read the film as broadly sympathetic to – and in some sense a metaphor for – the humanitarian ideals of Roosevelt's policies than as making a critical point about the 'second New Deal'. Certainly the communist press did not interpret the film as critical of the New Deal; the *Daily Worker*, for example, praised the film.[31] (The contemporary schemes – admittedly federal – to provide low interest loans to farmers' cooperatives for the purpose of building power lines, seem in general harmony with the Deeds plan.) In addition, had Capra intended to make a critical point about current administration policy, it is difficult to believe that he would have allowed Deeds' New York mansion, from where he dispenses his fortune, to resemble so closely the architectural layout of the White House.

In terms of American political tradition and what has been called its 'ideological project', it is Deeds' pilgrimage to see Grant's tomb that is most central.[32] Here Deeds tells Saunders that only in 'a country like America' could a small Ohio farm boy become a great soldier, and then president. Gary Cooper perfectly expresses the mixture of innocence and rugged individualism that Deeds brings to the world of the city. Quoting Thoreau, he remarks that New York has grand palaces without the noblemen to put in them. Capra's film in no sense challenges capitalism, but endorses a humane, and human, practice of it; Saunders and Deeds discover the similarity of their small-town roots, and the Deeds spell works on Saunders' opportunism and cynicism, while undermining her independence. Capra votes for a 'kinder and gentler America' – at least for those who are deserving – while endorsing both the economic system and the political tradition.

Many of the elements of *Mr Deeds* are repeated in *Mr Smith Goes to Washington* (1939), but the latter film uses its explicitly political locale to explore much further into the nature of power. James Stewart is another innocent, although he is a less convincing man of the west than Gary Cooper, and seems too diffident to put out forest fires single-handed. Innocence is suggested not only by the hero's idealist vision of American political values, but also by the role played by children in the film. Through montages the key relationships that make up the power structure are sketched, and although this structure is of power at the state level, the spectator is often reminded of the fact that Paine – and more crucially Taylor – have their eyes on the White House. From the beginning 'Youth Leader' Smith is viewed as a man of nature (an expert on wild game and animals) and as a patriot who can recite from Lincoln, Washington and Jefferson, but it is on the train journey to the capital that the nature of the film's hero is revealed. (The scene was apparently written by Capra himself.)[33] Smith's father was a 'champion of lost causes' who – as a publisher and editor of an independent newspaper – took on a mining syndicate on behalf of 'one small miner who stuck to his claim'. Had this film been made at Warners, Clayton Smith's death – shot in the back because he stood up to the syndicate – would have left its marks on his son. But, defying psychological truth, Jefferson Smith is – at this stage of the film – totally without bitterness, and he brings to Washington both a naivety and a shining vision of the American constitution. Into his bill he tries to put the 'Capitol dome', and the fight is on between reality and the individual's own vision and resources.

Sidney Buchman's contribution to the film has already been mentioned. In the later *Talk of the Town* (Columbia, 1942) the story also concerns the nature of American democracy. Professor Lightcap specialises in the principles of law but needs to be humanised – and not only by the ubiquitous Jean Arthur. Only when Lightcap recognises his own social obligations – acting outside the law to rectify an injustice done to his friend – is he fit to take his place on the Supreme Court bench.

Reflecting in part Buchman's concerns, *Mr Smith Goes to Washington* is more explicitly *about* American society than *Mr Deeds*. While the later film is more sentimental, with its smiling page boys, and with Jean Arthur's conversion less convincing and motivated than before, it reflects Capra's passion more powerfully through Stewart's performance. Further, and in part because of Buchman's involvement, the mechanisms of power are given greater detail and weight. There is even a defence of compromise and of its importance to the politician's art. When Smith discovers that his hero, Senator Paine, the fighter for lost causes alongside his father, has been taking Taylor's advice on how to vote for twenty years, he goes to see him in his Senate office. Paine tells him that he has been living in a boy's world, and that he ought to stay there; 'This is a man's world, Jeff, and you've got to check your ideals outside the door like you do your rubbers.' Paine defends his years of compromise – 'so that all those years I could sit in that Senate and serve the people in a thousand honest ways'. He defends his work in helping his state secure the lowest unemployment and the highest federal grants: '. . . but, well I've had to compromise, I've had to play ball. You can't count on people voting – half the time they don't vote anyway. That's how states and empires have been built since time began, don't you understand.'

Paine's dialogue is interesting because it cuts across the main drive of the film, the belief that the 'innocent' ideals of American democracy must and can be applied to the adult and real world of American politics. The realist discourse seems to triumph when Smith is accused of corruption and is discredited, even in the eyes of children. He makes one final, despairing visit to the Lincoln Memorial before intending to return to his boy's world, 'away from the words, and the monuments and the whole rotten show', but Saunders convinces him to make a final rally for his beliefs. She tells Smith, referring to Lincoln's example, that 'all the good that ever came into this world came from fools with faith like that'. Appealing to his faith in 'plain, decent, everyday common rightness', she inspires Smith to his final effort, his filibuster speech.

Lincoln is invoked as a sacred presence to inspire Smith's passionate last effort, but the forces of reality are still strong, and, as has been pointed out, Smith is again reduced to despair, to denying his beliefs, before Paine's last-minute *volte-face* gives the film its 'happy ending'. The film portrays a dialectic between American ideals and reality in which, for the hero, echoing the British amateur sporting ethic, it is the 'taking part' that is most important. Capra's vision cannot be divorced from his experience of and concern for the public realm. Capra's idealism – his affirmation of what he sees as the rational, or at least the ideal, over the 'real' – is as political as that of Herbert Marcuse, who made the same distinction central to his own work in the 1960s. (Marcuse, in his critique of American society in the mid-1960s, argued that the 'assimilation of the ideal with reality testifies to the extent to which the ideal has been surpassed'.) The distinction between ideas and reality in American politics also recurs in the 'Why We Fight' series of films that Capra supervised and often directed during the war years for the US Government. In *War Comes to America* (1945), for which Capra claims to have written the script, the commentary talks of Americans fighting both for a country and for an idea: 'The idea bigger than the country – without the idea the country might have remained only a wilderness, without the country the idea might have remained only a dream.'[34] In the wartime propaganda film no contradiction is intended between idea and country; in *Mr Smith Goes to Washington* the gap between ideal and performance is the crux of the film.

Social meaning was quickly thrust upon the film after its high-profile first showing for senators; while Washington insiders were hostile, critics and moguls defended the film, which a recent writer has seen as part of Hollywood's contribution to the 'renewal of national political sentiment' at the time.[35] In *Mr Smith Goes to Washington* Capra moved from the rather flat villains of the earlier film to a greater analysis of the penetration of political by economic power. The ideals of American democracy are associated with that icon of thirties documentary literature and culture, the common man and woman, but the narrative revolves around a particular representative of 'the people', the middle-class man as an innocent abroad. While agrarian and small-town values are preferred to those of the metropolis, and the emphasis is on morality rather than ideology, neither film allows a contemplation of collective action for change or permits within the narrative of the film any challenge to the key economic structure.

CAPRA AND THE FORTIES

In the later films the personal vision disappears or is watered down, and the individual vision is incorporated into the normal politics of corporate America. While Capra gives us his personal vision in *It's a Wonderful Life* (1946), in *Meet John Doe* (1941) and *State of the Union* (1948) there is not even a rhetorical victory for the values of good neighbourliness. In the 1941 film there is no individual vision – other than a final refusal to be used – while in Capra's last major film the worlds of vision and of power are separated. Capra's films exhibit a belief in the manipulative power of the mass media that the new post-war students of the media and politics were beginning, in what was to be the conventional wisdom for twenty years, to deny. Just after being asked to make the wartime 'Why We Fight' series of films, Capra had been shown *Triumph of the Will*, and he later recorded that the film was 'lethal' as a propaganda weapon.[36]

Capra began the 1940s aware of his reputation for Capra-corn, and this image may have distracted audiences from the cutting edges of his 1930s films. The sentiment, the screwball romance and Capra's speciality, the reaction shots of authority figures, all help to reassure audiences that happy endings are in sight. For their next project Capra and Robert Riskin established an independent company, and they attempted a harder, more realistic product that would convince critics as well as audiences. The film, *Meet John Doe* (1941), originally announced as 'The Life and Death of John Doe', was made on the Warner Bros lot, but was substantially financed by a Bank of America advance to Frank Capra Productions.[37]

In Capra's films of the 1940s his heroes are undefeated, but hardly victorious. *Meet John Doe* deals with the making of American myths and, as Carney suggests, it prefigures the age of the media event. Long John Willoughby (Gary Cooper), the hobo hired by tycoon and mass communications baron D.B. Norton (Edward Arnold, expanding his role in *Mr Smith Goes to Washington*), is a passive symbol of a movement of social clubs on which Norton intends to base his authoritarian political ambitions. When Willoughby realises his role as a stooge in the Norton operation he tries to speak up, but, at a political convention designed to launch a John Doe party, he is pre-vented from doing so by strong-arm tactics. Capra testified to disliking crowds, and his treatment of the convention indicates his fears that the masses could easily be swayed. Capra and Riskin at no point agreed on an ending to the film, and several endings were filmed. In one of the endings that was filmed but not used Willoughby does commit suicide, in line with the working title of the project; to Capra it was a powerful ending, but 'you just can't kill Gary Cooper'.[38] In the ending that was finally selected the despairing Willoughby/Doe, threatening to deliver on his promise to commit suicide on Christmas Day by throwing himself from the top of City Hall, is persuaded not to do so by a group of members of John Doe clubs who suggest that the movement can have a new life, separate from Norton.

Meet John Doe was Capra and Riskin's distinctive contribution to the pre-war cycle of films relating to the international threat of fascism. It was influenced by what Capra saw as the emergence of little 'Führers' in America.[39] Yet the film drew on elements of the Capra formula. Norton is not only a nascent fascist, but the basis of his economic and ideological power is made clear. (There is no humanisation of the Edward Arnold character, as occurs in *You Can't Take It with You*.) The John Doe clubs offer good neighbourliness, and a private employment service that takes people off relief, but they are all based on a lie – that John Doe is a real person. The small town is no longer insulated from mass culture as it seemed to be in *Mr Deeds Goes to Town*, something that in real life owed much to the national impact of the cinema itself. Denied a leader at the convention the people seem to turn into a mob. Willoughby is a cipher who never finds an authentic vision, and cannot even commit suicide because Norton's men will, in the tradition of totalitarian leaders of the era, cover up the tracks. The Capra protagonist does find a dignity and independence, a realisation of the implications of his passive and self-interested performance, but the indication at the end of the film that the people are similarly made aware carries little weight. The last words of the film, 'There you are, Norton. The people. Try and lick that', do not really put to rest the doubts raised by the film. The problem, however, concerns the extent to which Capra and Riskin are complicit in the phenomenon they describe, and warn Americans about. There seems to be no role for an authentic politics in the film, apart from the moralistic 'John Doe' clubs, which seem so dependent on their leader that they are hardly distinguishable from the threatening totalitarianism of the Norton junta.

To Andrew Sarris *Meet John Doe* showed Frank Capra crossing the line between 'populist sentimentality' and 'populist demagoguery', while Richard Corliss identified Robert Riskin with 'populist demagoguery', and Sidney Buchman with 'democratic republicanism'. Riskin had been one of the primary founders of

Screen Playwrights, the organisation formed in 1936 to oppose the Screen Writers Guild; in his writing his conception of politics seems limited. In *Mr Deeds* there is no politics beyond the implicit threat that the assembled farmers represent at the sanity hearing. Herbert Biberman, reviewing *Meet John Doe* for *New Masses* at the time, criticised Capra for the tendency that he detected in the film – and to some extent in *You Can't Take It with You* – for politics to be seen as of no use and for 'unpolitical organised neighbourliness' to take over.[40] Certainly, as already discussed, the most sophisticated treatment of politics appears in *Mr Smith Goes to Washington*, and it is in this film that the grass-roots support for Capra's protagonist is demonstrated, inadequate as it is to defeat the power of the machine. In *Magic Town* (1947), which Riskin wrote and produced, there is again little sense of local politics as something independent of the manipulations of a 'leader' from out of town.

In *Meet John Doe* and *State of the Union* the individual victory is muted or non-existent. In *It's a Wonderful Life*, Capra's first Liberty production, the director examines a small town from which a 'hero' never departs. Instead of inheriting a fortune or taking on a political office, the protagonist lives a life of constraint and frustration. George Bailey's life is powerfully affirmed as 'wonderful' in a seven-minute happy ending to end all happy endings, but what has gone before indicates a life that has fallen far short of Bailey's greatest and best hopes. As Robert Sklar points out, the life of George Bailey was really only 'wonderful' in contrast to the double hell – revealed to us by the angel Clarence – of Bedford Falls as it would have been had Bailey not been born. The 'happy ending' strengthened the stereotype of Capra as an archetypal old Hollywood director, dispenser of dreams, but the darker vision is surely there for all to see. As Ray argues, it was the glimpse of the 'utter emptiness of American life that remained despite the film's happy ending'.[41] For this or other reasons the returns at the box office were disappointing.

Packed with contemporary references, and adapted by Anthony Veiller and Myles Connelly from a play, *State of the Union* (1948), was Capra's second and final film for Liberty. Again, Capra's hero is manipulated, and he finally chooses defeat rather than be complicit in the 'new politics' and the fabrication of his image. When the doctoring of his real personality also spreads to his home, he draws the line. That businessman Grant Matthews (Spencer Tracy) has a vision seems more significant than the nature of that vision – an amalgam of traditional Capra motifs, a distrust of the key intermediate institutions of business and labour, and some internationalist ideas. The last of Capra's important films, it is consistent with the rest of the films of his central period in its picture of ideological controls on the individual.

To Capra *State of the Union* was 'my last Frank Capra film, my last burst of autumn colours before the winter of artistic slavery to the major studio hierarchy at Paramount Pictures'. Capra's two post-war films perhaps mark the end of the great hopes and dreams of the 1930s. What is left at the end of both films looks suspiciously like defeat, and resignation. Capra also reported a campaign of innuendo against his political affiliations which began while he was making *State of the Union*. (The film starred Katharine Hepburn and Adolphe Menjou; in the year the film was made Hepburn had spoken to a rally on behalf of Henry Wallace, while Menjou had been one of the most conservative of the friendly witnesses to testify to the House Committee on Un-American Activities.) The innuendo led in 1951 to Capra being vetoed for a Defense Department assignment, and to John Ford writing to the department on his behalf.[42]

In retrospect there seemed to be little scope in Capra's formula for further development, although the political accusations, which took two years to dismiss, and the feeling that the ending of Liberty represented a failure of courage, hardly encouraged him to try to seek new public metaphors for his feelings about the individual and society. In the light of the House investigation and the blacklist, the studios were likely to look suspiciously at ideas that could be construed as critical of existing institutions and 'normal politics', whether they were intended as such or not.

Capra's path continued to cross with those of liberal and left writers. At RKO Dalton Trumbo and Clifford Odets had worked on the script for what would become *It's a Wonderful Life*, before Liberty purchased the original story, and the scripts, in September 1945. Only a small section of the Odets script survived in the final script, on which Michael Wilson also claimed to have worked. The final credits for the script were given to the liberal Jo Swerling, to Capra himself, and to the team of Frances Goodrich and Albert Hackett. Late in the 1950s Harry Cohn contemplated Capra as a director for Clifford Odets' major, doomed project, *Joseph and His Brethren*.[43]

One of the objectives of the House Committee was to associate the popular culture of the Popular Front, and of anti-fascism, with the apparent threat of communism. In early 1948 William Wyler commented that a film such as *The Grapes of Wrath* could no longer be made, and a writer talked of the difficulty of making Westerns given that staple elements of their plots, including foreclosing bankers, were no longer acceptable. Capra's analysis of corrupt elites, however disguised by happy endings, seemed less welcome in the emerging age of the military industrial complex. Warners lost faith in the common man, while some left writers such as Albert Maltz, whose contributions to *Mildred Pierce* (largely unused in the completed film) and *The Naked City* had a broadly populist slant, became victims of the blacklist. The breakup of the Popular Front and the emergence of anti-communism as the central issue of the times, further discouraged such motifs. Affirming the system by criticising it was a strategy that was decreasingly favoured by post-war circumstances. To Ceplair and Englund the films of the 1950s displayed little of the 'populist spirit' that had been evident in 'the most notable thirties and forties films'.[44]

By the 1950s the notion of the regeneration of corrupt elites by the spirit of the people was seen by 'vital center' liberals as dangerous to the fabric of liberal democracy. Such liberals were instead to put their faith in the value of elites, and in the checking of popular passion by the proximate concerns of multiple group involvement. (Capra's *Meet John Doe* seems, unconsciously on the director's part, to dramatise the assumed danger of a politics without strong intermediate institutions, including parties and pressure groups.) Capra's formula was one that was suspicious of elites, and of the 'normal politics' of parties and pressure groups; by the 1950s these were seen as central to the American system. (Did not a politics of morality and passion threaten to sweep up the masses in a movement that might endanger institutions which guaranteed American liberties?) While the 'visions' in Capra's films contain right- and left-wing elements, and the contradictions inherent in populism, his work was often seen as part of the Popular Front consensus of the late 1930s, and of the war years. By 1950 it was Joseph

McCarthy who used a form of populist rhetoric as part of his anti-communist campaign. The ideological context of Capra's formula had been passed by.

To Carney the 'crisis that effectively concludes Capra's career is that he becomes unable to maintain his earlier belief in the expressive power of the individual'.[45] Yet Carney's detailed explorations into the structures of Capra's films seem compatible with, and even demand, a more social interpretation. This chapter has suggested the linking of Capra's work not only to a broad and contradictory populist tradition, but also to the dominant political currents of the time. The post-war decline of 'populist' cinema seems to provide some evidence of its political and 'public' significance. Capra's individualism was surely always related to social responsibilities, and the recurring vision of his middle-period films seems concerned with the social constraints on what Odets saw as the 'human possibilities'.

Chapter 3

Liberals, radicals and the wartime agenda

HOLLYWOOD AND THE COMING OF WAR

Whereas the studios were used to working within the framework of the Production Code, they generally saw this as essential in warning off political interference at the national or state level. The very apolitical nature of the Hollywood product – the much-expressed distaste for sending messages – was seen as the guarantee of the continued autonomy of the studios from government. Yet the right of the film industry to be left alone was already being challenged prior to Pearl Harbor, while international and national factors were beginning to inch the industry towards an interest in politics as a film subject.

The monopoly conditions of film production had caused concern in Washington at various times in the 1930s; the five major companies owned the first-run theatres in the largest cities, and various interests persisted in their attempts to outlaw practices – such as block-booking – which perpetuated their control over the market. It was in 1938 that the antitrust division of the Department of Justice made its move, beginning court proceedings against the major companies under the Sherman Antitrust Act. This legal move led to an agreement in 1940 which preserved the status quo, as far as the fusion of production and exhibition was concerned, in exchange for limited concessions by the companies.[1]

The sociology of Hollywood had changed considerably in the late 1930s, in particular with the period of the politicisation and unionisation of studio personnel, especially writers. Yet despite the intense political activity in Hollywood, the interest of the studios in the march of fascism in Europe as a subject for their films only increased in direct proportion to the closing of foreign markets to American film product. With *Confessions of a Nazi Spy* (April 1939), made by Warners in the face of disapproval from the Breen Office, and over a year before Germany banned American films, the gates began to open to films which dealt with the European war. Co-writer John Wexley, together with the European émigrés involved in the project, saw the idea in terms of educating the public about the threat of pro-Nazi organisations in America. The same year Fred Zinnemann, hired by MGM in 1937, was the director of a 'Crime Does Not Pay' one reeler that dealt with espionage in America directed from outside, and implicitly from Nazi Germany.

In 1940 a number of anti-Nazi films were released, most notably *Foreign Correspondent* and *The Great Dictator*, in August and October. At a time when, from the summer of 1940, Edward R. Murrow's radio accounts of the London blitz were making such an impact, *Foreign Correspondent* and *Arise My Love* both used stories of American journalists in Europe to urge greater awareness and preparedness on the American public. *Foreign Correspondent*, directed by Alfred Hitchcock for Walter Wanger, is a comedy thriller; the plot revolves around the kidnapped head of a 'European Peace Party' and a secret treaty clause – a classic MacGuffin which allows the director to concentrate on the set piece scenes and ideas that interested him. The speech at the end of the film, in which Joel McCrea (as Huntley Haverstock) broadcasts to America from a London suffering its first air-raid, was written by Ben Hecht at the particular urging of independent producer and liberal activist Wanger. Haverstock calls on Americans to rearm, and to 'hang on to your lights' as death and darkness come to London.[2] *Arise My Love* (November 1940) is a Paramount romantic comedy in which two individuals, played by Ray Milland and Claudette Colbert, find themselves in Europe – he because he volunteered to fight in Spain, she out of journalistic ambition. They fall in love before deciding that their obligations to the war are more immediate than those to each other. Without breaking the rather unreal world of Paramount romance – including the romance of newspapers and of war – the film does introduce the notion of how most Americans (and perhaps particularly the middle classes) are lucky to be cut off from the miseries and responsibilities of the Europe of the time. Thus after drinking a toast of farewell to their roles as the 'crusader' and the 'career woman' on a ship bound for the safety of America, a sudden torpedo attack sets off the events that lead them to return to the fight, first in Europe, and then in America.

The most well-known of the political films of 1940 was *The Great Dictator*, released in October, in which Charlie Chaplin not only laughed at the fascist leaders but stepped out of character to make a closing speech in support of a better world. In the body of the film Chaplin plays both the Hitler figure, Hynkel, and the poor barber who, with the other ghetto Jews, is terrorised by storm troopers. At the end of the film, in a case of mistaken identity, the barber gets to give the formal address to the soldiers instead of Hynkel. In the three-and-a-half minute speech Chaplin blames greed for poisoning men's souls, and calls on everyone to unite in the name of democracy to fight for a new, decent and free world. Much less prominent was *Three Faces West*, directed by Bernard Vorhaus at Republic Studios in the same year. The film deals with two groups of refugees, a doctor and his daughter in retreat from European fascism and a community of farmers suffering from the ravages of the American Dust Bowl. The marriage that ends the film combines the themes of anti-fascism, New Dealism and the populist spirit of the Joads.

The Dies Committee conducted hearings in the summer of 1940, finally clearing a number of prominent stars from suspicion of being sympathetic with the Communist movement. The next year the increased flow of pro-intervention pictures led to furious complaints from isolationist Congressmen that Hollywood was creating war hysteria and producing propaganda in support of those who wanted a stronger American involvement in the European war. In 1941 Warners released the enormously popular *Sergeant York*, while Twentieth Century-Fox released *A Yank in the RAF* and *Man Hunt*, two films that 'called unambiguously for American involvement'. Lowell Mellett noted in March 1941 that 'Hollywood patriotism could be attributed in part to the industry's fears about the Justice Department's anti-trust suit'. But the vogue for Americanism led in 1941 to what a recent study of wartime American films has called 'a steady, one-sided dose of interventionist propaganda in various guises'.

A subcommittee of the Interstate Commerce Committee held

hearings on a resolution that combined the issues of propaganda in motion pictures and that of monopoly in the motion picture business. Isolationists attacked Hollywood's role in supporting what they saw as Roosevelt's interventionist policies, while Harry Warner and Darryl F. Zanuck, as well as the attorney for the studios Wendell Willkie, defended the industry. In part the key members of the subcommittee were discredited by their anti-Semitism and lack of knowledge about the films concerned, and the hearings were abandoned following Pearl Harbor. The argument of Koppes and Black that the 'oligopolistic structure of the movie industry produced a monolithic political product' raises questions about what isolationist films would have looked like in 1941 – as distinct from apolitical films – and who, under whatever industrial structure, would have produced them.[3]

WRITERS AND DIRECTORS: POLITICAL PARABLES

The period of the Nazi–Soviet pact seemed to have little impact on the enthusiasm of Communist writers to contribute to anti-Nazi films. John Howard Lawson, chairman of the Hollywood Party, produced a strongly anti-fascist script for Fox's *Four Sons* in 1940, while Robert Rossen worked on two parables of resistance to autocratic power during that period. In *Four Sons* the emphasis is on the sombre story of a Czech mother who suffers from the effects of the Nazi Party, and who finally starts life again in America with her only surviving son.[4]

Edward G. Robinson said of his role in *The Sea Wolf* (1941) that the character he played – the tyrannical captain Wolf Larsen – 'was a Nazi in everything but name'. The Jack London novel, the rights to which had been purchased by Warners in 1937, has been viewed as part of the first wave of London's attack on American capitalism; in the book the story is told by Humphrey Van Weyden, a gentleman writer who accidentally finds himself aboard Larsen's boat, and the mood of his account is captured by his remark that 'Life had always seemed a particularly sacred thing, but here it counted for nothing, was a cipher in the arithmetic of commerce.' After several abortive outlines had been written, and after John Wexley had turned the assignment down, Robert Rossen was given the task of producing a new version in mid-1940, and by building up a minor character in the novel he introduced a familiar Warners motif of the social fugitive, a character played by Rossen's friend and collaborator at Warners, John Garfield. Leach (Garfield) is on the run from the police in San Francisco, and his struggle displaces the novel's emphasis on a Hobbesian war of all against all on board the *Ghost*. Leach tells Ruth (Ida Lupino), who Rossen has also made a fugitive from justice, that they are both struggling for dignity, and that 'There's a price no man will pay to keep on living.' Thus the story becomes a parable of the struggle of the nobodies of society for survival and dignity in an enclosed world dominated – in the tradition of mutiny-at-sea stories – by an autocratic captain.[5]

The Sea Wolf illustrates Warners' disciplined style of film-making. The director Michael Curtiz had been at the studio since 1926 after working in Hungary, Germany and Austria. The art director Anton Grot had been at Warners since 1927, and in 1940 he had created a machine – used first in making *The Sea Hawk* – to create weather and light effects on water within a studio tank. The ripple machine contributes to the enclosed feeling that the film has, and to the effectiveness of the lighting. The visual style of the film reflects Wolf Larsen's preference for an enclosed world in which he can 'reign secure' – studio effects, including fog and angled photography, enhance the feeling of a world without escape. The film is opened out to some extent by Rossen's writing for John Garfield and Lupino, and by their intense performances, bringing into the film feelings of helplessness associated with the Depression years, and a sense of optimism and struggle – class struggle rather than London's emphasis on social darwinism – reflecting the resistance to fascism. After the revolt against Larsen has failed Leach tells the men that Larsen 'needs you to break your backs for him; maybe someday you'll get wise to that'. (A less sympathetic assessment of *The Sea Wolf* can be found in Nick Roddick's book on Warners in the 1930s.)[6]

Thematically, *The Sea Wolf* can be placed with the other pre-war and wartime films dealing with questions of commitment, and of resistance to evil. In *Casablanca* Rick (Humphrey Bogart) commits himself to a cause that in 1943 America was totally involved in, but in 1940 there was less unanimity about the correct American response to the march of Nazi Germany. The Communist Party of which Rossen was a member had officially abandoned its Popular Front policy following the Nazi–Soviet pact and had joined with conservative isolationists in opposition to American involvement. In *The Sea Wolf* it is the common man, the Depression fugitive, who leads the fight against tyranny; the novel's emphasis on Van Weyden and his struggle with his manhood is replaced by a social feeling that had clear relevance in 1940 and 1941.

Out of the Fog opened in New York a month after *The Sea Wolf*, in June 1941. The Group Theatre play by Irwin Shaw had had its run in 1939, and was then seen as a call for a united front against fascism. In the play two despairing and dignified old men, a Jew and a Greek, are persecuted by a racketeer, before they decide on a plan to fight back. They are successful, but Shaw pointed out in his preface to what he called a 'fairy tale with a moral' that the meek do not always triumph in real life. (A *Motion Picture Herald* review referred to a 'screen foreword' that related the events of the film to contemporary politics, but no such foreword now appears on prints of the film.) The film mixes Odetsian drama – the daughter who dreams of a new life – with elements of the Warners gangster and social outcast genres. Jerry Wald and Richard Macaulay completed a first adaptation and Robert Rossen rewrote the script with John Garfield and Ida Lupino – successes in *The Sea Wolf* – in mind.[7]

At Paramount, Lester Cole fought a losing battle to establish a radical social context to a story that was an amalgam of Southern gothic and social melodrama. Even without evidence from production files it is possible to see the loose ends of the screenwriter's social concerns, articulated more fully in earlier versions of the script, in *Among the Living* (1941). The story concerns twin brothers, sons of a businessman who built up a Southern town 'from a bunch of shanties to what it is today'; John Raden returns for his father's funeral and discovers that his brother Paul is still alive, and – turned mad by his father's tyrannical mistreatment of his mother – has been kept locked up for twenty-five years. The family doctor falsified the death certificate in return for money to develop the 'Dr Benjamin Saunders Medical Foundation', the 'finest free institution of its kind in the south'. Paul escapes and commits two murders, but the audience has some sympathy for the pathetic figure, naively innocent of the passions and prejudices of the townspeople. John Raden and Dr Saunders remain silent about their knowledge of Paul's existence and likely responsibility for the murders, and it is only when Raden agrees to offer a $5,000 reward for the capture of the murderer that Paul is discovered. The climax of the film then turns on a temporary confusion between the twins as a mob of townspeople threaten to lynch the wrong man.

The loose ends suggest a partially obscured social context. Employment in the town revolves around the mills owned by the Raden family, yet they are not open, for reasons that are not explained. We see men standing on street corners and outside the closed mills, and it is tempting to connect this with the 'madness' that overwhelms the town when the reward is announced. Immediately groups of men with guns rush in all directions, and innocent transients – most prominently a black man – are set upon by mobs. There are also references to poverty and race which were apparently more extensive in earlier script drafts. The cinematographer, Theodor Sparkuhl, had worked on several German films in the 1920s, and two scenes – an expressionistic and disorienting view of 'modern' life in a café through the eyes of the newly liberated murderer, and a chase at night – point towards the later *film noir* cycle. In Cole's first draft script John Raden Snr was a German-born Nazi sympathiser who both caused and covered up his son's insanity, but this complicating reference to contemporary events did not appeal to Paramount. While the film also reflects the studio's notion of the horror genre, Cole has left his mark in the half-obscured context of small-town Southern politics.[8]

In May 1942 Warners released *In This Our Life*, John Huston's second film as director, with a script by Howard Koch. Koch was a progressive independent of the Communist Party, although Ceplair and Englund call him a communist in everything but name. A playwright and radio scriptwriter – he was the author of the Orson Welles broadcast of H.G. Wells' *War of the Worlds* – he joined Warners as a scriptwriter on the recommendation of John Huston, in 1939. Koch looks back to the early 1940s in Hollywood as a high point in his life, a time when, with Roosevelt in the White House and 'the Depression in back of us', everything seemed possible. Koch, who was consistently interested in social and topical issues, recalls that he turned down assignments in which he had no interest, and that writers in the early 1940s were 'involved in the struggle against fascism, in whatever form it appeared, and in working for a more democratic society, economically and racially'.[9]

In This Our Life, one of the top Warner Bros box office successes of 1942, was primarily a vehicle for Bette Davis, but here again the director, John Huston, and the screenwriter, Howard Koch, were aware of social nuances in the story, from a Pulitzer Prize-winning novel by Ellen Glasgow. The script revolves around Stanley Timberlake (Bette Davis), one of two daughters of a contemporary Southern family suffering from declining fortunes. While there are again some night-time scenes prefiguring *film noir*, Stanley as played by Davis is a melodramatic 'bad girl' more than a *femme fatale*; she makes her sister's life a misery before killing a child in a hit-and-run car accident and attempting to blame a young black law student, Perry Clay (Ernest Anderson). Clay, whose mother objects to his aspirations to raise himself, stands up for himself and is cleared, before Stanley is herself killed – in a car accident which follows Hays code conventions. Bosley Crowther commented on the frank allusion to racial discrimination, and on the distinctive 'definition of the Negro as an educated and comprehending character'. In 1942 Walter White wrote to Jack Warner – mentioning that he was speaking as well for Wendell Willkie – praising *In This Our Life* as a 'high water mark to date of honest treatment of the Negro as an integral part of the people of America'.[10]

Other radical writers of the time – Sidney Buchman and Ring Lardner Jr – may have deepened the social content of two George Stevens-directed comedies of 1942, although it is difficult to trace their precise contributions. In both these cases the screenwriters use existing conventions but adapt them in ways that seem to reflect their social perspective. At MGM Lardner, a party member since 1936, and Michael Kanin gained approval for their script – which became *Woman of the Year* (1942) – through the good offices of Katharine Hepburn, a friend of Kanin. The script opposed an ambitious woman news journalist and an easy-going male sports reporter, and producer Joseph Mankiewicz brought Hepburn and Spencer Tracy together for the first time on the screen in these roles. The film reverses the usual sexual conventions, with Sam Craig (Tracy) continually waiting for an audience with the careerist Tess Harding (Hepburn). Harding's obsession with work finally

drives Craig to leave her; the climactic and inevitable reconciliation is broadened in the film by the addition of an ending that
Mankiewicz approved in response to a desire for Harding to get
a more dramatic 'comeuppance'. Thus Stevens improvised a
breakfast scene – from an addition to the script by John Lee
Mahin – in which Harding, moved by watching her mother's
wedding ceremony, returns to Craig's house in the early
morning and attempts, and spectacularly fails, to cook breakfast.
Whether or how much this final humiliation of the would-be
independent woman unbalances the feminist thrust of the
Kanin/Lardner script is a matter for debate, although the
dialogue describing the final compromise – in which Harding
agrees to Craig's suggestion that she be not Tess Harding or Mrs
Sam Craig but Tess Harding Craig – is retained from the
original script.[11]

The same year George Stevens also directed, as well as
produced, *The Talk of the Town*, at Columbia, from a screenplay
by Sidney Buchman and Irwin Shaw. Buchman had been a
writer at Columbia since 1934 and a communist since 1938.
Much of the film is set in a house in the country in which a
distinguished law professor, Michael Lightcap (Ronald Colman)
is planning to write a legal treatise. Yet hiding in the same house
is Leopold Dilg (Cary Grant), a 'troublemaker' since childhood
and – as the opening of the film establishes – a man on the run
from prison after being accused of arson. The woman in the
middle is Nora Shelley (Jean Arthur), whose unwitting role –
related to that in her two Capra films – is to effect a compromise
between the natures and principles of the two men. In
the background is a social context in which, contrary to the
professor's constitutional principles, power is concentrated in
the hands of one man. As in Buchman's script for *Mr Smith Goes
to Washington* the reality of power similarly undercuts the high
principles of national democracy, and it takes a 'dreamer' –
Dilg's description of himself – to humanise and rejuvenate the
great principles.

At first Dilg hides his identity by assuming the character of
Joseph, a gardener. 'Joseph' and Lightcap talk, and the dry
intellectual from the city is contrasted to the simple man – with
a biblical name – who, unlike the professor, is a man of the
world. Lightcap is informed that he is to be appointed to the
Supreme Court, thus achieving a lifetime ambition, but this only

increases the pressure on him, as he begins to suspect that Dilg/ Joseph is a victim of injustice. The professor is humanised by a growing attachment to 'Miss Shelley' and along with this development comes a willingness to break the law to save Dilg from a mob incited – in the manner of *They Won't Forget* – to take the law into their own hands. After some increasingly hectic plotting the truth comes out and the professor, now fully humanised by his efforts as investigator, takes up his seat in Washington, talking of the need for the law to be 'engraved on our hearts' and leaving Dilg and Shelley to return to Sweetbrook.

In This Our Life was John Huston's second film as director, following the success of his first, *The Maltese Falcon*, in 1941. During the pre-war period and the war years a number of the New York group discussed earlier began their Hollywood directing careers. Jules Dassin began as an observer at RKO in 1940, before rather fortuitously making a short film at MGM, and so graduating to feature films. Joseph Losey spent two years at MGM in the late war years, contributing one of the 'Crime Does Not Pay' shorts, before being offered *The Boy With Green Hair* by Dore Schary at RKO. In 1944 Elia Kazan, who as a successful Broadway director was in a stronger bargaining position, negotiated a contract with the studio head most committed to a post-war film industry that would deal with the major social issues, Darryl F. Zanuck. Beginning work on *A Tree Grows in Brooklyn*, Kazan brought Nicholas Ray west with him as assistant director.

For some, like John Berry (in 1942) and Cy Endfield (in 1940), the transition was difficult. Endfield gained experience at RKO, working for Jack Moss, business manager of the Mercury Theatre unit at the studio, but it was not until October 1942 that he gained his first assignment, to a short subject at MGM. The subject, and the title, was *Inflation*, and the director remembers that the finished product was enthusiastically received by both the studio and the Office of War Information. The film attacked companies that were evading the administration's anti-inflationary policies, with Edward Arnold playing a businessman as a devil figure. Endfield also remembers thanking Jerry Bresler, the head of the MGM short subject department, for the high-quality assignment, and being told that 'I always figured it needed some kind of a communist to direct it'. But just before the short was to have a nationwide showing, MGM president Nick Schenck cabled the studio from New York to report that the US Treasury had requested that the film not be shown, following an unfavourable reaction from the Chamber of Commerce. Cy Endfield was not to make another film in Hollywood until after the war.[12]

Yet by far the most dramatic introduction to Hollywood was that of Orson Welles, who was hired by RKO in 1939, at the age of 24. George J. Schaefer, the studio's new president, was primarily interested in Welles as an actor, and in the Mercury Theatre as a possible independent production unit. But when Welles signed for RKO he was given unprecedented artistic freedom, although the studio retained the right of story refusal, and the contract was supposed to preclude ideas that were 'political or controversial'. Maland sees in *Citizen Kane* (1941) and *The Magnificent Ambersons* (1942) a complexity and an ambiguity of outlook that 'provided a rearrangement of the Popular Front mental categories', and also departed from Hollywood filmmaking conventions sufficiently to defy the expectations of both producers and audiences. In alliance with Herman Mankiewicz, whom Pauline Kael saw as representative of the Broadway and Algonquin wits who set the cynical tone of much of the best 1930s film writing, Welles produced a film that drew on the career of the notorious enemy of the left, William Randolph Hearst. Asked in 1960 about the film's status as a 'social document', Welles replied that 'I must admit that it was intended consciously as a sort of social document, as an attack on the acquisitive society, and indeed on acquisition in general.' While the theme of *Citizen Kane* has echoes of the Group Theatre staple of a man who gains the world but loses his soul, the dramatically unusual style and structure of the film conveyed a more distanced portrait, defying easy identification or moral judgement. After the war the French critic André Bazin was to see the film – and Welles's work with cinematographer Gregg Toland – as a turning point in terms of the use of depth of field to suggest greater ambiguity, and to invite a more active role from the spectator than that possible under the 'montage' conventions of either classical Hollywood or 1920s Soviet filmmaking.[13]

Kane was light years from D.B. Norton in *Meet John Doe*, and at the Congress of the League of American Writers, in June

1941, Welles' film was criticised as a 'romantic tale of personal frustration' which induced 'sympathy in the audience for what is basically a career of social crime'. (John Howard Lawson's later judgement was that the film 'inherits the class consciousness of the thirties in its portrait of a millionaire who is a prototype of American fascism'; but he felt that the film treated Kane 'with ironic sympathy, ignoring the implications of his conduct'. *The Magnificent Ambersons* fits even more clearly into Maland's notion of Welles's early work as 'close to the thought of many post-war American liberals', with its distanced view of progress and change. The failure of the 131-minute cut of the film at previews, with Welles in Brazil, led to the massive changes, including the addition of a happy ending, that are part of the mythology of Welles's career. At home Welles involved himself with the issue of discrimination and racism against Mexican Americans, and in Brazil he worked on the RKO documentary, *It's All True* – originally *Pan American* – that was partly sponsored by the Inter-American Affairs Committee, headed by Nelson Rockefeller. His work on the ill-fated documentary has been seen as challenging 'the racial conventions of Hollywood film-making', and provoking widespread opposition from RKO, the Brazilian elite and Rockefeller. Welles emphasised the Brazilian black culture in his work in Brazil and he 'wanted to show Brazilian heroes, not North American stars against Brazilian backdrops'. The film was never completed, and in June 1942, following the ousting of Schaefer from the studio, Welles's RKO contract was terminated. (Welles later spoke in Roosevelt's re-election campaign and wrote a series of editorial articles for the liberal and internationalist magazine *Free World*; on the Soviet Union he wrote in 1944 that the country deserved criticism but that 'just now we can't afford to be critics'.)

While no one in 1940 could match the unprecedented freedom that Welles secured from RKO for the making of his first film, there is evidence elsewhere of tension between the smooth and seamless system of studio production and the aspirations of some individuals to express themselves. Warner Bros has been seen as the most factory-like of the major studios of the thirties, but even here the process of production began slowly to loosen. In 1940 John Huston had unusual freedom to direct *The Maltese Falcon* and the completed film arguably reflects something of the greater moral complexity towards its characters that Maland detected in *Citizen Kane*, and which was also characteristic of several films of this period that were later to be seen as early examples of *film noir*.[14]

OWI, THE PROPAGANDA ROLE AND WARTIME LIBERALISM

Pearl Harbor transformed the nature of Hollywood's social concern, and criticism of government information services in the first half of 1942 led the President to create one unified body, the Office of War Information, from three existing agencies. Lowell Mellett, a close friend of and adviser to the President, became head of the Bureau of Motion Pictures (BMP), part of the OWI's domestic branch. In the same month, June 1942, the administration issued a *Government Information Manual for the Motion Picture Industry*, a document written by Mellett's appointee Nelson Poynter and his staff in the Hollywood liaison office of the BMP. The manual has been seen as 'the clearest possible statement of New Deal, liberal views on how Hollywood should fight the war'. It stressed that the 'people's war' was not just a fight of self-defence but also a fight for democracy and the 'Four Freedoms' against the forces and values of fascism; it also encouraged Hollywood to publicise the efforts of the Allies and of resistance groups in Norway, Yugoslavia and elsewhere in occupied Europe.[15]

By late 1942 the manual began to have an impact on studio production. But in June 1943, following the drastic cuts in the OWI's budget imposed by Congress, Poynter, who believed that Hollywood could show domestic problems if it demonstrated 'how democracy solved them', left the Bureau of Motion Pictures, along with Mellett. Thereafter, Ulric Bell, who had moved to the Hollywood office of the BMP in November 1942 as the representative of OWI's overseas branch, exercised what Koppes and Black – authors of the definitive study of the OWI's impact on Hollywood – have called 'an influence over an American mass medium never equalled before or since by a government agency'. But from an emphasis in 1942–3 on the major themes of the *Government Information Manual*, the impact of government in the later years of the war was much more to rule out or tone down themes which might imply criticism of American society or institutions.[16]

An example of the early influence of the government on Hollywood is the case of *Action in the North Atlantic*, released by Warners in 1943. A treatment for the project, written by Guy Gilpatric and entitled 'Torpedoed', was reviewed by the Hollywood office of the BMP in July 1942. The reviewer commended the feeling in the outline that 'American crews, like America itself, are a composite of the best of all nations, races and creeds', but he criticised the patronising air in the characterisation, the emphasis on the antipathy of the merchant captain towards the Navy, and the negative characterisation of a negro pantryman.

John Howard Lawson was granted the major writing credit, although both A.I. Bezzerides and W.R. Burnett felt that Lawson's powerful position had helped him win arbitration decisions concerning credit for the film. An OWI reviewer commented in September 1942 that the screenplay retained the best features of the original story and corrected all the previous mistakes. The black character, for example, had been written out of the final script, and of the film. The release print was reviewed in May 1943, and the film was recognised as a well-deserved tribute to the Merchant Marine, and as an effective dramatisation of the idea of the United Nations. The review concluded that from the perspective of the overseas branch of the Office of War Information the film 'will be powerful and heart-warming proof to foreign peoples that Americans are delivering the goods, that our power and determination will prevail against the enemy and all his weapons, and that we are truly a working, fighting part of the United Nations'. Further-more Poynter, from Hollywood, informed Lowell Mellett in Washington that he felt that the film would be particularly useful for showing as a 'morale booster' in all the cities with war plants.[17]

While primarily a film of action, achieving an impressive, semi-documentary quality in the opening scene in which a merchant ship carrying oil is torpedoed, it also contains significant reflections on the home front. At the hiring hall the men who have been rescued after eleven days in a lifeboat sit round a table – all of them prominently displaying their union badges – and play cards. When one man (Pulaski) complains bitterly about not being able to see his young son, and announces that he intends to get a shore job instead of signing for a new ship, a Jewish character at the table tells him about the much greater suffering of the Poles and the Czechs, who are 'lined up in front of guns digging each other's graves'. A seaman rips off Pulaski's union badge, a gesture that eventually shames the man into reversing his decision and signing on again. Unions also became a patriotic symbol in two other Warners films of 1943 – *Edge of Darkness*, written by Robert Rossen, and *Destination Tokyo*, co-written by Albert Maltz. In *Tender Comrade*, the 1943 home front drama written by Dalton Trumbo and directed by Edward Dmytryk at RKO, the central women characters – 'five women engaged in an experiment in collective living' – refer to themselves as a 'union local'.[18]

To the writer Donald Ogden Stewart, an ardent anti-fascist activist, *Keeper of the Flame* (1942), which he adapted from the novel by I.A.R. Wylie, conveyed 'the most about fascism that it was possible to say in Hollywood'.[19] Again it is a reporter who unearths the truth about the threat of fascism in America. Stephen O'Malley (Spencer Tracy) sets out to write the story of the revered figure Robert Forrest, who dies in a car accident as the film begins, and he only gets at the truth when he breaks down the reticence of Forrest's widow Christine (Katharine Hepburn). O'Malley is cynical at one point about an advertising firm's ability to 'manufacture rousing affirmatives' about people like Robert Forrest, and he finally succeeds in confirming his suspicions about the 'great American hero'. O'Malley confronts Christine Forrest with evidence that she let her husband be killed when she could have saved him, and she finally admits her guilt and justifies her action by speaking of the real nature of Robert Forrest and the Forward America Association. In the long speech that she makes the thinking of the OWI and the convictions of the screenwriter merge to produce the only real political analysis of the film. Christine Forrest describes her husband's fascist organisation, and how they 'painted it red, white and blue and called it Americanism'; she shows O'Malley a store of articles designed to exploit hatreds against various groups in America including Jews, Catholics, Negroes, city dwellers, labour and trade unions. And she explains the financing of the organisation by a few rich men who were unable to attain power democratically, and the appeal to other disaffected groups including World War I patriots who subsequently failed in business. However timely – as Ogden Stewart later argued – the speech calls attention to itself as a message reflecting the particular nightmares and concerns of liberals of the time; Lowell Mellett was shocked to find that 'the propaganda sticks out disturbingly'.[20] Nowhere else in the rather conventional film is there any comparable analysis of the nature of the Forward America Association, or of the reasons for the great esteem in which Robert Forrest is held.

Reviewing the results of its activities in early 1943 the BMP considered that there had been a decided change in the outlook of the industry in the period since the Hollywood office had opened in May 1942. From regarding the war primarily as a 'dramatic vehicle upon which to build successful box office productions' leading producers came to consider first of all the effect of their films on the task of winning the war.[21]

Warners in particular were prominent in the field of war propaganda, and their production policy drew on their 1930s reputation as the studio which was closest not only to the American working man but to the values of the New Deal itself. Writing in the *Daily Worker* in 1943 David Platt described Warners as the '100 per cent pro-New Deal studio' and commended a number of that studio's films. In 1943 Jack L. Warner, speaking for himself and his brothers, talked of dedicating the studio to the 'production of pictures which will help the people to understand the peace and the victory'. He cited *Casablanca* (1943), *Yankee Doodle Dandy* (1942), *Action in the North Atlantic*, *Edge of Darkness* and *Watch on the Rhine* (1943); on the way were *Air Force*, and then *Mission to Moscow*, a film, Warner argued, that would show 'that Russia is doing much more than just pouring out its blood to stop Nazis'. Those who worked on *Mission to Moscow* (1943), including the writer Howard Koch, believed that the venture had the specific endorsement of the President, but the distortions of the historical record, justified in terms of the need to bolster the relationship with the Soviet Union at a crucial period in the war, led to controversy at the time, and to the later, partial citing of the film by the House Committee on Un-American Activities.[22]

As late as 1941, in his survey of the Hollywood community, Leo Rosten had concluded that of all the groups involved in the productive process, writers were most frustrated by the 'constricting demands of producers, the public and censorship'. By 1943 liberal and radical writers set the ideological tone of a number of important films, while the Hollywood Writers Mobilisation, established and subsidised by the Screen Writers Guild to co-ordinate Hollywood writers in support of the war effort, increased the prestige of writers with government and public alike. This strengthened bargaining position may ironically have contributed to the increased tendency of writers to seek more creative independence by moving into production and direction. In addition the publication of a collection of *Film Plays* in 1943 testified to the enhanced prestige of the writer in the war years. In a contribution to the collection John Gassner, the co-editor with Dudley Nichols, drew attention to a new adultness in wartime cinema, and looked to a future that would see the production of 'works of greater inner penetration and intellectual force, devoted to the present world travail'.[23]

Robert Rossen had become chairman of the Hollywood Writers Mobilisation in 1942, while that year he had also begun work on the Warners contribution to a cycle of films on resistance movements in occupied Europe. Rossen welcomed an assignment to adapt a William Woods novel about the resistance movement in Norway, and he was able to work closely on the project with director Lewis Milestone. The resulting film, *Edge of Darkness* (1943), was described by Bosley Crowther as 'strong melodrama', but 'only a surface conception of the complicated tragedy of Norway', while David Platt found the film to be 'powerful propaganda for a Second Front'. Platt bracketed the film with *Mission to Moscow, North Star, Action in the North Atlantic, Watch on the Rhine, Hangmen Also Die, This Land is Mine* and *Sahara*, seeing these 1943 films as an advance in maturity in the Hollywood war film. Of the writers who gained screen credit on these films – respectively Howard Koch, Lillian Hellman, John Howard Lawson, Dashiel Hammett (from Hellman's play), John Wexley and Dudley Nichols – all but Nichols, a liberal activist, were radicals.[24]

Rossen worked closely on the novel to try to suggest the structure of the town of Trollness, where *Edge of Darkness* is set. The main characters are the middle-class doctor, reluctant to become involved, and his family; the owner of the local cannery, who explains his collaboration in terms of business self-interest; and the head of the fishermen's union, who is the leader of the resistance. The writer would have been aware of the discussion in radical circles of the 'correct' portrayal of the enemy. The Communist Party in Hollywood held regular writers' clinics, at which scripts were discussed in the light of Marxist theory and practice, and one such meeting dealt with the issue of the 'sympathetic treatment of our enemies' in relation to a script dealing with occupied Norway. David Platt criticised *The Moon is Down* (1943) for concentrating on the 'spiritual sickness of individual Nazis', while Paul Trivers, writing in *New Masses*, praised Rossen for adapting the novel so as to avoid this danger. To Trivers, as a result of Rossen's work, 'audiences recognise there is no escaping the struggle today, that there is no personal life apart from the struggle'.[25]

While Rossen would have been aware of such debates, the most pressing constraints on his work were those that sprang directly from the hectic Warners production system. The Warners files reveal something of the pressures on the writer and director from producer Henry Blanke, and from Jack Warner, who involved himself closely in the production process. Milestone apparently welcomed Rossen's suggestion that the script be written in a Jewish idiom, but such approaches had to be compatible with the casting of Errol Flynn and Ann Sheridan as the resistance leader and his girl – not to mention the 'casting' of Carmel as the Norwegian town of Trollness. Warner's earlier endorsement of the project as 'timely' did not prevent him writing to Blanke, insisting that he wanted 'a great big, schmaltz love scene between Flynn and Sheridan', and complaining to Milestone of a lack of 'over the shoulder shots of the stars', explaining that he had learnt from years of experience that 'the audience wants to be close to the stars'.[26]

The ending of the script and of the film is more affirmative than that of the novel. The film ends with an extract from a speech by President Roosevelt: 'and if anyone doubts the democratic will to win – again I say – let them look to Norway'. The OWI review of the release print found the film to make 'some excellent points for the Government's War Information Program': (1) 'The people of Norway are shown to be courageous, determined, united'; (2) 'The enemy appears in the story as a formidable foe, but one which can be defeated'; (3) 'Continuous resistance to the enemy is shown to be the only hope of eventual victory'; (4) 'Resistance, in order to be effective, necessitates a unified effort of all the people'. Nelson Poynter wrote to 'Colonel' Jack Warner, praising the film's contribution to the understanding of the war.[27]

Dorothy Jones, in her study of the film work of the Hollywood Ten, concluded that no communist propaganda could be found, but that the Ten had contributed to 'an impressive number of top-quality war films which made a positive contribution to the government's war information programme'. Albert Maltz, who had come to Hollywood in 1940, was hired by Warners when producer Jerry Wald wanted him to add anti-fascist and social content to Delmer Daves's first draft script for *Destination Toyko*. Like *Action in the North Atlantic*, *Destination Toyko* (1943) contains burials at sea, warnings against false heroism, atrocity propaganda, and an emphasis on the importance of teamwork between officers and men. It also includes such references to the enemy as 'Fried Jap in tartar source' and 'I'll take mine boiled in oil'. There is also a stab at appeasers, as an enemy bomb is found to have 'Made in the USA' stamped on it – 'the appeasers' contribution to the war effort'. The references to the Japanese enemy were, as Koppes and Black argue, part of Hollywood's perpetuation – against the advice of the OWI – of the racist stereotypes prevalent in American political culture.[28]

WAR, GENRE AND PREJUDICE

The circumstances of war had a powerful impact on Hollywood's traditional genres. While William Wellman made *The Ox-Bow Incident* as a personal project at MGM, foreshadowing the Westerns that dealt with social themes in the fifties, the major studios generally abandoned the genre to B-picture studios such as Monogram and Republic, who adapted it to anti-Nazi purposes. A script that Dore Schary wrote with Sinclair Lewis, in which the American west was a metaphor for the world at war, did not see the light of day at MGM.

The social problem film all but disappeared, becoming absorbed into propaganda films which affirmed American democracy. Even as late as October 1943 the majority of producers held to the dominant pre-war philosophy that Hollywood should avoid controversy and keep people's minds off their troubles. Walter Wanger, an independent producer who had not been afraid to criticise American society before the war, now turned to praising American capitalism. After the

OWI cuts in mid-1943, home front dramas risked transgressing the Office of Censorship code if they depicted class or racial conflict or provided ammunition for enemy propagandists, leading to a BMP recommendation that foreign distribution be banned. In August 1943 the State Department vetoed the inclusion of *The Grapes of Wrath* in a package of American films to be shown in European countries under the auspices of the OWI. At a time when communist writers were making a major contribution to propaganda films, the Communist Party was strongly opposed to open discussion of domestic conflict; they regarded John L. Lewis's call for a miners' strike as treasonable and saw the black 'Double V' campaign – against fascism abroad and Jim Crow at home – as disruptive. Late in the war the *Daily Worker* critic David Platt even praised King Vidor for *An American Romance* – although the true author was as much the OWI as Vidor – despite the director's earlier *Comrade X* and his early membership of the Motion Picture Alliance for the Preservation of American Ideals.[29]

At the Writers' Congress in the spring of 1943 – jointly sponsored by the Hollywood Writers Mobilisation and the University of California – Darryl F. Zanuck, who had recently returned to the studio from duty in the armed forces, committed his studio to the production of the adult films that he was confident the matured, post-war audience would demand. He urged Hollywood to 'begin to deal realistically in film with the causes of wars and panics, with social upheavals and depression, with starvation and want and barbarism under whatever guise'. But more immediately, attempts to deal with domestic problems were officially discouraged. For example, the studios came under pressure from welfare organisations to deal with the significant rise in youth crime, a phenomenon that was seen as a product of the disruption of family life caused by the war. Val Lewton, who achieved such remarkable things with his B picture unit at RKO during the war, wanted to make a film on the disruptive effects of the war on the American social order. Yet the project ran into considerable OWI criticism, and the film, *Youth Runs Wild* (1944), was finally heavily cut and re-shot over Lewton's objections. The OWI reviewer criticised the portrayal of the problem of juvenile delinquency without sufficient emphasis on the steps being taken to redress it by federal, state and community agencies.

One of the few efforts in this area at a major studio was undertaken by Robert Rossen at Warners. Rossen discussed a project on youth problems with various welfare professionals and produced a treatment in October 1943. The head of the Youth Corrective Authority in California wrote to Warners, expressing the hope that a film might 'take some community that has suffered from the war impact and show how the same energies and inclinations that get groups of boys and girls into trouble can be used, if intelligently directed, to make [them] a valuable asset to the community'. Rossen's treatment resolves around a 14-year-old girl who runs away from Arkansas in an attempt to find her parents in a warplant town. He envisaged a kind of *Grapes of Wrath* story concerning what he saw as the new 'American immigrants', the young people who went west to the warplant towns in California to find security. Yet while the treatment reflects these liberal sentiments, it contains scenes of violence and poolroom low life – a recurring Rossen interest – which might have caused problems with both the PCA and the Office of Censorship. In *New Masses* Rossen wrote of how his work on a home front picture had convinced him that the alienation and defeat of the 1930s had been replaced by a pattern of 'optimism and hope'; yet the difficulties of combining problem and solution proved insoluble, and the project did not reach script stage.[30]

There were signs even before the war that there was little scope for further development of the gangster genre; films such as *The Roaring Twenties* and *High Sierra* had seemed to mark the end of an era for the classical gangster genre. As with social criticism, any portrayal of corruption or gangsterism was seen by the OWI, and by writers who came to anticipate its judgements, as dangerously at odds with the wartime assertion of unity. Commenting on *Girls in Chains* (PRC, 1943) the OWI reviewer argued that at 'a time when the Nazi radio is trying to convince the world that America is a nation of gangsters and that the democratic process is helpless in its efforts to cope with crime, such a presentation could only serve to confirm fascist propaganda'.[31]

A test case came with the consideration by Warners of a proposal to adapt a 1941 play, *Brooklyn USA*, by John Bright and Asa Bordages. The play concerned the efforts of Brooklyn longshoremen to thwart the attempts of native born fifth columnists to help the Nazis. The character Albert Anaconda is owner of the Shipping Corporation and – covertly – of the stevedoring company; he is ostensibly a 'pillar of society' but in practice an 'American Fascist'. John Bright, a self-described 'uncompromising radical' and a founding member of the Hollywood Communist Party, had grown up in the Chicago of the 1920s and had co-written five key films for James Cagney, including *The Public Enemy*. Also working on successive treatments and scripts at Warners in 1942 and 1943, for producer Jerry Wald, were – apart from Bright and Bordages – radicals Alvah Bessie and Daniel Fuchs, and Jo Pagano. Yet despite these efforts, and Jack Warner's enthusiasm for the project, it ran up against the twin pillars of wartime censorship and 'advice' – the PCA and the OWI – and never reached the screen. The PCA objected to a script, to its background of 'national disorder, disloyalty and dissension', to the helplessness of the forces of law and order and to the suggestion of the existence of a 'class struggle' in America. Fulfilling its traditional function the Breen Office warned the studio of likely objections by political censor boards.

John Bright had consulted members of the OWI in an attempt to relate the topic to official war aims. In the 1942 script Anaconda heads a traitorous group of Americans who own property in Germany, and one character comments approvingly on their attempts to impede the war effort: 'If the war is slowed up enough and Russia is knocked out, this country will have to make peace with the Germans.' Nelson Poynter recognised that the story pointed up the issues, and 'what humble people are fighting for', but even he doubted whether such a picture would be good propaganda abroad, asking whether the script did not indicate that American municipal and federal authorities were 'unable to cope with a few racketeers who are sabotaging the war effort?'[32]

Radical writers played a significant role in the development of the wartime genres that emerged, in part in response to the encouragement of the OWI. Employed for their political expertise, these writers contributed to the shift of emphasis that such films exhibited, from the individual hero towards the collective effort and teamwork needed for victory. Dorothy Jones, in her 1956 study of the content of the films on which the Hollywood Ten worked, pointed out that they were almost twice as likely to work on war films as the industry as a whole, and that they were responsible for many of the war films with the highest reputation. Political knowledge and analysis was in demand, and radical writers, along with some liberals, were best prepared to respond by writing, in particular, about resistance and the enemy.[33]

Discussing the combat film, Basinger has pointed to the emergence of the 'unified group as the hero' as a central motif in war films, and this is evident in Lawson's script for *Sahara*, a 1943 film which related the European phase of the war to traditional notions of American character and 'builds a case for Allied Solidarity'. In John Howard Lawson's final wartime script – for *Counter-Attack* (1945), an adaptation of a play by Janet and Philip Stevenson – the offensive on the Russian front was dramatised, with emphasis given to Paul Muni's playing of the ordinary Russian soldier who outwits his German prisoners. While Lawson was 'cast' for his wartime assignments, in each case he brought to the project political expertise and a highly developed sense of aesthetics which limited the emphasis of each film on its 'stars'. The radical writers may not have had a radical aesthetic about film, or any significant power base within the studio system, but the interest of the Communist Party in the craft of the screenwriter, and the discussions in their writers' clinics, had some effect in a period when the new Hollywood interest in politics and messages increased the prestige and bargaining power of the writer.[34]

Opinion as to the worth of Hollywood war films has varied. In 1943, when some critics were praising the new batch of war films, James Agee saw only sentiment and lack of realism, and Hollywood mistrusting its audience. Koppes and Black, in their survey, echo this perspective. Other commentators, then and now, were and are more sympathetic to what they see as the portrayal of social life as a more collective and cooperative activity. In 1945 Dorothy Jones, who worked as head of the Film Reviewing and Analysis Section of the OWI, saw a revision in the 'stereotyped characterisation of minority groups', and a shift to greater realism; she looked ahead to the possibility of Hollywood – in time – assuming the 'progressive leadership of the nation'. The last year of the war saw a movement towards a less affirmative view of the war, with films such as *The Story of G.I. Joe* (which James Agee saw as 'a tragic and eternal work of art', and General Eisenhower saw as the 'greatest war picture I've ever seen'), *They Were Expendable* and *A Walk in the Sun*. All benefited from distinctive direction, from William Wellman, John Ford and Lewis Milestone respectively, while three radicals – Leopold Atlas, Guy Endore and Philip Stevenson – shared writing credit on the *The Story of G.I. Joe*. Milestone contributed $300,000 of his own money to help finance the independent production of *A Walk in the Sun*, and he continued his association with Robert Rossen, who faithfully adapted Harry Brown's short novel.[35]

To Thomas Cripps the 'combined operations of black activists, conscience-liberals in OWI, and Hollywood liberals, helped nationalise racism as a political issue'. What they did not do was allow racism, as an entrenched element of American culture, to be described or depicted. Walter White, who with Wendell Willkie had campaigned in wartime Hollywood against the traditionally stereotyped pre-war depiction of blacks on film, and against the tendency of producers to blame the prejudices of Southern censorship boards, detected some modest improvements until Willkie's death in 1944 seemed to reduce the pressure on Hollywood. Dalton Trumbo broke through the rhetorical emphasis on unity at the Writers Congress to attack the depiction of blacks in films. But OWI's attempts to change the portrayal of blacks came to an end with the pressure on the agency in 1943; thereafter the emphasis of war propaganda was to be on American democracy, and on unity against the fascist enemy, rather than on any articulation of the problem of racism. To Koppes and Black, 'Hollywood for the duration continued to treat blacks as a people essentially apart.'[36]

Despite this a few dignified, unstereotyped roles for blacks in wartime films (for example, *In This Our Life*, *The Talk of the Town*, *Casablanca*, *Sahara* and, arguably, *Lifeboat*) represented a sharp break with the past, and made wartime rhetoric about unity seem less hollow to many blacks. Jack Warner was for a time enthusiastic about a film to be based on a 'negro story' by Lillian Hellman, a story which did not shirk discussion of American discrimination and bigotry. The script has two blacks who, on the evening of a heavyweight title fight involving Joe Louis, discuss the reasons for a lynching that one of them has witnessed. Vincent Sherman worked on a script at Warners in late 1942 that was based on the Hellman story, and which also represented black doubts about the wartime rhetoric about unity, before affirming that unity. Yet there is no record of this short film being made, and in the later years of the war Hollywood was – encouraged by the purged OWI – even more wary of departing from wartime affirmation of American democracy. The short film about race that was completed, and which had a powerful impact, was *The Negro Soldier* (written by Carlton Moss, directed by Stuart Heisler and released in 1944), a film which excluded any reference to slavery or racial discrimination. The War Department film documentary was shown to service and civilian audiences and impressed the NAACP, and influenced post-war liberal efforts in Hollywood to raise issues of prejudice on the screen.[37]

The wartime liberal agenda is also evident in a limited number of films which portray heroic Jewish characters as part of the war effort, and in two films, *Mr Skeffington* (1944) and *Pride of the Marines* (1945), both of them made by Warners, and written respectively by Philip and Julius Epstein, and by Albert Maltz, which went beyond this in raising problems of anti-Semitism in an American context. (Maltz also wrote a short on religious intolerance, *The House I Live In*, released in 1945 and featuring Frank Sinatra.) There was little response, however, to pressure from the American Jewish Congress to get the studios to make a film which explained the German extermination of Jews. The avoidance of any explicit treatment of the Holocaust in part reflected the reluctance of the industry leaders to make a film that dealt only with Hitler's treatment of one group. Ilan Avisan refers to the 'striking avoidance of any explicit presentation of the Jewish catastrophe during the course of the war'. When Lester Cole's script for 'Lebensraum' – filmed as *None Shall Escape* (1944) – came before OWI, a reviewer, while accepting that the project was timely, wondered whether the film would not be '"preaching hate" at a time when we will be studying how to rehabilitate the whole German nation'. The low-budget film deals with the Nazi occupation of Poland and suggests the fate of Jews; a young German officer tells a local girl that 'anyway, those weren't people they were Jews'.

The extreme caution shown by the studios on issues of race is illustrated by accounts of the experience of Warners in producing a short film, *It Happened in Springfield*, about 'a method of promoting tolerance through education in the public schools'. The film continued to blame racism on pro-Nazis, and black children and teachers were apparently excluded because of fears that Southern exhibitors would boycott the film.[38] The persistence of the wartime concern with fascism is also reflected in the 18-minute film *Hitler Lives*, which apparently played in 81 theatres in major American towns and cities in the early months of 1946. The previous year Jack Warner had appointed a committee, chaired by Jerry Wald, and including Alvah Bessie, Emmet Lavery and Howard Koch, to work on a film about the dangers of fascism after the war. Bessie, Koch and Lavery produced a script, originally called 'The Ghosts of Berchtesgaden'. Koch, writing to Jack Warner in August 1945, suggested a prologue in which Warner would explain that the picture was aimed at exposing 'the attitudes and tactics of fascists' so that everyone might be on guard against tendencies that 'might be leading us in the same direction Hitler led Germany'. Koch felt that such films, together with feature films such as *Confidential Agent* (1945) – based on Graham Greene's novel and set in England in the late 1930s – might help to combat domestic fascists such as Gerald L.K. Smith.

It is uncertain whether changes were made in the script, which was finally credited to Saul Elkins. Bessie later argued that the film had never been made, and he suggested that this was because the screenplay 'pointed its finger at individuals and financial interests whose exposure might have embarrassed the financial octopus known as Warner Brothers'. In the released film the emphasis is mainly on the dangers of a revival of German imperial ambitions: 'The German lust for conquest is not dead. It's merely gone under cover.' Over pictures of gas ovens the soundtrack talks of 'human fertiliser' and 'typical German efficiency'. The film then turns to the persistence of the danger of fascism in America, with shots of crowds and rallies, and a commentary discussing 'race hatred', and 'persecution, hatred and violence'. A montage moves from a man speaking, to various shots of crowds, to a lynch mob and finally a lynching. These groups, the soundtrack suggests, hope for unemployment and a disillusioned America.[39]

TOWARDS PEACE

The broad consensus in favour of American participation in an international organisation designed to keep the peace, and in

favour of the ideal of international cooperation, is reflected by
the wartime efforts of Darryl F. Zanuck to make two films which
he hoped would strengthen this feeling in America. First
he committed his studio to making an expensive colour film
depicting President Wilson's struggle with Congress over
the League of Nations, and although Lamar Trotti's script
concentrated on the man and his family rather than the politics,
the film – released in August 1944 – may have made a contribution to the emerging climate of internationalism. Zanuck's
friendship with Wendell Willkie – a director of Twentieth
Century-Fox – led him to attempt to make a form of documentary drama film about Willkie's well-publicised morale-raising
world tour in 1942, a film that would also capture the ideas of
the politician's bestselling account of the trip, *One World*. Trotti,
a conservative, laboured to create an acceptable screenplay,
while Dudley Nichols was among other writers used, and Elia
Kazan (in 1944) and John Ford (in 1945) were also approached
as possible directors, or for advice. Yet while work on the project
survived the relative commercial failure of *Wilson* and the
sudden death of Willkie, by 1945, as Wiseman has explained,
the signs of an emerging 'cold war' made the 'One World'
concept increasingly anachronistic. The account of the failure
of Zanuck's project reflects both Hollywood's sense of its political
importance at the time, and the gradual movement of opinion
away from Wendell Willkie's outlook towards a different form
of American post-war internationalism.[40]

Parker Tyler has speculated on the emergence of psychological murder films at the end of the war, suggesting that
they were a response to the notions, aroused inevitably if
subconsciously in the public mind, of war as murder and of
murder as motivated by some form of madness or psychological
disorder. It is difficult to prove or disprove such explanations
of the connection between films and national psychology,
notions which were voiced at the time and which became
increasingly fashionable. Evidence is easier to obtain in relation
to notions of *film noir* emerging out of particular studio and
commercial practices. It has been pointed out, for example, how
the 'house style' of Universal shifted during the war, with the
expressionist tradition of horror films being continued in crime
and psychological dramas. *The Spiral Staircase*, produced by Dore
Schary at RKO with Selznick stars, was a powerful mix of gothic
horror and *noir* elements.

At RKO the B-picture unit under Val Lewton developed distinctive themes and styles without excessive interference from above or outside; among these low-budget films, made at the height of the period of wartime affirmation, was the dark and pessimistic *The Seventh Victim* (1943). In terms of A pictures the box office success of *Double Indemnity* led other studios to look for similar projects. At Warners Jerry Wald was influenced by the Paramount film, and particularly by its flashback structure, to make changes in *Mildred Pierce*, so that the result is as much *film noir* as woman's picture.[41]

Also of relevance to the emergence of *film noir* may be the absence of social problem films during the war years, and the beginning of a tension, from around 1943, about their reappearance. That year saw the height of Hollywood's concern with the war, and, with the Writers Congress in Los Angeles, the height of progressive optimism about the democratisation of American filmmaking, with writers in particular being the beneficiaries. Edward Dymtryk predicted that there would be a turning away from the problems of the enemy towards those of America. Yet it is also possible to date from that year the stifling in Washington of the reforming strand of the New Deal, and the emergence on the west coast – barely noticed in the affirmation and rhetoric of war – of domestic communism as an issue of the radical right.[42]

Chapter 4

Post-war Hollywood

In the immediate post-war period there were those on the left who saw the prospect of independent production opening up the possibility of greater co-operation between writer and director, and of reduced front office involvement in the production process. It was true that the Breen Office, administering the Production Code, still acted as a check on the filmmakers' efforts to reflect even the surfaces of American society more accurately, while falling box office returns after 1947 discouraged innovation. Adrian Scott referred in 1946 to industry censorship as 'a dreadful burden on the creators of films'. The year 1946 had been the peak year for admissions, following the wartime boom, but after that a decade-long decline set in, reflecting new educational and leisure pursuits, the post-war baby boom, and ultimately the spread of television. Yet from the perspective of the 1950s onwards the late 1940s seem to have provided considerable opportunities for more critical film styles and themes. Thomas Cripps has commented on post-war changes in Hollywood by suggesting that the congressional committees that investigated alleged communism in the industry 'may have constituted a conservative response to fears that the old virtues of Middle America were being subverted by liberals who seemed to have engineered a *coup d'état* in the media of mass communication'.[1]

Dorothy Jones, who had monitored Hollywood's wartime film work for the Office of War Information, raises the similar issue of the extent to which the attack by the House Committee on Un-American Activities on Hollywood was the result of a fear that the films were 'beginning to devote themselves seriously to an exploration of some of the social, economic and political problems of our time'. She comments on the increasing interest in social themes by Hollywood after the war, tracing this in part to the service experience of producers, directors and writers, and to the renewed interest in 'documentary technique'. Jones sees 1947, the year of the first congressional hearings, as the year when what she calls 'social document' films began to appear in number. She cites Production Code Administration figures for the first half of 1947 indicating that 21 per cent of Hollywood product was in the social problem category; thereafter there was a decline of this category to 16.5 per cent in 1948 and 1949, and to an average of 9.5 per cent in the first half of the fifties.[2]

The wartime alliance between liberals and radicals – itself a revival of the late 1930s Popular Front – had high hopes for the post-war years. The 1943 Writers' Congress in Los Angeles, commended at its opening session by a message from President Roosevelt, had reflected the wartime sensitivity of Hollywood to its public responsibilities and its aspirations to continue this role after the war. Dorothy Jones wrote in 1945 that with 'the best artistic talent of the country at its disposal, Hollywood may in time assume the progressive leadership of the nation'. Darryl F. Zanuck was one of the moguls who spoke to the conference and who, newly returned from service duty, committed his studio to the kind of adult pictures that he felt the war-hardened American public wanted. Despite the commercial failure of *Wilson*, Zanuck continued in the immediate post-war years to support a revival of the social problem film.

Both the *Screen Writer* magazine, and the scholarly *Hollywood Quarterly* gave considerable space to liberal and radical aspirations for better, more creative and more socially responsible post-war filmmaking. For many of the younger creative personnel in the industry the social perspectives were those formed in the 1930s, and the aspiration to make *better* films was linked to the desire to make more *progressive* films. At the very least it was assumed that the wartime moratorium on the social problem film – replaced generally by patriotic affirmation – would come to an end. There was a belief that the wartime responsibilities of the industry, together with the realism of service documentaries, could be continued in post-war Hollywood filmmaking. Yet the confidence of writers in particular was misplaced, underestimating the degree of continuity in studio methods of filmmaking, and in particular the extent that writers remained a Hollywood proletariat. Raymond Chandler's comments, in a 1945 article, are a necessary counter-balance to the optimistic voices. While he admitted that writers had made gains in prestige, he saw the producer-dominated system as incompatible with 'an art of the screenplay'; to Chandler the essence of the system was that it 'seeks to exploit a talent without permitting it the right to be a talent'.[3]

A number of immediately post-war developments led to the disintegration of the wartime united front between liberals and radicals. The political mood changed abruptly as Truman succeeded Roosevelt in 1945, and relations with the Soviet Union worsened. Republicans campaigning for the 1946 election drew on fears of spy plots and union infiltration to 'Red-bait' their opponents, and in early 1947 the President, taking Senator Vandenberg's advice, moved to rally support for interventionist policies by talking up the communist threat. Non-communist liberals, on the defensive because of their past associations, established their own organisation, Americans for Democratic Action (ADA), in response to the left's attempt to prolong the wartime progressive alliance through their own new body, the Progressive Citizens of America (PCA). President Truman instituted a loyalty programme as part of a general campaign against the left, while the House Committee on Un-American Activities, urged on by J. Edgar Hoover, threatened legislation outlawing the Communist Party and began its hearings on communism in Hollywood.

The Communist Party had itself shifted away from its collaborative wartime stance, following the criticism in 1945 by the senior French communist, Jacques Duclos, of the wartime communist leader, Earl Browder. The party had reconstituted itself as a Political Association in May 1944, but a year later Browder was overthrown and – at least officially – the party returned to the pre-Popular Front model of inevitable class conflict. As the Cold War deepened, from the Berlin Blockade in 1948 and the Soviet acquisition of nuclear weapons in 1949, the victory of the Chinese communists the same year, and the North Korean invasion of South Korea in 1950, the position of the American Communist Party became more beleaguered. In 1950 the vision of internal subversion by communists and fellow travellers became central to Senator Joseph McCarthy's assault on the New Deal tradition.

The progressive consensus was already losing its hegemony as the war ended, with the emergence within Hollywood of right-wing anti-communism in the form of the Motion Picture Alliance for the Preservation of American Ideals. The common purpose of military victory was no longer there to paper over the divisions between radicals and liberals in the Hollywood community, and the forces of reaction were to be strengthened by the emerging national politics of the Cold War. For the radicals, the dramatic change in policy following the Duclos letter and the replacement of Earl Browder caused much resentment and a feeling, even amongst those who supported its goals, that the balance between necessary discipline and respect for members' opinions had swung too far towards the former. Some radicals dated their adherence to the party to the early or later 1930s, others to the war years or the period when it became the Communist Political Association, and these differences in perspective were to be put under heavy strain during the congressional investigations.[4]

As the war ended there was much discussion in Hollywood of the increasing importance of independent production. In 1947 there were fifteen producing companies for every one operation that existed in 1940, and some of this growth in independent production was a result of efforts to avoid high marginal tax rates on personal incomes by new ventures in which payments could be claimed as capital gains, and thus be subject to considerably less tax. New production companies also seemed to offer more independence to writers and directors of the stature of Frank Capra, John Ford, Mervyn LeRoy, Preston Sturges, Dudley Nichols and William Wyler. If David O. Selznick, Walter Wanger and Samuel Goldwyn had been among the pioneering independent producers, post-war companies such as Liberty Films and Enterprise Productions seemed for a time to represent a stronger potential challenge to traditional Hollywood production techniques and to promise a more pluralistic commercial film culture. Writing from a British perspective in 1947 Fredric Marlowe warned against reading too much into the phenomenon, but concluded that 'its healthy and progressive manifestations are daily becoming more tangible'. Yet with industry profits for 1948 at half the 1946 figure independent producers were particularly hard-hit.[5]

Viewed in historical perspective the second half of the 1940s was a period when the traditional Hollywood system suffered a series of 'shocks', the most significant of which was the decline in audiences and profits, beginning in 1947. Least unexpected was the Supreme Court's decision, handed down in May 1948, in the *Paramount* case. This decision led to the divestiture by the majors of their theatre circuits within five years, thus opening up the exhibition market to greater competition. At the very least this development benefited smaller studios without theatre circuits such as Columbia Pictures and Universal, and the studio designed to distribute independently made films, United Artists. With the beginning of divestiture the major five studios also began to have a reduced ability to enforce the hidebound formulas of the Production Code. (While the Breen Office was attempting to hold the line in the late 1940s, broadly accepted by the industry because of the protection it provided from local and national censorship and the Legion of Decency, there was evidence that it was fighting a losing battle.) The psychological approach to sex and crime of post-*Double Indemnity films noirs* was not directly addressed by the code, while Breen Office objections to prestige productions such as *The Best Years of Our Lives* and *Gentleman's Agreement* were successfully resisted by Goldwyn and Zanuck.[6]

Another financial 'shock' concerned the post-war threat to Hollywood's heavy reliance on its overseas markets, which were said to have contributed approximately 40 per cent of the industry's revenue since the mid-1930s. Having co-operated with the war effort, and with a backlog of product, Hollywood after the war was poised to regain its world dominance. Will Hays, of the Motion Picture Producers and Distributors of America (MPPDA) – the Motion Picture Association of America (MPAA) from 1947 – appealed to the US Government to act against foreign 'unfair' tactics, including subsidies, taxes and all forms of protectionism. Yet most countries did start imposing restrictions on US imports after the war; in Britain it was announced in August 1947 that only 25 per cent of the rental receipts of American films would be allowed out of the country. An industry meeting in February 1949 heard that foreign remittances were down 33 per cent from 1946.[7]

More central to the post-war politics of the industry was the outbreak of violence on the picket lines in 1945 as conflicts over union recognition widened the political divisions in Hollywood which had been hidden by the unity of the war effort. Most liberals supported the position of the Conference of Studio Unions (CSU), while the dominant International Alliance of Theatrical Stage Employees had largely been discredited by wartime convictions of its leaders for extorting money from the studios. The IA had fought back through Roy Brewer, who was brought to Hollywood to direct its policy; Brewer joined the Motion Picture Alliance and accused the CSU leader Herbert Sorrell of following the communist line even before the end of the war in September released that party from its adherence to a no-strike agreement. In October violence took place outside the Warner Bros lot as studio guards reacted fiercely to a mass picket intended to resolve the issue, and there were further strikes the next year before the CSU effort petered out. Looking out on the picket line at Warners, Jack Warner is said to have declared that he was 'through making pictures about the "little man"'. While the exact effect on his studio's political stance is a matter of speculation, within two years Jack Warner was to give a rambling testimony to the House Un-American Activities Committee which played up to its garish portrait of the studio as a hotbed of communist influence. But the disputes were certainly important in dividing the Screen Writers Guild and, as Lary May has shown, helping to prompt the movement of the Screen Actors Guild away from its traditional pre-war support for the cause of labour.[8]

The emerging Cold War, Attorney General Tom Clark's talk of domestic communist plots, and the President's executive order of March 1947 establishing a loyalty programme for the executive branch, all helped to establish the agenda of internal subversion used by the committee, and to confuse in the public mind the roles of radical dissident, revolutionary and spy. Ten of the nineteen 'unfriendly witnesses' who were subpoenaed by the committee actually appeared before it in October 1947, and this group, the 'Hollywood Ten', were convicted of contempt of Congress in November, following the unexpected abandonment of the hearings. The same day as the full Congress voted on the Ten, executives representing the major producers met at the Waldorf-Astoria Hotel in New York and decided to dismiss the Ten and not to employ anyone who was believed to be a Communist. This was the origin of the covert Hollywood 'black-list', although the studios did not fully implement it until 1950, when the Supreme Court declined to review the test cases of John Howard Lawson and Dalton Trumbo, and when other events, including the perjury conviction of Alger Hiss, seemed to demonstrate a danger of domestic communism.[9]

The reasons for the Waldorf-Astoria decision – reached by a representative committee of executives that included Dore Schary, Samuel Goldwyn and Walter Wanger – have been much debated. Some have seen the producers as fearing that the public would avoid 'stigmatized films', although the sustained box office success of *Crossfire* (released in July 1947) seemed unaffected by the involvement of its producer and director in the events in Washington. Certainly there seemed to be no overwhelming public support for punishment of the Ten, and as many disapproved as approved of the investigation. While the liberal activist Philip Dunne has been critical of the strategy and tactics of the Ten before the committee, Abraham Polonsky, who like Lawson stresses the dominant impact of American foreign policy at the time, has suggested that decisions at the higher reaches of the federal government were responsible both for the blacklist, and for the intense pressure put on the 'stars' to dissociate themselves from the Committee for the First Amendment and other groups supporting the constitutional rights of the Hollywood Ten.[10]

The attempts to improve the image of the industry at this time only tended to give credence to the paranoia of the Alliance about communist influence. Eric Johnston, head of the main industry trade association, the MPAA, since 1945, and a businessman who had written advocating future industrial co-operation, had come dangerously near to the language of Ayn Rand's infamous 'Screen Guide for Americans' when in March 1947 he argued that 'We'll have no more *Grapes of Wrath*, we'll have no more *Tobacco Roads*. We'll have no more films that show the seamy side of American life.' To Lary May the events of this time were not so much the reactionary counter-revolution suggested by Cripps as a 'revolutionary effort sparked by corporate leaders who helped to convert national values and popular imagery away from doctrines hostile to modern capitalism'. Such an approach, linking the Red Scare to attempts to change ideology, again raises questions about the impact on film of the political generation under discussion. While notions of communist propaganda in film have rightly been dismissed, the impact of the more politically conscious members of the Hollywood community on the films that they worked on has generally been under-researched.

Looking at the crucial foreign markets, soon to be reopened, Darryl F. Zanuck wrote in 1945 of American films as selling not only 'bathtubs, telephones, automobiles and sewing machines' but the 'American way of life' as well. But, as Richard Maltby points out, the importance of these markets, and the industry's need for State Department help in exploiting them, hindered Hollywood's 'social conscience' by obligating 'an optimistic portrayal of the American way of life'. The development of what would later be called *film noir* – ironically by admiring French critics – was in the short term frowned on by the State Department as likely to give foreigners precisely the unflattering view of America that it wanted to redress. It is interesting to speculate on the effect of this on what Polonsky and others have seen as administration pressure on the industry leaders at the time of the congressional investigation in 1947 and the subsequent creation of a blacklist. Dore Schary, only three weeks before the crucial meeting in late November 1947, made a point of relating the 'sociological and political' content of films to the international situation. With the film industry being 'the sole representative of the United States' to much of the world, Schary felt that 'renewed thought must be given to [the] effect of our pictures abroad'.[11]

Despite such liberal films as *Crossfire* and *Gentleman's Agreement* in 1947, it has been argued that Hollywood's post-war economic problems delayed the continuation of the wartime cycle of liberal message movies, and that it was not until 1949 that 'Hollywood's fiscal affairs had stabilised enough that the studios undertook the risks involved in making political movies that might divide or alienate audiences'. Hollywood's belated recognition of the civil rights agenda may also have reflected President Truman's cautious commitment to the issue – his rhetorical endorsement of the recommendations of the Committee on Civil Rights and his executive order ending discrimination in the Armed Forces – in the previous year. To Carol Traynor Williams, citing *Variety*, a crucial factor was the unexpected re-election of Harry Truman in November 1948, and the view of this as evidence that 'liberal days were here again'. Cripps has argued that until 1949 the 'political vacuum in postwar cinema was filled by 16mm documentarists'. Certainly at the end of the war several writers at Warners, the producer Adrian Scott at RKO and even Orson Welles contemplated or advocated such productions, and a number of films, reflecting a variety of production circumstances, were made.[12]

Ralph Ellison saw the small cycle of liberal films dealing with race, at the end of the decade, as explained in part by the war experience, but also by the fact that 'the United States position as a leader in world affairs is shaken by its treatment of Negroes'. Discussing *Lost Boundaries, Pinky, Home of the Brave* and *Intruder in the Dust* – all released in 1949 – Ellison felt that only the last named 'could be shown in Harlem without arousing unintended laughter'. The conservative director Clarence Brown was attracted by William Faulkner's book, published in 1948, in part because of his own memories of witnessing a lynching in Atlanta as a young man. His bargaining power with Louis B. Mayer was strong, but he also needed the support of Dore Schary, then vice-president in charge of production at MGM. The project called for a leftist writer, just as had so many wartime propaganda films, and Ben Maddow wrote the screenplay. But Schary's rationale for the film was some way from the great hopes of 1945; he saw it as part of an obligation on the industry to be prepared for occasional commercial loss – the film fared poorly at the box office and received few Southern bookings – in making a 'distinguished picture that was really about something'.[13]

The blacklist instituted as a consequence of the 1947 congressional investigation was arguably the 'shock' that had the greatest impact on film content. The members of the Motion Picture Alliance publicised what they saw as the issue of communism in Hollywood, essentially inviting the Un-American Activities Committee in Washington to investigate. To the Alliance a number of films, including *The Best Years of Our Lives, The Strange Love of Martha Ivers, Mission to Moscow* and *Pride of the Marines*, contained 'sizeable doses of Communist propaganda'. HUAC had their own interests in the film industry as a subject for investigation. The anti-Semitic Representative John E. Rankin, a member of HUAC, had asserted in March 1947 that the motion picture industry 'needs a houseclearing and needs it badly'. The chairman of the committee in 1947, J. Parnell Thomas, had specialised, during his ten years as a

Congressman, in attempting to 'expose the New Deal as a Communist project and New Dealers as subversive *per se*'. For politicians the film industry offered abundant glamour and publicity.[14]

Dalton Trumbo, writing in 1953, argued that the House Committee attacked Hollywood for three reasons: to destroy the trade unions, to paralyse anti-fascist political action and to 'remove progressive content from films'. Trumbo quotes John Howard Lawson, in his book *Film in the Battle of Ideas*, as speculating that following the congressional investigations and the blacklist there was to be 'no more talk of human aspirations and national social objectives'. This raises the question of the extent of the effect of the Hollywood radical community on film-making, both in the war years, which clearly encouraged anti-fascism as a theme, and after. Abraham Polonsky has identified a broader grouping of what he calls 'social radicals', influenced by the work of the Hollywood Writers' Mobilisation, and he also sees this social movement as being cut off by the triumph of McCarthyism. Polonsky characterised the social-film movement in the United States at that time as a 'generalised political awareness existing in a number of people who were trying to make films that reflected this in one way or another when they had the opportunity to do so'; elsewhere he says that left wingers 'did pictures with humanist content and the flavour of democracy'.

John Howard Lawson stressed, as essential to an under-standing of Hollywood, the Marxist distinction between the economic base of society and the superstructure of institutions and ideas erected on it. He depreciated the wartime Hollywood output of 1942–3, arguing that the 'democratic content' of the films was 'limited by shallow characterisations, cheap sentiment, racist stereotypes'. Lawson drew a straight line between the interests of the American bourgeoisie and the post-war foreign policy, arguing that 'the development of an aggressive plan for the United States to control the world by military force after the end of World War II required a rapid reorientation of the dominant culture'.[15]

To Polonsky the post-war period in Hollywood was a time of 'interesting ideas'. Although the Hollywood production system had generally been seen as neutralising any overt political content in film, as well as imposing a uniform and politically conservative aesthetic on the industry's output, it is arguable that the disruption to the usual pattern of the industry after the war in some way increased the opportunities for different kinds of film, and for a reduction in the number of levels of control over the work of Hollywood's creative community. But the anthropologist Hortense Powdermaker, writing at the end of the 1940s, presented a generally pessimistic view of Hollywood's development, seeing it as representing the totalitarian aspects of both business culture and mass communications. Instead of seeing positive changes in the industry she perceived in Hollywood film a continuing cynicism about the public, and a structural inability to reflect the real human condition on the screen. By 1949 a series of articles in the liberal *New Republic* was also generally pessimistic; writers pointed to the dip in profits in 1947 and the drastic effect of this on independent production. Lewis Milestone pointed to the collapse of the foreign market and the 'fear psychosis' created by the 'witch-hunts', while bemoaning a state of 'No pictures with messages'.

Also in 1949, when *Life* magazine gathered together a round-table panel consisting of 'the younger and more progressive movie-makers', the impression given by their debate was of a rather beleaguered group, committed to making more 'adult' Hollywood films but very aware of the restraints on such work posed by such factors as industry self-censorship, the tyranny of exhibitors, the star system and audiences in thrall to it, and a small-town mentality constantly critical of the incursions of metropolitan culture. The group included, as well as educators and financiers, Joseph L. Mankiewicz, Hal Wallis, John Huston, Robert Rossen, Dore Schary, Jerry Wald and Fred Zinnemann; the failure of Zinnemann's *The Search* was seen as indicative of the problems faced by films – however well made – without stars. This same frustration with audience taste was reflected by a critic from Richmond, Virginia, who bemoaned the poor local turnouts for *Another Part of the Forest* (1948), *Odd Man Out* (1946), *The Naked City* (1948) and *Ride the Pink Horse* (1947), relative to the success of *Up in Central Park* (1948), *Welcome Stanger* (1947), *The Perils of Pauline* (1947), *Road to Rio* (1947) and the 'Blondie pictures'.[16]

Some of these debates are illustrated by attempts at 'social' filmmaking within the studios, as war gave way to peace.

RKO

During the war years RKO had recovered from the crisis of 1942, and record profits were made until 1946. Production chief Charles Koerner – who died in 1946 – supported projects such as Clifford Odets' *None But the Lonely Heart*, but is best remembered for the films made by producer Val Lewton. Edward Dmytryk, a former film editor and a director since 1939, rose to prominence during the war with *Hitler's Children* (1943), a melodramatic account of the effect of nazism on German youth, which cost $200,000 and returned gross rentals of $3.5m. This led to his first A-grade picture, *Tender Comrade* (1943), from a script by Dalton Trumbo, and to his subsequent four-film association with producer Adrian Scott and writer John Paxton, beginning with *Murder My Sweet* (1944). Scott and Dymtryk both joined the Communist Party late in the war years, at around the time that the party began its year-long manifestation as the Communist Political Association. Dymtryk had lectured for the People's Educational Center during the war, and he saw the party as 'the only ones doing anything'.

After *Murder My Sweet* Dymtryk and Scott worked on the anti-fascist drama *Cornered*, the first script of which was written by John Wexley in early 1945. Wexley's plot involved a captain in the Canadian RAF who – on being liberated by the Free French from a Vichy prison, attempts to track down the sadistic state prosecutor. The hunt leads him eventually to Argentina, and here he finds Nazi influence becoming covertly entrenched through the ownership of several large industrial concerns. The man that the captain is seeking turns out to be a figurehead for this trust, although he is posing as a Belgian banker. (In his script Wexley referred to Siemens as operating through various fascist fronts throughout Latin America.) Yet the Wexley script was considered unsatisfactory – in part, possibly, because it violated the Good Neighbour Policy – and the liberal writer John Paxton was also put on to the story, and he wrote a more conventional manhunt drama which included nothing of Wexley's concern with the mechanics of Nazi control over industrial capital. Wexley complained unsuccessfully to a Screen Writers Guild arbitration committee about Paxton's sole credit, and in addition there were two meetings at Dmytryk's home at which Wexley, supported by several communist writers, argued that the changes to the original script had destroyed the anti-fascist message. The second meeting, attended by Albert Maltz and John Howard Lawson, was inconclusive, but Dmytryk later traced his own disillusionment with the party, and even Maltz's article in *New Masses*, to the episode.[17]

In the late 1930s the writer Adrian Scott had attempted unsuccessfully to make a documentary film on aspects of the fight against tuberculosis. In 1945 Scott, now a producer, first raised the issue of a film about anti-Semitism. In a memorandum to Charles Koerner and William Dozier he proposed a film, based on a novel by Richard Brooks, which could be made for $250,000 – it actually cost twice that – and shot in 21–25 days; the film would be about 'personal fascism as against organised fascism'. To Scott, anti-Semitism was not declining, despite Hitler's defeat, and 'anti-semitism and anti-negroism will grow unless heroic measures can be undertaken to stop them'. The film was to be one such measure. On returning from working on *So Well Remembered* in England, Scott received general approval from Peter Rathvon, who for a time was in charge of production following the death of Charles Koerner; he then gained approval for John Paxton's script from Dore Schary, the new chief of production, who had been appointed by RKO owner and chairman Floyd Odlum in January 1947. Schary, who remembered that Koerner and Rathvon had turned down the project, would have been aware of the announcement, the month before, of the forthcoming production by Twentieth Century-Fox of a film of Laura Z. Hobson's *Gentleman's Agreement*.

The Jewish son of immigrants from Russia, Dore Schary became a Hollywood writer in the 1930s and had a major success with his script for *Boy's Town*, in 1938. He was involved in the liberal and anti-Nazi political causes of his day, but although he taught a course on screenwriting for the League of American Writers, meeting radical and student writers such as Carl Foreman and Paul Jarrico, he clearly dissociated himself from the communist position. During the period of the Nazi–Soviet pact Schary emphasised his differences with communists by first breaking with Hugo Butler over the pact and then refusing to sign a petition proposed by John Howard Lawson which attacked Roosevelt's Latin American policy. In 1941 Schary crossed the line into management, accepting Louis B. Mayer's invitation to him to take charge of MGM's B pictures. After that he worked for Selznick, where he produced *Till the End of Time*

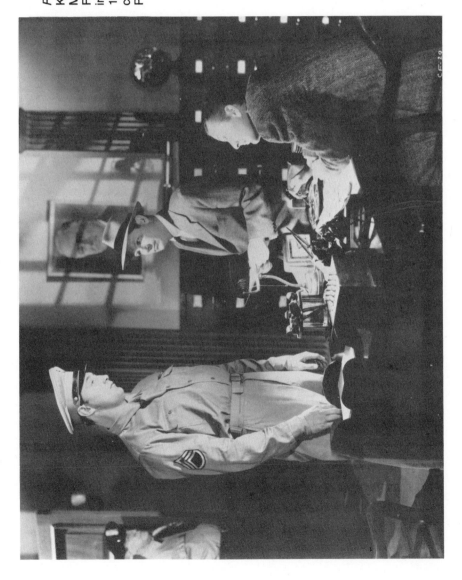

Plate 3: Sergeant Keeley (Robert Mitchum) and Captain Finlay (Robert Young) in *Crossfire* (RKO, 1947). Reproduced courtesy of BFI Stills, Posters and Designs.

(1946) for RKO. That film – directed by Dmytryk and written by Allen Rivkin – had dealt with the problems of returning soldiers, while, in one scene, showing how wartime solidarity was also needed to defeat a fascist veterans' organisation. On his appointment at RKO *Crossfire* (1947) was one of the first films that Schary approved.[18]

The social purpose of *Crossfire* is contained – or even possibly subverted – by the crime thriller, or *film noir*, form. The story follows the investigation, conducted by a tired and reluctant detective, Finlay, into first one, then two murders. The suspects, and some of the witnesses, are veterans, waiting in a Washington DC hotel for final release into civilian life. There is an emphasis on tension, as the men wait in a limbo between wartime certainties and the renewal of peacetime responsibilities and relationships. While low-key lighting adds to the mood of uncertainty, and the script casts doubt on some of the 'evidence', a number of elements relate the film to post-war political debates. Siegfried Kracauer interpreted the tiredness of the detective in *Crossfire* as illustrative of the fact that liberalism was receding in the late 1940s. In Finlay's office, to which the film regularly returns, are signifiers of progressive political thought. There is a prominent portrait of Roosevelt, while later on a framed picture of the Declaration of Independence is also clearly visible. At the beginning Finlay's office is in darkness, while later, as Finlay reveals his knowledge of the murderer's identity, and explains his plan to trap him, the view of the Capitol building from the window seems to shine into the room. (The filmmakers, like Capra, bring the capital dome into their film.) Whatever the ennui of the characters, this effect – linked to Finlay's comparison of the murder of a Jew in 1946 to that of his Irish Catholic grandfather in 1848 – affirms, towards the end of the film, the increasingly beleaguered Popular Front agenda. (However, the final scene of the film – the gunning down of Montgomery, the murderer/fascist, by Finlay – rather undercuts the sense of a victory for ethical rationality.)

To Colin McArthur *Crossfire* is best considered in terms of the essentially metaphysical, rather than social, meanings of *film noir*. Yet what he calls the 'dark and monstrous world constructed by *film noir*' is combated in the film by the light of progressivism and social inquiry. Liberal authority in the film may be tired, but it is arguably strong enough – and effectively represented in Robert Young's understated performance as Finlay – to justify reading the film as drawing on both forms.

Adrian Scott defended the different approaches of *Crossfire* and *Gentleman's Agreement*. He saw the RKO film, with its emphasis on 'lunatic fringe' anti-Semitism rather than what Paxton's script refers to as the 'You can't join our country club' kind, as confronting the reality of the 'native American fascist', and the danger of authoritarianism if depression returned. Scott called for co-operation from those in the industry in order to make a programme of films on anti-Semitism and minority prejudice; he proposed a series of documentary shorts – costing around $10,000 each – which would be designed for different audiences, and which would be made available freely to exhibitors, schools, and labour and social organisations. 'To destroy a mass prejudice', he wrote, 'a mass instrument is necessary.'[19]

Dore Schary also presided over another film that dealt with discrimination and prejudice, at a time when such a subject was given a wide berth by the studios. It was Schary who purchased a short story by Betsy Beaton, dealing in religious terms with a boy whose hair changed into grass, and brought Joseph Losey to RKO from MGM to work on the project, his first feature film, with 'hot' producer Adrian Scott. Politically, Losey has seen himself as 'engaged' in the late 1930s, and as being associated with the Communist Party in Hollywood before he joined it, 'briefly', in 1946. Scott wrote a first version of the script, and intended making the film in 16mm and Eastman Color to save cost, but by the time the project was given the go-ahead by Schary, in late 1947, Scott, as one of the Hollywood Ten, was no longer the producer, and the film was to be made in Technicolor. While the basic story concerned discrimination, Losey remembered that 'we all felt so strongly that there must be a world movement for peace' that this became an additional theme, one that was to be even more controversial when the film was completed, after a thirty four day schedule, in late March 1948. Ben Barzman and Al Levitt, also on the left, wrote the script, the basic structure of which had been agreed earlier with Scott. Barzman remembers the film in terms of a boy who wakes up with green hair and comes to identify this with a mission to warn people 'that there must not be war'.[20]

While arguments over the film, and the departure of Dore Schary following Howard Hughes' takeover of the studio, delayed its completion, *The Boy with Green Hair*, released in early 1949, essentially followed the original intentions (although Losey's inexperience and his frustration with studio norms meant that the film looked more conventional than he intended). The film deals in flashback with the experiences of a 12-year-old boy, Peter (Dean Stockwell), as he grows up an orphan in a small town. The sensitive boy is brought up by his Gramp (Pat O'Brien), a kindly if melancholic 'singing waiter' who – in a rather brief fantasy sequence – we see through Peter's admiring eyes as a king holding court. What Barzman remembers as a 'small miracle' – the change to green of the boy's hair – takes place when Peter is upset by a series of Refugee Appeal posters at his school, starkly depicting the plight of war orphans. In another 'unreal' scene – which Losey wanted to shoot on location – Peter steps into a glade inhabited by such children, and discovers his mission, and a meaning for his green hair, in terms of the need to warn of the effects of war.

The green hair thus signifies both differentness and the cause of peace, as Peter carries out his mission to explain, and is shunned by the townspeople because of his hair. In what seems in retrospect – to further overload the symbolism – a metaphor for the blacklist, parents complain to the school board of the danger of contamination, while the milkman complains of lost trade because people blame Peter's complaint on the milk. Even his Gramp betrays him by bowing to public pressure and getting the boy to shave his head, something that, in a final post-flashback scene, he regrets.

The film is a strange mixture of aesthetic experiment, social protest and studio sentiment, but the prominence of peace as an issue in the film led to attempts to change and even reshoot it in the ten months between the completion of filming and release in January 1949. There were attacks on the film, and pressure for changes to be made, after Howard Hughes had begun his eccentric management of the studio, following his purchase of Odlum's controlling stock in May 1948. Barzman remembers opposition from 'establishment filmmakers' and 'representations to the heads of RKO', while also recalling that he refused to make changes that he felt would have 'watered down' the film. Efforts were made to rewrite dialogue even before Dore Schary resigned from the studio on July 1, 1948.

One such sensitive scene – at a time when, in Losey's words, 'peace was a dirty word' – took place in a grocery store, when a number of women customers discuss the threat of war. Several lines of dialogue that show the women as cynical of the toll of war on the young and suggest that a new war is likely, were described by ex-Chairman Floyd B. Odlum in a letter to Rathvon – about to take over from Schary, briefly, as production chief – as 'subject to wrongful interpretation'. Odlum suggested that they be 'tempered somewhat', and lines were written to balance the voices hostile to war with others suggesting the need for preparedness. Losey remembers notes of suggested changes coming from the 'Hughes office', and Rathvon himself contributed to the efforts to change the grocery store dialogue.

Some changes in dialogue – where characters are off camera – were made, but even if reports of $200,000 being spent on rewriting and reshooting were correct, in the end the film was released in what was substantially the original form. Producer Stephen Ames, a stockholder in Technicolor, helped to defend the film, and the studio management was no doubt reassured by a preview that produced, of 644 comment cards, not one reference to 'reds or fascism'. The extent of the debate and controversy generated by discussion of these changes indicates something of the sensitivity of the studios to the danger of political attack. Losey commented at the time: 'I hope we don't have to preface it with a title reading "This picture is opposed to war, but we don't mean war with Russia".' To some reviewers the emphasis on peace distracted attention from the effectiveness of the film as a comment on racial prejudice. Yet *Ebony* magazine voted the film 'the outstanding 1948 film fighting against race hatred', and saw it as a 'powerful message for tolerance'.[21] The *Hollywood Reporter* praised the film as a 'warm and sensitive fantasy drama', while *Daily Variety* noted the film's charm, but felt it was 'not quite the epic of pity and unreality which great fantasy should be'. Other critics found that the scene involving war orphans was melodramatic. The reviewer for the *Daily Worker* praised the speeches on peace and reconstruction while finding the treatment of the boy over-sentimental and 'cute'. Yet he felt that the film was interesting and important for its 'glimpses of intolerance in American life', and that it went 'against the grain of "pure entertainment"'.

While the debates on the film reflect pressures at the time, the significance of the film can also be seen in terms of its cautious innovations, and its portrait of small-town fear and intolerance. While Losey's ambitions were restricted by his inexperience and by studio procedures, the production history reflects the shared perspectives and the collaboration between producer, directors and writers which flourished for a time with Schary's encouragement. The film itself was remarkable, if not for its content, for its 'look', cutting across the traditional Technicolor norms by emphasising muted colours, particularly browns and greys. Losey's next proposed project for RKO, already planned, was cancelled as part of the Hughes economy drive, and Losey left the studio at his own request in March 1949, with six months of his one-year contract to run. Before leaving the studio Schary sent Losey a bound copy of the script as filmed, inscribed with the message that 'in these days it's comforting to hear good words from good men!' The Schary era at RKO is also reflected in such films as Nicholas Ray's *They Live By Night* (1949 – delayed for two years during the Hughes regime), *Out of the Past* (1947), *The Set-Up* (1947) and *The Window* (1949). But by 1949 RKO was in terminal decline.[22]

TWENTIETH CENTURY-FOX

Twentieth Century-Fox enjoyed spectacular profits during the war years, but with other studios it faced a number of problems in the post-war period. Independent companies formed to take advantage of tax concessions competed with the studios for scarce and expensive studio space, while rising production costs encouraged the search for economies. In the second half of the 1940s the minority of Fox films with social relevance fell into the social problem or semi-documentary categories. Through these films the studio, which had few stars, differentiated its product, in particular with the high prestige films that were personally produced by Zanuck.

Zanuck's interest in topical stories and in films of broad social concern can be traced back to his period at Warners in the early 1930s, while *The Grapes of Wrath* has been seen by Russell Campbell as a model for a series of post-war films of 'social consciousness'. Zanuck was proud of his record with *I am a Fugitive from a Chain Gang*, *How Green Was My Valley* and *The Grapes of Wrath*, and he explained what he saw as the failure of *Wilson* and *The Ox-Bow Incident* by the fact that they were 'not good movies'. He continued to combine the roles of studio and production head, and he saw it as part of his role to agree a script with his writers before involving the director, and to work with the film editor.[23]

Elia Kazan, who signed a five-year, five-film contract with the studio in 1944 – after considering a similar deal with Warners – was able to begin with A pictures, given his status as a successful Broadway director. He learnt the craft of filmmaking within the supportive, if restrictive, studio framework, while maintaining an ambition to make more personal films. It was the smaller budget, 'semi-documentary' productions, that gave him more autonomy, rather than the 'social problem' epics, *Gentleman's Agreement* and *Pinky*, that he made for Zanuck. What Kazan brought, even in these early films, was his particular affinity and ability with actors, and his first film, *A Tree Grows in Brooklyn* (1945), was praised in particular for the performances of James Dunn, as the 'pipe dreaming' father of the family, and Peggy Ann Garner, as his daughter. The film is a humanist, sentimental, set-bound drama of a puritan mother ('The tree ain't going to put no pennies in the bank') and an inadequate but life-affirming father. James Agee disliked the deadness of the sets, however exact, and the too neatly 'tagged' characters, but felt nonetheless that the film represented 'the respectable beginning at least of a return toward trying to represent human existence'.

The first and classic Fox social problem picture was *Gentleman's Agreement*, from the Laura Z. Hobson bestseller. Zanuck supervised Moss Hart's script closely, and ensured that it followed the book. Book and film explore domestic, rather than neurotic, anti-Semitism, using the device of a gentile journalist, Phil (Gregory Peck), who poses as a Jew in order to discover a new angle on anti-Semitism. But the sugar on the pill for the audience is the love affair between Phil and a society woman, Kathy (Dorothy McGuire), whom he meets on his assignment. In a classic 'happy ending' – too neat for modern audiences and for some in 1947 – the 'problem' is forgotten, as Phil embraces Kathy, despite evidence of her own prejudice. In a letter to director Kazan, Zanuck noted that Kathy 'betrays herself so completely that it is difficult to know why Phil comes back to her and forgives her'. Yet the film won commercial and critical success, and for Kazan, still essentially a stage director, the Academy Award for 'Best Direction'.[24]

The success of *Gentleman's Agreement* led to a decision to go
ahead with a film on the race issue, based on a bestselling but
rather inadequate novel that had been purchased by the studio
in 1946. The problems of agreeing a final script took a year,
from May 1948. In successive script conferences Zanuck stressed
that the film, to be called *Pinky* after the central character,
should be focused not on the problem in general but on the
personal adventures of the girl at the centre of the story: 'Once
we try to make it the story of the white–black issue in the south
we are not going to have a good movie'. The political problems
involved in the project were pointed out early on by Philip
Dunne, who warned Zanuck that 'There is no question that you
will be attacked by the professional leftists as by the professional
negrophobes'.

The plot of the film concerns a young black woman who
has 'passed' for white in the North, returning to see her
grandmother in a small Deep South community. At the end of
the film, in which she faces up to the hardships and indignities
of being black, she spurns the request of a white doctor, who
has followed her to the South, that she comes north, marries
him, and lives as a white. The early drafts of the script, by
Dudley Nichols, involve a representative of a campaigning black
organisation trying to persuade Pinky to join the fight. Dunne,
who subsequently worked on the project, later interpreted this
script as 'a slap at the NAACP'; at the time he recommended
that the emphasis be placed on the decision by Pinky – like that
of Zanuck's friend Walter White – to reject the option of passing
as white. Zanuck, taking advice from White, and from White's
daughter, continued to stress that the story was 'not a story
particularly about race problems, segregation or discrimination',
but about why the central character, 'as an individual, finally
decided to be herself – a Negress'. Director Elia Kazan, stepping
into the breach when John Ford dropped out, has seen *Pinky* as
lacking the pain of real drama, and as being handicapped by the
central casting of the white actress Jeanne Crain as Pinky, the
granddaughter of Aunt Dicey (the black actress Ethel Waters).
However, to one recent writer Crain's implausibility is 'out-
weighed by her effectiveness in getting white audiences to
imagine how altered their lives would be if they were black'.[25]

On another film that Zanuck personally produced, *No Way
Out* (1950) – a film that Zanuck wanted to divorce from any

notion of 'Hollywood' or 'movie' – he made a similar point: the theme of prejudice should be the background and foundation of the film, but 'never at any time do I want the problem to become bigger than the story'. He was prepared to recognise that the intention was to produce a picture which was 'powerful propaganda against intolerance', yet this should be achieved by telling the story 'in terms of entertainment, excitement, melodrama and characterisation'. Worrying about the proposed race riot in the film Zanuck mentioned that he expected to 'lose about 3,000 accounts in the South who will not play the picture under any circumstances'; 'It is time for us to be courageous, but we must also be sensible, and not too courageous with other people's money.'

Zanuck was also wary of the semi-documentary genre. In the early 1940s Fox had taken over distribution of the 'March of Time' series of semi-documentary newsreels, and the former 'March of Time' producer Louis de Rochement had joined the studio. Zanuck was clearly concerned that this innovatory form of film might place factual accuracy above drama. In a memorandum he claimed that he originally vetoed the idea of 'telling a story in the "March of Time" vein' when Louis de Rochement brought the idea to him, but that subsequently they devised a way of blending fact and drama. In casting it was agreed that the featured roles were to be played by qualified actors, while other roles were played by non-actors. De Rochement's first production was *The House on 92nd Street* (1945), dealing with the story, based on FBI files, of a German spy ring in Washington. Zanuck had criticised the first draft script as lacking in drama, conflict and suspense; he urged that screenwriters make an entertaining picture out of the story or 'just turn the material over to the MARCH OF TIME and forget about making a picture out of it'.[26]

Zanuck was similarly sceptical about the dramatic possibilities of the first draft script for *Boomerang* (1947); while he admired the technique of following police procedure in the case of murder in a small town, he urged that writers 'get some "movie" into it'. Shooting the film entirely on location allowed Kazan, working directly with writer Richard Murphy – a former literary editor with little Hollywood experience – to exert a greater influence. The film is as near to the tradition of Frontier Films as to that of *House on 92nd Street*, and it presents a critical view of community power that conflicts with the early expectations – produced by the sentimental 'Anytown' opening and official-sounding introductory narration. The scenes of suspects being arbitrarily picked up, and of the falsely accused Waldron (Arthur Kennedy) being given the third degree, are anything but text-book civics; more expressionist and low-key staging and lighting could easily have transformed such scenes into *film noir*. The theatrical ending, the emergence of a 'villain', and the emphasis in the closing narration on how the story was based on events in the early life of an American Attorney General, Homer Cummings, all undercut but hardly cancel out the generally cynical perspective of the political pressures on police and the legal system in a representative American town. (Kazan was sufficiently relaxed to use his uncle, Joe Kazan, the hero of *America America*, in a small part, along with other local citizens of Stamford, Connecticut and several Actors Studio members-to-be.)

With one of the most well-known of the Fox 'semi-documentaries', *Call Northside 777* (1948), based on a real case in Chicago, the Production Code Administration objected to the 'questionable portrayal of the police' in the first draft screen-play. The story is of a reporter (James Stewart) who re-opens an eleven-year-old case of an imprisoned man whose mother believes him to be innocent. The reporter and his editor take up the case, and the final release and vindication of the imprisoned man is a triumph for police procedure and new technology. Along the way, despite the at times tedious obsession with police techniques, the film emphasises its real locations, including bars in the Polish district, poor homes and a prison. Zanuck again, in his conference remarks, was worried about the lack of drama, and suggested that his writers should read the scripts of *Kiss of Death* and *Nightmare Alley*. Perhaps prompted by the comments of the Breen Office, the final dialogue emphasises that in some countries a reconsideration of such a miscarriage of justice would not be possible.

Zanuck similarly supervised one of the first anti-communist films which coincided with the era of the House Un-American Activities Committee investigations. But as Leab shows, Zanuck was motivated more by commercial than by ideological con-siderations. As with the other semi-documentaries, *The Iron Curtain* (1948) closely followed the facts – in this case those of

Igor Gouzenko, a Russian who had exposed espionage and subversion in Canada on defecting from his post as a code clerk at the Soviet Embassy in Ottawa.[27]

WARNER BROS

In 1945 Jerry Wald presided over a committee at Warners which discussed, apparently at the suggestion of Jack Warner, ideas for films that would combat American fascism. Howard Koch wrote to Warner about the danger of Gerald Smith, who, under the banner of 'Christian Nationalism', was trying to divide and confuse the people by appealing to their prejudices. Yet this agenda would be short-lived, and in addition many of the writers associated with the tradition of social concern at the studio would move on after the war.

In October 1945 the Warner Bros studio became a central arena for the bitter industrial dispute between the IATSE, favoured by the producers, and the Conference of Studio Unions. A union cartoon of the time showed a woman, representing 'Democratic Unionism', nailed to a cross which resembles the Warners shield. In his testimony in 1947 to the House Committee on Un-American Activities, Jack Warner argued that Warners had been chosen as the first studio to be picketed because it was expected to be in support of the strike. In fact it was the Warners chief of police who ordered the use of tear gas and high pressure fire hoses on around a thousand people assembled as pickets outside the studio. In a Western Union telegram to Jack Warner three days later, on October 8, 1945, a number of writers and others protested at what they saw as the 'Outrageous violence perpetrated by hired thugs and police' at the studio. The telegram was signed by Lewis Milestone, Dalton Trumbo, Frank Tuttle, Robert Rossen, Howard Koch, Rex Ingram, Irving Pichel, John Howard Lawson, Sidney Buchman, John Garfield, Earl Robinson and John Wexley. Whatever the truth of the story of Jack Warner's renunciation of the 'little man' as a subject for filmmaking, the disputes seemed to contribute to a movement by the studio away from its 1930s and wartime concern with the working man.[28]

Alvah Bessie recalls hearing that he and Howard Koch were held by Jack Warner to be responsible for the 1945 CSU strike. In June of that year both writers, along with Emmet Lavery, had completed a first draft of the officially approved post-war anti-fascist film *The Ghosts of Berchtesgaden*, (later *Hitler Lives*). The studio did not take the option to renew Bessie's contract, while Koch, disenchanted with the studio for some time, was allowed to leave following the protest telegram quoted above. Koch, discussing the immediate post-war period felt that the material being submitted to writers was 'carefully avoiding the significant themes' with which the studio had previously identified.

The end of the war meant a reduced demand for the political knowledge of left-wing writers, and in addition the studio was to cut back its production of films. In terms of its working methods, a crucial change had come with the departure of production chief Hal Wallis at the end of 1944 to set up an independent company with Joseph Hazen, making films for Paramount distribution. Robert Rossen left the same year, and Mark Hellinger departed in 1945, leaving only Jerry Wald of the trio cited by Buscombe as contributing to the 'nexus of crime, working class life and radical politics' apparent in several pre-war Warners films. James Cagney left the studio to form an independent company, as did the much suspended John Garfield, when his seven-year contract ended in 1947.[29]

In May 1947 Jack Warner was the most garrulous and irresponsible of the friendly witnesses who gave informal testimony to the House Committee on Un-American Activities, when it held executive sessions in Los Angeles as part of its 'investigation' into Hollywood communism. Referring to a question about communist influence on films, Warner told the committee that he had noticed 'that type of writing coming into our scenarios', but he had cut out such material. In his original testimony he identified fifteen writers as communists whom he had dismissed, although in his public testimony before the committee in October he withdrew four names. In October Warner also referred to *Mission to Moscow* as a film that was 'made only to help a desperate war effort and was not for posterity'. Later Warners became known as one of the studios that were most strict in responding to the blacklist – more so than MGM – and in checking the backgrounds of potential employees.[30]

One writer turned director who remained at the studio until 1947 was John Huston; he had worked as a screenwriter at the studio before getting his first directing assignment, *The Maltese*

Falcon in 1941. Furthermore, Huston had widened his film-making horizons during the war years by making a series of combat documentaries, of which the last, *Let There be Light*, dealt with those who suffered mental damage in the service and how they could be helped by psychiatric treatment. Whatever the effect of the direct experience of war – a period which changed the work of some directors, notably George Stevens – Huston returned to Warners and picked up the project that he had instituted at the studio just before the war, and which had been 'saved' for him – B. Traven's novel, *The Treasure of the Sierra Madre*. Huston, while still technically in the army, had written much of the script – uncredited – for *The Killers*, made for Mark Hellinger at Universal-International, and he also worked without credit on scripts for *The Story of G.I. Joe* and *The Stranger*.

Huston's liberalism, and his social concerns, are shown most strongly in his films of the late 1940s. As James Naremore points out, something of Huston's sympathy with the ethos of 1930s Popular Front literature can be gauged from his pre-war choice of *The Maltese Falcon* to direct, and his interest in *The Treasure of the Sierra Madre*. Huston's wartime experience may have influenced his decision to make *The Treasure of the Sierra Madre* (1948) entirely on location in Mexico, and to present the central actors, and particularly Humphrey Bogart, Warners' biggest star, so unglamorously. James Agee, who saw Huston's late 1940s work as representing the best hopes of American cinema, wrote admiringly of the film, although he argued that the fable of men and gold was to him undermined by the character of Dobbs (Bogart), as written and played. To Agee it was too easy to conclude that 'if only a reasonably restrained and unsuspicious man were in his place, everything would be all right'.

In 1947 Huston threw himself into the protest against the House Committee hearings, becoming, with Philip Dunne and William Wyler, one of the triumvirate that organised and led the Committee for the First Amendment. Huston continued to provide liberal support for the Hollywood Ten, even after the blacklist policy had been instituted and rank-and-file support for the CFA – including that of Humphrey Bogart – had evaporated. (Huston was an early member of the PCA and, according to Agee, sponsored Wallace in 1948, but voted for Truman.) Huston determined to put something of his feelings

about the course of events in post-war America into *Key Largo*
(1948), which he wrote with Richard Brooks, drawing on a
thirties verse play by Maxwell Anderson. To Huston the central
figure, a war-hero major, Frank McCloud, to be played by
Bogart, was intended to be 'a disenchanted, if not embittered
idealist', who was seeing the dashing of his hopes for the peace.
Huston later referred to the slipping away of the 'high hopes
and idealism of the Roosevelt years' and to his sense, which he
wanted to convey in the film, that the underworld was again on
the move, 'taking advantage of social apathy'.[31]

In the film the war hero visits a beach hotel on the Florida
keys, only to be kept hostage, along with the hotel owner,
Temple (a disabled Rooseveltian character played by Lionel
Barrymore) and Nora (Lauren Bacall), the wife of Temple's son,
who died in the war. The hostage takers are the remnants of a
pre-war gang, led by Johnny Rocco (Edward G. Robinson). The
major – Bogart, playing on his famous wartime roles – declares
that he is no longer interested in anything or anyone beyond
himself, but by the end of the film he has recovered his
confidence, routed Rocco's gang and seems set to claim Bacall,
in an ending derived from Hemingway's *To Have and Have Not*.

At the time Huston was excited by the idea of using a
quotation from Roosevelt in the film – something which, in a
contemporary letter to Margaret Case, he said 'amounts to
treason nowa-days'. (The lines, about the fight to 'cleanse the
world of ancient evils, ancient ills', do appear as part of McCloud's
early statement of his wartime goals.) In the same letter Huston
expressed his belief that *Key Largo* would be 'one of the most
daring pictures ever made', and doubted that the Warners
knew 'what they are saying through it', but the extent to which
these intentions are or were readable in the completed film must
be questioned. Something of this reading was seen at the time,
for example by Peter Ericsson, writing for the British film
magazine *Sequence*. Ericsson saw the gangsters as 'being forced
to adopt new tactics', and he detected an 'unexpected bitterness
and disillusion in the script's commenting on the general chaos
and aimlessness after the war, and the corruption of American
politics'.

Compared to *Casablanca*, however, Bogart's post-war cause is
much less clear. Stephen Jackson, of the Production Code
Administration, called for the injection of 'some "law-abiding"

elements in the story', and then emphasised the office's objections to the portrayal of the Robinson role as 'definitely a gangster surrounded by his henchmen and his kept women'. Jerry Wald, the film's producer, was particularly frustrated by the Breen Office attitude, which he saw as part of a 'piling up of continuous censorship'. In response to this pressure, according to Richard Brooks, references to Rocco's involvement in vice and dope were dropped, references that might have made clearer the post-war developments that Huston had in mind. Instead there are rather lame references to the return of prohibition, and the object of liberal anger is merely the familiar and villainous 'gangster' – with Robinson's presence recalling the character's past glories rather than any powerful post-war stature.[32]

After these two films Huston, also less happy at the studio after the war, left when his contract came up in 1948, forming an independent company, Horizon, with Sam Spiegel. As for Warners, Edward G. Robinson's farewell to the Warners gangster genre was followed a year later by James Cagney's, in his return to the studio for *White Heat* (1949). Viewing the latter film in a federal prison, following the failure of the appeals of the Hollywood Ten, John Howard Lawson was shocked by its 'antisocial message'. The psychopathic killer of *White Heat* – whose crimes were unrelated to environment or class – was further evidence to the decline of the 'social' tradition at Warner Bros.[33]

Chapter 5

Post-war: new directors and structures

Writers in particular were confident that they would play an important part in the filmmaking of the peace, as they had in war-time production. Dalton Trumbo and Gordon Kahn were the first editors of the journal *The Screen Writer*, which aspired to become the voice of the Screen Writers Guild. In an editorial in the first edition they included a ringing declaration, affirming their 'primary convictions that the motion picture is the most important of all international cultural mediums and that the screen writer is the primary creative force in the making of motion pictures'. One young writer referred to the experiences of writers in wartime documentaries, and to the expectation that, if this experience could be transferred to the post-war feature film, more honesty, realism and maturity on the screen might result. An editorial in the first issue of *Hollywood Quarterly* declared that the '"pure entertainment" myth', which had encouraged 'social irresponsibility and creative impotence' on screen and on radio, had been an early casualty of the war.

Yet the social responsibilty that had been encouraged as a feature of the industry's wartime filmmaking, was not easy to translate into post-war circumstances. Divisions on the subject emerged in Hollywood, and are reflected in a public debate, reported in the October 1945 edition of *Screen Writer*, about the issue of whether Hollywood should make films designed to influence public opinion. On one side of the argument was James McGuinness, chairman of the newly formed Motion Picture Alliance for the Preservation of American Ideals, and previously a supporter of the Screen Playwrights during its brief existence in the late 1930s, as a company union designed to defeat the Screen Writers Guild. McGuinness emphasised the role of pictures in supplying 'balms for the spirit', while on the other side Robert Riskin pointed to the already considerable role of censorship, and argued that the failure of Hollywood to deal with world problems would be akin to it 'debasing itself artistically', and 'would represent an unforgivable disregard for its obligations to the public'.

The president of the Screen Writers Guild, Emmet Lavery, claimed in 1945 that no group in Hollywood had been as 'sincerely and vigorously interested in upgrading motion pictures as the screenwriters'. Robert Sherwood, returning to the film capital after the war to write *The Best Years of Our Lives*, also commented on the greater recognition given to the writer after the war, but felt that the 'position of the screenwriter in the Hollywood hierarchy is still lamentably low'.[1]

Directors and would-be directors also had hopes for the post-war period. Frank Capra felt that few directors in the 1930s had much independence in terms of choice of subject matter and their ability to work on scripts. Writing in 1946 Capra anticipated that the growth in independent production following the war would improve the quality of films, and widen opportunities for producers and directors to transcend what he saw as the 'aura of sameness which inspired the phrase "a typical Hollywood product"'. William Wyler, newly signed up as a member of Liberty Films, referred to the effect of the war on his co-directors at the independent company, and anticipated that they would have unprecedented personal control of their films. He commented that his colleague George Stevens was 'not the same man for having seen the corpses of Dachau', and that the competition with European filmmakers, who 'approach their work with a simplicity and directness which eludes many of us in Hollywood', would force the American industry to change.[2]

Many of the creative hopes were related not only to wartime idealism, and the leadership role played by the left, but to the moves towards independent production at the end of the war. New companies were formed, and the majors began to offer 'semi-independent status' to previous employees. Yet the growth of independent production was to be a slow one, hampered by the downturn in attendances and profits that began in 1947, and there was no sudden increase in creative autonomy. Frank Capra's feelings about the impact of the failure of Liberty Films have been previously discussed. In 1946 Capra, William Wyler,

George Stevens and business manager Samuel Briskin signed an agreement to create Liberty Films, and to release nine independently made films through RKO, which would also advance certain production costs. But the stock of the new company was acquired by Paramount Pictures in May 1947, a development that Stevens and Wyler, and ultimately Capra, regretted, and which would seem to have contributed to Capra's decline.[3]

The success of *The Best Years of Our Lives* (1946), directed by Wyler as the last film of his pre-war contract with Goldwyn, was interpreted as evidence of a move towards adultness and realism. The archetypal film on post-war 'readjustment' dealt sensitively with the problems of three returning veterans, while Gregg Toland's 'deep focus' cinematography – with its supposedly democratic implications for the spectator – won wide praise. The $3m production was, and is, an easy film to like, and it brought in $10.4m in North American rentals, but critics on the left were quick to point out the limits of its social analysis. Robert Warshow saw the film as concealing the reality of politics by presenting 'every problem as a problem of personal morality', while Abraham Polonsky, writing in *Hollywood Quarterly*, was also critical, particularly of the easy resolution of the problems of Fred Derry (Dana Andrews), the 'junked bombardier', following his walk in the 'graveyard' of discarded wartime planes. A more striking example of the potential of filmmaking outside the usual channels came with the long anticipated release of Chaplin's post-war film. To Charles J. Maland, American audiences were unprepared for Chaplin's own role in *Monsieur Verdoux* (1947), and for a film which suggests, contrary to Hollywood practice, that 'larger social and economic forces, particularly economic depression and war, determine the fates of individual people'.[4]

United Artists had distributed *Monsieur Verdoux*, although ironically the company was in financial decline, as the major studios were now competing with it to provide financing and distribution to independent productions. One of the most well-publicised and genuinely independent of the new production companies was Screen Plays, Inc., created in 1947 by Stanley Kramer and other wartime friends, most of them with experience of filmmaking in the Army Signal Corps. Financing for two low-budget films, which were both successes when released by UA, came from private 'risk' capital. Both were written by Carl Foreman, who had come to Hollywood in the late thirties and who claimed to have been influenced by Dore Schary at a pre-war film school organised by the Los Angeles branch of the League of American Writers. To Foreman the new company, in which he and others owned stock, was dedicated to the idea that 'in film the story is the thing'.

Carl Foreman had been in the Communist Party for around four years from 1938, and he later claimed that, in the 1940s, 'a considerable amount of my thinking remained of a "Marxist" nature'. Foreman wrote and Kramer produced *Champion* and *Home of the Brave*, both of them highly successful at the box office in 1949 and also critically well received. Foreman remembers attempting, in adapting the Ring Lardner story 'Champion', to draw 'a parallel between the prize fight business and western society or capitalism in 1948', while Kramer remembers that 'I desperately hated the fight game'. *Champion* was shot in twenty days at a cost of £500,000. It tells a story of a young man, played by Kirk Douglas in his first screen role, whose poverty and sense of grievance drives him to boxing success. Foreman clearly attempts to provide an environmental rationale for Midge Kelly's ruthless rise – orphanage, cold and hunger, etc. – and there is the same emphasis on an alienated world of money and sex that is prevalent in *film noir*. At one point Kelly tells his brother that the fight game is 'like any other business – only the blood shows'. Yet while the film is relentlessly powerful, with fast montages and fight scenes, it lacks the darker tone of *film noir* – apart from the opening and closing scenes – that might broaden the critique beyond boxing. No social alternative to the fight game melodrama – in which the film's rousing music seems complicit – is available, as it is in *Body and Soul* and even in *The Set-Up*. The same team, including director Mark Robson, rushed *Home of the Brave* into production, so that it would become the first of several planned films on the race issue to be released, in 1949. Adapting the Arthur Laurents play about anti-Semitism, the film explores the effects of racism on a black GI during a wartime special assignment. The racist character in the film seems rather overdrawn, creating an easy target, and, as Roffman and Purdy argue, the neurosis of the black character is played up so much that 'his problem seems as much his own fault as that of racist America'.[5]

In 1948 John Huston set up an independent production
company, Horizon, in partnership with Sam Spiegel. Spiegel
had come to America in 1935, having been born in Austria and
worked in the film industry in Berlin, before leaving Germany
in 1933. Huston was interested in a story in a book by Robert
Sylvester, dealing with revolution in Cuba, and with Spiegel
he arranged financing and distribution at Columbia Pictures.
Budgeted at $900,000, the film was substantially shot on location
in Cuba, and written by Huston and Peter Viertel. The result,
We Were Strangers, was a strange concoction for 1949, and one
that predictably resulted in attacks on Huston from the right.

The story concerns a Cuban-born American, Tony Fenner
(John Garfield), who becomes involved in a revolutionary plan
to assassinate the corrupt and oppressive Cuban leadership. The
opening scenes of the film, while 'placed' in the Cuba of 1933,
can also be read as an oblique comment on the Washington
hearings and the blacklist, events that Huston regarded as
'obscene'. A man is shot down for distributing leaflets, while
scared parliamentarians are shown being pressured to outlaw
public assembly. An opening title relates the action of the film
to 'the White Terror under which the island of Cuba cowered
for seven long years, until its freedom loving heart found its
heroes in 1933'. In addition to this romantic, fable-like agenda
for the film, a further opening caption relates the events to
follow to the American ideals of Thomas Jefferson, and his
maxim that 'Resistance to tyrants is the word of God.' (In one
sense God and Jefferson were probably seen as useful insurance against criticism of the film's broadly sympathetic view of
revolution.)

The reference to heroes presumably is to Fenner, China
Valdes (Jennifer Jones) – who is politicised by the murder of her
young brother – and the other conspirators, although their plan
to plant a bomb may kill a hundred innocent people, friends
and relations of the 'hyenas', along with the guilty political
leadership. The moral ambiguity of the plot is an element of the
story, but the plan is never carried out, and at the end of the
film the police close in on the group, and after a battle, Fenner
dies in China's arms. Confusingly, but in line with the fable
suggested by the opening titles, this 'defeat' for the plot that
forms the central action of the film comes at the same time as
'victory' is proclaimed for a wider, popular uprising against the

regime. (Shots of leaders hanging upside down emphasise the broad support within the film for necessary violence against evil.)

Whatever the morally dubious nature of their scheme, it is difficult not to see the central figures as successful revolutionaries. Before his death Fenner talks despairingly of returning to the ordinary people of Spanish Harlem who raised the money for the fight, but after his 'heroic' death China's speech suggests that Fenner is to be seen as part of the struggle against oppression. (The speech almost suggests a 'Zapata'-like afterlife, except that minutes after his death his cause is proclaimed as victorious.) Gavin Lambert, writing for *Sequence*, related *We Were Strangers* to wartime films such as *They Were Expendable* and *A Walk in the Sun* which had embraced 'a collective study of men in crisis'.

There are clearly other readings, particularly of the ending, about which Spiegel was apparently unhappy. While the above reading finds the film to be surprisingly positive about violent action to remove dictatorship, Robert Sklar points to a film that 'abhors tyrants but is decidedly ambivalent towards movements that oppose them, and is most interested in the tragic fate of Americans who get in the way'. Both readings ultimately turn on the interpretation of Fenner/Garfield; it has been suggested here that Garfield's intensity, his commitment to the 'cause', makes him more than a stray American, while the action that he leads is less an example of the 'bad', 'terrorist' way forward than a constituent part of the fable's final popular revolt. Myron C. Fagan, of the Cinema Educational League, saw the film as 'Communistic', while, as Sklar shows, the *Daily Worker* was unimpressed by the film's treatment of Wall Street–Cuban relations.[6]

Thom Andersen includes *We Were Strangers* in the group of post-war films that he relates to *film noir*, and in which he sees John Garfield as a key signifying figure. (The stark and dramatic lighting of Huston's film was contributed by Russell Metty, who was accomplished in *noir* cinematography, and who is perhaps best known for his work on *Touch of Evil*.) More than any other 'star' of the time Garfield was both close to liberal-left circles, and also, in pre-war films such as *Four Daughters*, *Dust Be My Destiny* and *The Sea Wolf*, identified with some form of alienation from and rebellion against established society. To Abraham

Polonsky, the writer of Garfield's two key post-war films, *Body and Soul* and *Force of Evil*, the tragedy of Garfield's life is simply put: 'The Group trained him, the movies made him, the Blacklist killed him.'

Huston, like Welles, had begun his directing career in Hollywood before the war. Other directors of this generation began either in the war years, or in most cases in the immediate post-war period. The following sections examine the early work of a number of liberal-left directors in this period. Jim Cook and Alan Lovell discuss the interaction between their group of thirties artists and Hollywood in terms of the notion of 'negotiation', allowing for various types of accommodation between artist and the changing industrial and aesthetic structures and conventions of Hollywood at the time. Other writers have pointed to the lack of work on directors, relative to screenwriters, in terms of the impact of liberal and left ideas on Hollywood film. The limited attempts at independent production may not have had much impact on the bureaucratic and financial context of filmmaking, and at times greater autonomy was balanced by severe budgetary constraints. But the examples above and below suggest that new production structures did sometimes provide opportunities for the 'interesting ideas' seen by Abraham Polonsky as in the air at the time, especially given the new fashion for location shooting. This period can be seen as a time of interaction between individuals – part of a wider institutional practice – who viewed Hollywood's major role as the efficient production of entertainment, and a generation, influenced to a greater or lesser extent by 1930s and wartime political ideas, who were often conscious of the artistic and sometimes political judgements of their peers – generally outside of the industry – on their new work.[7]

JULES DASSIN AND ALBERT MALTZ

After the war, and his MGM apprenticeship, Jules Dassin worked twice with Mark Hellinger, who had left Warners and become an independent producer at Universal International. Hellinger had been a prominent Hearst press crime reporter in New York, and had contributed the story for Warners' epitaph to the gangster era, *The Roaring Twenties*, as well as producing Warners' films such as *They Drive By Night* (1940), *High Sierra*

(1941), and *Manpower* (1941), dealing with crime and working-class life. A product, in 1946, of a merger of International Pictures, created in 1943, and Universal, which wanted to exploit its wartime prosperity to achieve 'big five status', Universal-International was to make A pictures exclusively – with budgets rising towards £1m – and to become a home for independent producers, including the Mark Hellinger unit, and Diana Productions, involving Walter Wanger, Joan Bennett and Fritz Lang. With the beginning of the market downturn, super-vision of productions was tightened in 1947, and Universal returned to a low cost 'assembly line strategy' in 1949.[8]

To Jules Dassin the working environment at Universal was not easy, and their 'laws, their values and above all their money, weighed heavily on you'. Hellinger produced *The Killers* (1946), and then two other 'social' dramas, both of them directed by Jules Dassin. The first, *Brute Force* (1947), a social *film noir*, introduced the wartime anti-fascist and collective theme into a domestic, prison drama. Written by Richard Brooks, the film achieves a distinctiveness within the rather clichéd prison genre by its violence and intensity. The final revolt of the prisoners is led by Joe Collins (Burt Lancaster) in the knowledge that it is doomed to failure; the prison is portrayed as a fascist state, with the liberal constitutional authorities powerless to check the dictatorial power of the senior guard, Capt. Munsey (Hume Cronyn). Although there is mention and depiction of over-crowding this is less a social problem film than a film about men who are left no option but to revolt, doomed as that revolt must be. (The film contrasts with the more sociological *Riot in Cell Block 11*, written by Richard Collins for Walter Wanger.) For Collins and most of the inmates of cell R.17, catharsis comes only with death. In the final scene of the film the camera retreats to view the ineffectual liberal doctor (Art Smith) looking out of the bars of a cell: 'Nobody escapes,' he says, 'nobody ever really escapes.' Siegfried Kracauer cited Art Smith's humanistic doc-tor, fighting the good but losing fight, as a further example of how the immediately post-war films, from *Crossfire* to *Boomerang* and *The Best Years of Our Lives*, show liberalism on the defensive.

After *Brute Force* Dassin directed *The Naked City* for Hellinger. Malvin Wald, a young writer with wartime experience of work-ing on training and documentary films, suggested a semi-documentary story, to be based on New York Police Department files. Dassin expressed an interest in the idea, and Albert Maltz was hired to work on Wald's first draft script. The result was a screenplay that emphasised the routine, unglamorous nature of police work, and also examined the social and economic contrasts of life in the city. As Colin McArthur points out, the social criticism in the film is a product of the script rather than Dassin's directorial contributions. The script stresses each character's economic status, from the dead girl's aspiration to be rich, to her Polish-American parents and their hardships in the Depression. The chief suspect, Frank Niles, plays bridge with Park Avenue friends and takes a 'flyer on the stock market on inside tips'; veteran detective Dan Muldoon (Barry Fitzgerald) comments that Niles spends as much in one night as he does in a week supporting his wife and three kids.

The film was shot entirely on location in New York in the summer of 1947, and to Dassin his freedom was increased by the fact that the Universal executives 'didn't know what I was doing'. But to Dassin, when the film opened in New York in March 1948 its 'humanist' vision – emphasising the contrasts in wealth in the city – had been 'ripped out of the film, because Albert Maltz had just been named'. The decision of the studio executives not to employ the Hollywood Ten, including Maltz, and the death of Hellinger, in December, both increased front-office sensitivity to the film.

Whatever the extent of the cuts, the film retains enough location footage to reflect some of the original emphasis on a progressive populism. The film begins with an extended montage of shots of New York at night. The man sleeping outside on a fire escape, the night worker at a power station and a woman sweeping up at a railway station are balanced by a scene of dinner-jacketed revellers at the Trinidad Club, 'rounding off', as Hellinger's narration explains, 'an evening of relaxation'. Much of the film is on the margins of *film noir*, and the location shooting seems less effective than in *Call Northside 777*, hardly living up to the reference to the photographs of Wegee implied by the title. Nor is there anything of the frustration with police work shown by Lee Cobb in *Boomerang*. There are brief shots of life on the streets interspersed with long static scenes in which Lieutenant Muldoon perches on the edge of desks, albeit real New York desks, while co-ordinating the search for the murderer. Only in the final chase does the city reappear as a major actor; to James Agee the result, barring this 'majestic finish', was 'mawkish and naive'.[9]

Albert Maltz's work had been much in demand during the war, while in 1946 he became involved in what became a notorious affair, following his article in *New Masses*. The debate followed the replacement of Earl Browder as head of the American Communist Party at the end of the war. Browder had dissolved the American Communist Party in 1944 and re-formed it as the Communist Political Association, but a year later the French communist Jacques Duclos denounced the new body, seeing it as betraying revolutionary principles. The Communist Party was reconstituted following the debate on the Duclos letter, with William Z. Foster at its head. To Polonsky the new policy was 'absurd', and was one of 'ramming an arbitrary revolutionary policy down the throats of American communists'. Maltz's article argued that too strict an adherence to the notion of art as a weapon had narrowed and restricted artistic activity on the left; he made the heretical point that an artist could be great without 'being an integrated or a logical or a progressive thinker on all matters', and that writers should be judged by the work, rather than by the committees that they joined. Maltz's position was fiercely attacked in the *New Masses* and *Daily Worker*, and he eventually admitted the errors of his position in a subsequent article of April 9, 1946.[10]

But Maltz was effectively blacklisted after the Waldorf statement in November 1947. Zanuck had purchased a new Maltz novel, *The Journey of Simon McKeever*, and planned a film with direction by Dassin and a script written by John Huston. But consultation with New York, and pressure from the Alliance for the Preservation of American Ideals, led to the cancellation of the project. When Fox producer Julian Blaustein asked Maltz to write a script based on an Elliott Arnold novel, *Blood Brothers*, Maltz's blacklisted status led him to agree with his friend Michael Blankfort that Blankfort would front for him, and that he would receive Blankfort's fee. The resulting film, *Broken Arrow* (1950), was endorsed by the Association of American Indian Affairs as one of the first films to attempt 'a serious portrayal of the Indian side of American history'. Maltz's responsibility for the script was revealed publically only in 1991.

Instead of the film of the Maltz novel, Dassin made the first of two films at Fox, before he also became a victim of the

blacklist and moved to Europe. *Thieves Highway* (1949), from a
script by the proletarian writer A.I. Bezzerides, echoed the
concerns of *They Drive By Night*, which was also based on a
Bezzerides novel about the struggles of truck drivers. Bezzerides
remembers being frustrated by Zanuck's demands for script
changes, and the resulting film was less documentary realism
than – in Barry Gifford's review – 'a typical proletarian melodrama that pits one earnest man against an exploitative, corrupt
businessman attempting to control a marketplace'. The script at
times suggests a broader critique, but also provides a villain –
the 'produce dealer', played by Lee J. Cobb – who divides and
rules, but whose eventual downfall contributes to the reassuring
ending. Dassin points up the excitement and *film noir* exoticism
but, as Colin McArthur argues, he adds little to any thematic
statement implicit in the script.[11]

JOSEPH LOSEY

Losey recounts how he had lost some of the sense of optimism
and struggle that he felt in the 1930s. Although he was a
member of the Communist Party only briefly, after the war, his
left-wing reputation had led him to be vetoed during the war
by both the Air Corps and the Navy. He later recollected that
after Hiroshima, 'after the death of Roosevelt, and after the
investigations, only then did one begin to see the complete
unreality of the American dream'. Following his contract at
RKO, where he worked on *The Boy with Green Hair*, Losey briefly
followed Dore Schary to MGM. But the writer and former
journalist Daniel Mainwaring – who often wrote under the name
Geoffrey Homes – cleared the way for Losey to work on a
project for an independent unit at Paramount. Losey, who
recalls telling Schary that he was making a mistake by going to
MGM, chose the relative freedom, within a drastically limited
budget, of the William Pine and William Thomas B-picture unit,
despite the fact that he found the producers to be 'monsters'.
(They were known as the 'dollar Bills', in recognition of their
consistently successful commercialism; their films were generally
produced for less than $300,000.)
    In terms of *The Lawless* (1950), it was Mainwaring who insisted
on a story that allowed discussion of discrimination against
Mexican-Americans in California, an issue that had first come

to public attention in the war years. Mainwaring's script for the film, which Losey was to direct, provoked an unusual reaction from the Breen Office when it was submitted in October 1949. While Breen found the script to be compatible with the Production Code, he also found the story to be a 'shocking indictment of America and its people'. He argued that the 'over-all effect of a story of this kind made into a motion picture would be, we think, a very definite disservice to this country of ours, and to its institutions and its ideals'. Breen warned against further steps towards a film based on the material submitted, and urged that the matter be raised with 'the responsible executive of your company'. The Breen Office was eventually satisfied, and the film was shot in 21 days at a cost that Losey remembers as only $150,000. One critic described the completed film as dealing with 'a hysterical man-hunt for a Mexican youth mistakenly accused of attacking an Anglo-Saxon girl'. Newspaper reporters play up the case and a mob breaks into a newspaper office and destroys a printing press, before the riot nearly ends with the lynching of the boy. Jewish and black reviewers saw the film as a valuable defence of minority interests; a writer for *Ebony* in particular welcomed 'the penetration of the racial theme into the B picture class'. The film is arguably characteristic of Losey's work of this time in its criticism, not only of the rich, but of the ordinary people, the 'square' guys – to use Bud Crocker's language in *The Prowler* – of small-town and suburban America; the story of *The Lawless* also seems to connect with other films of the time, including *The Sound of Fury* and *Ace in the Hole*, as well as with the later *Invasion of the Body Snatchers* – also written by Mainwaring.

Losey next signed with Sam Spiegel (then calling himself S.P. Eagle), to direct *The Prowler* (1951), based on a script by Dalton Trumbo and Hugo Butler. (Only Butler was credited, because Trumbo had been blacklisted.) There are elements of *Double Indemnity* in this *film noir*, but where Wilder is cynical, a more coherent, if not necessarily more powerful social critique can be found in the later film. To Losey *The Prowler* is 'a film about false values': '"100,000 bucks, a Cadillac, and a blonde" were the *sine qua non* of American life at that time and it didn't matter how you got them – whether you stole the girl from somebody else, stole the money and got the Cadillac from corruption'.[12] The plot concerns a police officer, Webb Garwood (Van Heflin) who is called to a house to investigate a suspected prowler, and first meets Susan Gilvray (Evelyn Keyes), the lonely and frustrated wife of a successful, but impotent, radio broadcaster. On the first of Garwood's recurring visits to the baroque house, the relationship between sex and money as objects of his desire is emphasised. Garwood's partner recommends that Susan pull down her blind, while telling her that banks do well to keep the counting room well out of sight. Bored by his unambitious police friends – shades of *In a Lonely Place* – Garwood is attracted as much by the prospect of social success as by greed and sexual passion. His facination with her and the life she represents – a pre-credit sequence briefly allows the audience to share this perspective – connects with her desperation and gullibility; his resulting murder of the husband leads ultimately to the retreat of the couple from modern civilisation, and to the desert location where the law finally tracks them down.

The Breen Office was at the time trying to hold the line against the emergence on the screen of wartime and post-war changes in values and behaviour. The verdict on the first script was negative, with Breen finding 'a story of extremely low moral tone, with emphasis on almost animal-like instincts and passions'. In order to give greater stress to the punishment of sin, Breen suggested that scenes of police activity be injected at various points 'so as to strike a note of impending doom and ultimate tragedy', an interesting example of the influence of censorship – or self-regulation – on the *film noir* form. Both the Breen Office and Losey and his writers had a moral tale to tell; Breen insisted that Garwood later become a 'voice for morality' by showing contrition, but the emphasis at the end of the film is as much on Garwood's resentment that he is to be caught for behaviour that others regularly get away with. He tells his wife that 'I'm not any different from those other guys – some do it for a million, some for ten, I did it for 62,000'. A lengthy vetting process did not prevent the Censor Boards in Maryland and Massachusetts making some dialogue cuts, in particular concerning the paternity of the baby. Sam Spiegel, an accomplished producer – if not always very quick to pay his writers – commented on the problems with the Production Code, noting that 'we fought it out and won', and that the 'woman sort of atones for it by suffering'.

Losey had arranged to work with Foreman, George Glass and

Stanley Kramer, in their new unit at Columbia Pictures. But before that, in 1950, Losey worked at that studio on a faithful remake of *M*, the Fritz Lang film of 1931. Losey cast David Wayne as M, the child murderer, and emphasised the extent to which M was a victim, persecuted by an equally disturbed society. The police are like the gangsters, if less ruthless and efficient, while the script, primarily written by Waldo Salt according to Losey, emphasises the role of the murderer as a scapegoat. When someone remarks that the killer will 'burn' when he is caught, the Inspector (Howard Da Silva) comments: 'That's right. That will fix everything.' The drunken lawyer who speaks up for the murderer, as he is threatened with lynching by a mob, asks whether a blind man should be lynched because he cannot see. As with his other American films, Losey uses the new opportunities to film on location, in this case in the older parts of Los Angeles, with particular effectiveness.

Losey's last film in Hollywood was *The Big Night* (1951), a film produced independently by Philip Waxman, for a United Artists release. Shot for $300,000, the film contains melodramatic elements, but is directed in a generally restrained manner. The story concerns a young boy, George La Main (John Barrymore Jr), who, on his seventeenth birthday, sees his father being ritualistically beaten and humiliated. The boy takes a gun and sets off to exact revenge on the perpetrator, a sports journalist called Al Judge. What follows is a quest that takes the young boy to a boxing arena and to a series of clubs, bars and nightclubs haunted by the criminal, the desperate and the lonely. Again, there is something of Losey's recurring interest in false social values; George feels that his gun gives him adultness, while, after paying a compliment to a black nightclub singer, he thoughtlessly, and to his immediate but futile regret, adds the remark, 'Even if you are . . . ' The climax of the film comes when George confronts Al Judge, and learns a more complicated explanation of his father's beating.

From one perspective the film can be compared to *Force of Evil*; one critic sees Losey's film as about a child who learns to accept society's guilt, and his own complicity in it, and who 'therefore takes a decisive step towards his own general emotional maturity and freedom'. Whether the conclusion to the film – in which George confronts his father with the truth and takes responsibility for his actions – has this impact is rather doubtful. Losey's intended flashback structure, however, was replaced by a chronological one, when the director, fearing the imminent delivery of a subpoena, left America to work on a new film in Italy. Losey's trip turned out to be the beginning of his long exile in Europe.[13]

ABRAHAM POLONSKY AND ENTERPRISE STUDIOS

After the war Polonsky returned from service with the Office of Strategic Services to Paramount, the studio where he had signed a contract in 1939. Polonsky, from what he saw as his primary world of writing and universities, became fascinated by the movies, but realised quickly that the creative power lay with the director. In early 1946 David L. Loew, Charles Einfeld (previously an executive at Warners) and A. Pam Blumenthal secured a revolving credit of £10m from the Bank of America to establish Enterprise Studios. Studio lots were leased, and distribution was arranged, first through UA, then MGM. Established stars were attracted away from the major studios by the chance to participate in the profits, and into the studio came another company set up jointly by John Garfield, whose contract with Warners had expired, and his former business manager Bob Roberts. Their company, Roberts Productions, began by providing Enterprise with *Body and Soul*, which cost $1.8m and grossed $4.7m, becoming the studio's one major commercial success from its nine productions, released between 1947 and 1949.

While Enterprise aspired to make all types of films, it attracted to it a number of radical or liberal artists, including Garfield, Abraham Polonsky, Robert Rossen, Arnold Manhoff, John Berry and Robert Aldrich. Screen Plays also made their first film for Enterprise, *So This is New York* (1948), from a Carl Foreman script. Robert Aldrich wrote of Enterprise as embodying a 'communal way to make films', but he admitted that 'there was nobody at the head of the studio to bring us all up short'. By mid-1948, with the failure of *Arch of Triumph*, which had cost over $4m, the studio was in deep financial trouble. To Polonsky Enterprise was a 'grand new idea'; the problem was that 'they didn't make very good pictures'.[14] John Berry, who worked at Enterprise, and was an interim director on *Caught*, is generally referred to in accounts of the liberal – or humanistic, or

Plate 4: Filming *The Naked City* (Universal, 1948) on location in New York. Reproduced courtesy of BFI Stills, Posters and Designs.

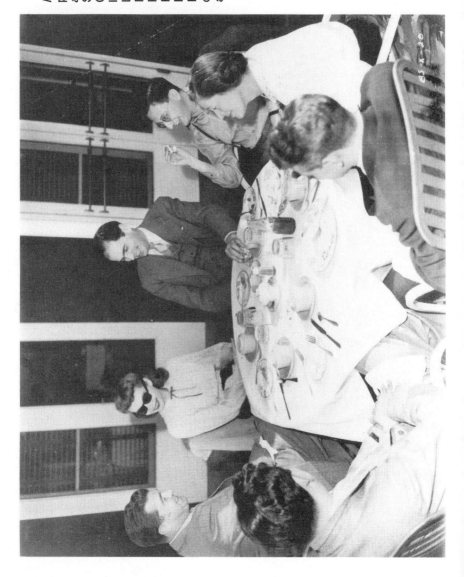

Plate 5: During production of *Body and Soul* (Enterprise Studios, 1947). Clockwise from top left: Robert Rossen, Lilli Palmer, Gottfried Reinhardt, Abraham Polonsky, Ann Revere, Joseph Pevney, John Garfield. Reproduced courtesy of BFI Stills, Posters and Designs.

Plate 6: Ben Tucker's office, in *Force of Evil* (Enterprise Studios, 1948). Making the calculations: Joe Morse (John Garfield). Reproduced courtesy of BFI Stills, Posters and Designs.

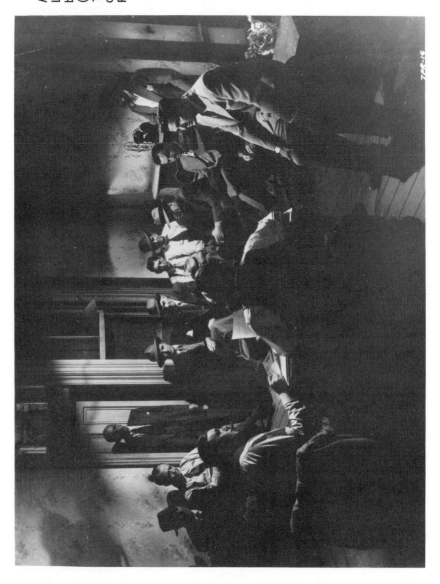

Plate 7: In contrast, Leo Morse's numbers bank in *Force of Evil* (Enterprise Studios, 1948). Reproduced courtesy of BFI Stills, Posters and Designs.

Plate 8: Martha Ivers (Barbara Stanwyck) and Iverstown in *The Strange Love of Martha Ivers* (Paramount, 1946). Reproduced courtesy of BFI Stills, Posters and Designs.

sometimes radical – movement in Hollywood. His first film, for RKO, *From This Day Forward* (1946), had dealt unusually with the everyday problems of a married couple during the Depression, although the result was generally sentimental, and undermined by Joan Fontaine's star casting. His last film in Hollywood before he left for Europe was *He Ran All the Way* (1951), which was produced by Bob Roberts for UA, and which was also John Garfield's last film.

Polonsky moved to Enterprise from Paramount to write the original script for *Body and Soul* (1947), and Robert Rossen, who had just directed *Johnny O'Clock* at Columbia, was suggested as director. Rossen had written for Garfield at Warners, but the fact that Rossen was a communist was also a positive consideration in the decision to give him the chance. Polonsky remembers a conference attended by both David Loew and Charles Einfeld at which Rossen was hired, subject to his agreeing not to change a line of the script, and that the director was held to that pledge under the threat of being fired. Also employed on the film were assistant director Robert Aldrich – who became Polonsky's lifelong friend – and cinematographer James Wong Howe, who also had a long association with 'social' filmmaking.

Throughout, Polonsky's script for *Body and Soul* places the fable of the streets in the context of a system of business, of a capitalist system, that is more powerful and all-pervading than any individual character in the film – except, ultimately, Charlie Davis. Davis' story is told in flashback, following an opening sequence in which he prepares for a fight which he has contracted to lose for $60,000. The audience sees how, as an energetic young man from the East Side slums, Davis only took up boxing after watching his mother humiliated by the questions of a charity worker; she tells him to 'fight for something, not for money'. Once a fighter, Davis is soon advised to cut in Roberts, a promoter who is described as 'the dough, the real estate, everything – the business'. Davis (John Garfield) achieves success but becomes himself obsessed by money, leaving or betraying his friends, including the black boxer Ben, who dies following a bout with Davis – who was not told that he suffered from a blood clot. Only at the end of the film, with his triumphant victory in the ring, a victory which bankrupts him and is sure to threaten his life, does Davis act on the self-knowledge his success has brought him. He wins the fight, and affirms not only himself, but his parents, his best friend, his social roots, his girl friend and Ben. As Polonsky's shooting script expresses it, at the end 'the neighborhood swallows Charley up'.

Polonsky remembers that Rossen wanted to end the picture by having Davis suffer the consequences of his action, being shot by the mob, and falling into a barrel of filth and garbage. Polonsky's version ended with Davis' defiant words, echoing the phrase used by Roberts throughout the film: 'What are you going to do – kill me?', he tells Roberts, 'Everybody dies.' After viewing both endings Rossen accepted Polonsky's more affirmative version. To Polonsky, Rossen's ending was heroic, but was 'totally against the meaning of the picture, which is nothing more than a fable of the streets'. The point of interest is Davis' eventual spiritual growth and his romantic return to his roots, while what may follow, the ending that Rossen favoured, is not part of the fable.[15]

Garfield and Roberts then offered Polonsky the chance of directing a 'melodrama', and Polonsky chose Ira Wolfert's book, *Tucker's People*, and worked with Wolfert on the script. Enterprise had serious financial problems at the time, in 1948, but the Bank of America extended its loan to allow the film, and two others, to be completed. *Force of Evil* cost $1.15m, and was released in December 1948, by which time Enterprise Studios had disbanded. Polonsky has described Wolfert's book as a melodrama about the numbers racket, but in reality about 'everything else in the world, including the nature and structure of finance capital and its effect on people, and the way in which the numbers racket was a kind of symbol of the capitalist system'. Within the gangster genre, which hid the film's social critique, *Force of Evil* drew an explicit parallel between corruption and racketeering and the 'normal' operation of American business. The film failed in its objective to reach large audiences, but was recognised by a minority as both distinctive and experimental. A review in *Sequence*, the British film magazine, saw it as a 'writer's film', but praised the assimilation of the dialogue, with its 'almost poetic, incantatory effect', into the action. Polonsky remembers an appreciative letter from Lindsay Anderson, a co-editor of *Sequence*.[16]

Force of Evil begins with shots of Wall Street from above, and with Joe Morse (Garfield), who is both narrator and central character, contemplating the making of his first million dollars. A lawyer for a 'corporation' run by an ex-gangster, Ben Tucker,

Joe's brief is to work for a smooth transition of the company's 'numbers racket' operation into a legal lottery. Joe Morse's peace of mind is only disturbed when his obligations to the combination bring him into renewed contact with his older, less successful brother, Leo. Leo runs a small, dingy 'collection office' which is – the narrator explains – like a bank, in that money is deposited there, but unlike a bank because of the infinitesimal chances of withdrawing, or winning. As Tucker's people plan the racket – the fixing of a winning lottery number – that will strengthen the combination, Joe Morse explains the strategy: 'Tomorrow night every bank in the city is broken. And we step in and lend money to who we want while we let the rest go to the wall. We're normal financiers.'

The plot turns on Joe Morse's guilt about his brother, Leo Morse, and his relationship with Leo's former secretary, Doris Lowery; another of Leo's employees, the bookkeeper Bower, informs on the organisation, and this leads ultimately to the death of Leo at the hands of the old-fashioned gangsters who are seeking an alliance with Tucker. With his brother's death, and his increasing complicity in violence, Joe Morse decides to help the special prosecutor who, although never seen in the film, is investigating the rackets. The dialogue, while sharply related to this narrative, more importantly suggests a world in which alienation and despair are conditions of the system. Unlike a 1930s Warners Bros story, the authorities here are passive, suggesting that there is no 'cure' for the 'problem': the police are only activated by tip-offs, while the special prosecutor is never seen, and no decisive change is suggested by the ending.

It is the dialogue that immediately distinguishes the film, without in any way diminishing the credibility of the characters. In *Body and Soul*, as Charlie Davis prepares for the big (fixed) fight, the smooth, business-suited Roberts tells his boxer how things are: 'You know the way the betting is, Charlie. The numbers are in. Everything is addition or subtraction. The rest is conversation.' Polonsky suggests that language is both determined – that it frequently disguises and obscures reality – and free, a form of revolt against how the world works. Money talks, but so, poetically and sometimes subversively, do individuals. These lines capture much of Polonsky's play with language, its infinite and lyrical possibilities, and also suggest its 'superstructural' evasions and limitations. In *Force of Evil* Joe Morse knows that his brother will ultimately join the combination, while clinging to his delusions that his small-time numbers bank is a public service, while Doris Lowery will also turn up for the job that he can promise her. All, including himself, have – to paraphrase another of Joe's lines – enough strength to fight for a piece of corruption, but not enough to resist it.

As has been shown elsewhere, characters in the film constantly refer to criminal activity as normal business. Leo Morse sees his previous businesses, real estate and a garage, as petty larceny, while the unseen special prosecutor is seen as part of this world: 'Hall is the business', Joe Morse says, 'and Ben Tucker is his stock in trade.' Even Polonsky's richest lines, closest in feeling to Odets, are related to the narrative and theme. When Joe Morse is moving towards greater self-awareness, increasingly guilty that his brother is paying the price for his success, he expresses this to Doris by telling her, 'My trouble is, Miss Lowery, that I feel like midnight, and I don't know what morning will be.'

Joe descends to the river at the end of the film, to find his brother's body, thrown away 'like a dirty rag nobody wants'. He has already announced his decision to co-operate with Hall, something which is well motivated, given the murder of his brother, but which may have been influenced by Production Code pressures. (The PCA were shocked at the depiction of the police, and objected to the 'completely anti-social basic theme of this story, which presents wrong as right and right as wrong'.) In his voice-over Joe tells how he 'turned back to give myself up to Hall because if a man's life can be lived so long and come out this way, like rubbish, then something was horrible, and had to be ended one way or another. And I decided to help.' The music is quietly affirmative, suggesting a kind of moral awakening on the part of Joe Morse, rather than any 'solution' to a problem. The root causes suggested in Polonsky's film are clearly beyond the remit of a special prosecutor, although Polonsky does suggest, through his central character, how the fetters of the system can be broken by self-knowledge.

Polonsky regarded what he called post-war 'social radicals' as covering a wide spectrum of opinion, with traditional Communist Party attitudes at the centre, but also encompassing liberal democrats, socialists and others. He saw his artistic and political interests as without contradiction, and his two key films of the 1940s suggest his Marxist thinking, about the nature of capitalism, while they also attest to his belief in the possibilities of artistic and political autonomy, for his characters and himself. Polonsky was to write one further script, before his long Hollywood exile began.[17]

NICHOLAS RAY

During the war Nicholas Ray had been assistant to John Houseman, who was then head of the OWI's Voice of America. In 1944 Ray came to Hollywood with Elia Kazan, and was assistant director on *A Tree Grows in Brooklyn*; in 1945 he worked with Joseph Losey in staging a Roosevelt memorial event at the Hollywood Bowl. To Houseman, a friend of Ray since the mid-1930s, Ray had 'been taught to regard hardship and poverty as a virtue and power as evil'. Ray had written an adaptation of Edward Anderson's Depression novel, *Thieves Like Us*, on the suggestion of Houseman, who was a producer at RKO. Schary then approved Houseman's project, with ex-Mercury Theater contributor Charles Schnee as the scriptwriter and Ray – again on Houseman's urging – as a first-time director. The resulting film, the release of which was delayed by Howard Hughes' takeover of the studio in mid-1948, was *They Live By Night*.

The tone of the film is announced immediately, by the close-up of the lovers, while a caption explains that they 'were never properly introduced to the world we live in'. Bowie (Farley Granger) is the driver for a gang of robbers who cannot break away from his life of crime; when he marries Keechie (Cathy O'Donnell), they become doomed lovers, clutching for normality. We both identify with first the gang, and then the fugitive couple, by watching from inside the car, and we also view them from above, in sequences shot by helicopter. In the original book one of the robbers described the bankers, ever ready to exploit a robbery by suggesting that more money had been stolen than was the case, as 'thieves just like us'. There are suggestions of this metaphor in the film. When the two lovers get married they purchase a licence for $20 from a rather pathetic man who earns a living from catering to fugitive lovers, and he tells Bowie that he is a thief just as Bowie is. When Bowie finds it impossible to leave the gang, another member, T-Dub, tells him that their partnership to 'charge' banks is a business; 'so to speak, you're an investment, and you're going to pay off'. But the emphasis is on the irony of the two lovers, trying to attain a normality that is often belied by the cynicism and vindictiveness of what is shown of 'adult' society. The pay-offs, the $20 marriages and the public taste for lurid tales are contrasted to the 'innocence' of the central couple. They are at their happiest drinking Cokes in their car, and they dream of holding hands at the movies. As Biskind suggests, the film offers more of a sentimental affirmation of the unlucky and the misunderstood, than any very consistent critique of society, still less of capitalism.

Ray's next film, *Knock on Any Door*, was more conventional than his first, but more unambiguous in its attack on the social causes of crime. The source book was originally purchased by Mark Hellinger, and following his death the company formed by Humphrey Bogart and others, Santana, took on the project, and the film was produced by Robert Lord, late of Warners. (Robert Rossen also made a bid for the property.) The National Probation and Parole Association acted as technical advisers. Bogart plays a liberal lawyer, Andrew Morton, who has pulled himself to success and respectability from a beginning in the slums of Chicago. Reluctantly, and at a cost to his career, Morton agrees to defend a young Italian American delinquent, Nick Romano (John Derek), against a charge of murdering a police officer during a robbery. Most of the film covers the trial, but during Morton's defence testimony there are flashbacks which illustrate the young boy's life of crime, from the first time Morton met him.[18]

Romano's father died in prison because of legal incompetence, for which Morton feels partly responsible, and when the young man steals a car he is subjected to a brutal regime in a reform school. There are signs of a desire to break the mould, particularly when he gets married, but Romano, whose motto is 'Live fast, die young and have a good-looking corpse', seems unable to avoid the course laid out for him. Morton is convinced that he is innocent, but at the end of the case, and of the film, Romano breaks down after sustained questioning by the prosecuting attorney, and admits his guilt. This allows Morton to make a passionate statement to the judge, before the sentence is read, in which he blames the selfishness and stupidity and blindness of 'society', and in particular the 'solid citizens of this community', for the generic problem of which Nick Romano is one example. Morton's appeal for mercy fails, however, and the final scene is of Romano's long walk to the electric chair.

ROBERT ROSSEN

Rossen's career in the 1940s illuminates many of the changes in the industry structure in that decade, and in particular the growth of more autonomous production units inside and out-side of the studios. By 1944 Rossen had left Warners, and he spent a year in New York, disturbed, according to his later friendly testimony to the House Committee, 'by a great many things that were going on in the party, and my own work'. Memos from Warners at the time seem to suggest Rossen's impatience or frustration with the production system, while he worked on a number of uncompleted projects. He later testified that he began to believe that writers could only 'function in a complete entity', if they had the opportunity to direct their own work.[19]

When Rossen returned to filmmaking he wrote screenplays for two films directed by Lewis Milestone. After scripting Harry Brown's novel for the film *A Walk in the Sun* Rossen signed a contract with Hal Wallis, who had established his own company on leaving Warners. (Paramount bought a partnership in Hal Wallis Productions, and partly financed and released its films.) Under this contract Rossen wrote the script for *The Strange Love of Martha Ivers*, from a short story by John Patrick. Since the story covered little more than the prologue of the final film, the script is an interesting reflection of the writer's concerns. The emphasis is on the relationship between three individuals who, as children, had apparently been witnesses to a murder. (A prologue to the film shows Martha striking her dictatorial aunt, leading to her death, in the presence of Walter and – apparently – Sam.) When one of that group, Sam Masterton (Van Heflin), returns to the town by chance some sixteen years later, he discovers the other two have become the town's power elite, and his arrival sets off the melodrama.

When Sam comes into town he finds, in what a roadside placard announces as 'America's Fastest Growing Industrial City', a town dominated by the massive industrial plant owned and managed by Martha Ivers (Barbara Stanwyck), Sam's childhood friend. It was Rossen's idea to make Martha, and her alcoholic husband Walter (Kirk Douglas), who is running for the post of District Attorney, wrongly suspect that Sam had returned with the intention of using his knowledge of the murder for the purpose of blackmail. Sam Masterton, a war veteran and gambler, meets up with a parolee, Toni (Lizabeth Scott) – a typical Rossen loser from, like Sam, the wrong side of the tracks – and this leads to an intertwining of the characters that is eventually resolved by the revelation of past secrets and the double suicide of Martha and Walter.

The fact that Martha Ivers is a successful business executive and Walter O'Neil a District Attorney encourages connections to be made between their distorted personalities – they have let an innocent man hang for the murder of Mrs Ivers – and their positions of power. The company town is presented as mean spirited, as if everyone is a party to the deceit and false values on which power rests. The prologue shows Walter's father to have been obsessed by Mrs Ivers' wealth and social position, while the grown up Walter O'Neil's perspective is reflected in lines from the final script which were not used in the film, but which suggest the alienated, contractual relationships that recur in *film noir*. Walter tells Martha: 'You are my father's estate. His gift to me. He brought me up to believe that it's a son's duty to protect his inheritance.' In the film Walter does ask Martha to accept that the unsolved murder was a threat to the 'power and the riches that you'd learned to love so much, and that I'd learned to love too'.[20]

Sam is tempted by Martha, who at one point encourages him to kill Walter and to replace him as her partner in a contract to suppress the truth, but Sam finally walks away, leaving town for the west, and marriage with Toni Marachek. Working closely with Lewis Milestone, Rossen was able to set much of the tone of the film, although Hal Wallis had not renounced the close involvement in filmmaking that he exercised at Warners, and the close-ups of Lizabeth Scott, and Miklos Rozsa's elaborate and near-continuous score, reflect his notion of a Hal Wallis Production. How much the social context of the personal melodrama was noticed is open to question, although John R. Lechner, executive director of the Motion Picture Alliance for the Preservation of American Ideals, was merely pointing the way for the House Committee, and ultimately the studios in their blacklist, by citing the film, with others, as containing 'sizeable doses of Communist propaganda'. Neither the Alliance nor the Committee provided analysis of film content, but merely associated films with FBI and other information on the political affiliations of individuals.

Rossen's first experience of directing came when he was called in by Harry Cohn at Columbia to write the script of *Johnny O'Clock*, and when Cohn and the star, Dick Powell, asked him to direct. Abraham Polonsky has noted that Rossen's talent as a director was expressed as 'force applied everywhere without let-up', but Bernard Tavernier has argued, discussing *Johnny O'Clock*, that the film exhibits a 'directorial grace', and an invention, not shown in Rossen's later career. Tavernier saw the film as reflecting Rossen's 'Jewish pessimism and idealism', a combination that was 'perfect for *film noir*'.[21]

Johnny O'Clock (1947) concerns a gambling outfit that is profitable, and which seems to operate at the edge of the law. Johnny O'Clock (Powell) manages a casino and is a junior partner to Guido Marchettis (Thomas Gomez); he has an affluent lifestyle, and at the beginning of the film he is also a 'business associate' of a corrupt cop called Blayden. When a gambler is killed by Blayden, apparently resisting arrest, O'Clock's world – and the narrative takes place around a small number of studio sets – comes under investigation by Kotch (Lee J. Cobb), a cynical and hard-bitten detective. O'Clock resists Kotch's inquiries, and seems entirely selfish and invulnerable – an echo of Bogart's wartime pose. The abbreviated, mean-spirited dialogue is an analogue to cautious, calculating behaviour. Blayden describes O'Clock's interest in a girl in terms of his having 'the first mortgage', while other characters explain their loyalty, or lack of it, in terms of pragmatism and profit. When O'Clock is finally forced into a confrontation with his partner Marchettis, who is guilty of the two murders, he remarks: 'Twenty years together down the drain.' Marchettis replies: 'There was nothing between us but cash'.

Here again relationships are reduced to a nexus of cash and sex. O'Clock and Nancy Hobson (Evelyn Keyes), sister of the murdered hat-check girl, develop a relationship, but it is only at the end of the film that this experience begins to break down O'Clock's code. When O'Clock stalls Kotch he sneeringly asks him, 'How much money have you got'; Kotch's response is to ask O'Clock how much 'time have you got – to live'. In O'Clock's predatory world, which is largely the world of the film, only in the park are rich and poor equal: 'on a hot night', O'Clock tells Nancy, 'anyone can sleep on the grass'. O'Clock, he tells her, is 'no fool'; he will pay off Marchettis at a time of his choosing: 'I'll pick the spot and I'll pick the time. And I'll get away with it. All my life I've operated that way. And all this time I've won.' Yet, not for the last time, a Rossen protagonist has finally to reconsider the meaning of winning. He confronts Marchettis only to collect his share of the business profits, before planning to run, and he kills his partner only in self-defence. He seems ready to shoot Kotch too, but – vulnerable now – he gives himself up, breaking his code.

Rossen's world is pessimistic, and there is no explicit affirmative vision, as in Polonsky's work. Yet there is a romanticism in the last scene, and an alternative vision is present, buried deep in Cobb's world-weary performance. Rossen's detached protagonist finally joins society. Every scene of the film is directed with care and imagination, and the musical score also undercuts the dominant tone of the film, hinting at the romanticism beneath the surface, the reluctant altruism that Michael Wood sees as characteristic of the hardboiled American film of the period.

The modest success of *Johnny O'Clock* led to the approach by Roberts Productions, including John Garfield, to direct *Body and Soul*, and this in turn led to Rossen signing a contract with Columbia Pictures. This contract gave Rossen considerable autonomy (including the responsibility of producing and directing) over every alternative film he made at the studio. Rossen's services were in demand at this time, in 1947, and he also acted in what he later called an 'advisory capacity' in the scriptwriting stage of the production of *Ruthless* (1948), a film that was directed by Edgar Ulmer, and which presents precisely the negative view of business that was currently disturbing Eric Johnston. Alvah Bessie's colourful account of Rossen's role indicates something of the influence that the left – as a kind of fraternity – could have at the time, in the lower budget reaches of filmmaking.[22] For Columbia – his contract with Wallis was left in some dispute – Rossen produced *The Undercover Man*, directed by Joseph H. Lewis, and he was then able to write, produce and direct for the first time, choosing Robert Penn Warren's 1946 bestseller, *All the King's Men*, as his property.

At this time Rossen had contributed to the post-war discussion of the proper direction of American filmmaking, and he was particularly impressed with the British and French films that were honoured by the New York critics in 1946, including *Open City*, *Brief Encounter*, *A Matter of Life and Death* and *Henry V*. By contrast he depreciated the 'cinderella stories' that Hollywood producers favoured, and praised *The Best Years of Our Lives* as the only 'realistic' American picture of 1946.[23]

Rossen's contract with Columbia Pictures, using his own production company, enabled him to make *All the King's Men* entirely on location. Robert Parrish's account of the prolonged editing process, in which over an hour's material was cut, indicated that Rossen strove to film the bulk of the story material of the book. To the biographer of Huey Long, T. Harry Williams, the thesis of Robert Penn Warren was that 'the politician who wishes to do good may have to do some evil to achieve his goal'. But politics in the book was seen only as a framework for Warren's wider speculations. In the film, in part because of the drastic cutting, following several unsuccessful previews, the emphasis is on the rise and eventual fall of Willie Stark, only partly mediated, as in the book, through the consciousness of the intellectual, Jack Burden.

While Burden's consciousness is central to the book, the narrated scenes in the film, in which Burden reflects on his own life, as well as his involvement with Stark, only partly detach the viewer from the political events that are vividly displayed. Yet the detachment provided by the character of Burden is important in assessing the meaning of the film, and was arguably attractive to Rossen. Burden is a fellow traveller, dissatisfied by the remoteness of the upper-class world of Burden's Landing from the lives of ordinary people in the state, and impressed first by the honesty of Willie Stark, and then by his strength of purpose and commitment to progressive change. The Stark campaigns connect this scion of the defeated Southern aristocracy to history and to change.

Shooting in available light in real locations, indoors and out, Rossen produced a film of great vividness and power. The fact that Burden remains with Stark's team until his death helps to involve the audience with the use of power for democratic purposes, and although the misuse of power is shown, the audience has no alternative source of identification, and is continually reminded of Stark's programme of change, and of the mass support for such change. At the time the *Hollywood Reporter* saw the film as 'an arresting celluloid study of the effect of a demogogue on the mass mind', but, reviewing the film at some distance from the political climate of the late 1940s, Tom Milne argues that Stark 'is not so much corrupted by power as unable to maintain his balance of incorruptibility while wielding it'.[24]

Stark becomes a hero to the people from whence he came, just as Charlie Davis is a hero to the people of the Lower East Side. Yet Stark is corrupt, both in his personal life, and in his public efforts to break the opposition of Judge Stanton – efforts that finally drive the judge to suicide. Burden seems prepared to leave Stark, but, after his boss's speech in front of the state legislature, following the defeat of the impeachment motion, the two men seem again to be on good terms. Burden's speech to Anne Stanton at the end of the film, after Stark's death, in which he suddenly calls on her to help him make people see Willie Stark as Adam Stanton saw him, seems uncharacteristic of Burden and an effort to give the film a neat concluding message.

Willie Stark's final speech raises the dilemma of Rousseau-esque democracy, that political scientists of the 1950s were often to see as at the heart of totalitarianism. Stark tells the crowd: 'Remember it's not I who have won, but you. Your will is my strength, and your need is my justice.' To Paul Rotha the 'basic weakness – and danger – of the film is that little attempt is made to show how the real machinery of democratic action in the hands of people educated in democratic ways of thinking could have worked'. There seems no alternative to Willie Stark. Yet the seductiveness of power, and its mechanics, have rarely been better shown, particularly with the performance of Mercedes McCambridge as Sadie Burke. And contemporary writers have stressed the film's portrayal of the potential of democratic authority, as well as the need for constraints on that legitimate power, once established.

Made for less than $1m, the film had considerable impact, and won three Oscars in 1949, including that for Best Picture, although its rental income of $2.4m was considered disappointing. While the portrait was to some extent placed in the past, and in the South – the by then traditional Hollywood whipping-boy – the film was seen as emphasising the dangers rather than the possibilities of mass political movements, in line with what was becoming the dominant ideology. Perhaps for that reason, the left seemed dissatisfied by the film, and Rossen's final break with the social milieu of the party may have come when the film was criticised at a party meeting. Rossen had been one of eight members of the group of nineteen 'unfriendly' witnesses who were not called on to testify in 1947. But in 1948, according to Richard Collins, Rossen sent a letter to Harry Cohn, attesting to his then non-membership of the Communist Party. Rossen worked in Mexico on *The Brave Bulls* (1951), for Columbia, but when HUAC resumed its hearings on the film industry in 1951 Rossen was named by several witnesses as a communist, and Columbia moved to break its contract with him.[25]

Chapter 6

Film noir and society

THEORIES AND APPROACHES

In the discussion of *Crossfire* in Chapter 4, Colin McArthur was quoted as viewing the meanings of *film noir* as metaphysical rather than social, and as dealing with '*angst* and loneliness as essential elements of the human condition'. Certainly the emphasis on fate and despair as themes in the literature on *film noir* can be cited as further evidence that social interpretations of such films are generally misplaced. Place and Peterson, for example, in their article on the visual characteristics of *film noir*, see the typical moods of such films as 'claustrophobia, paranoia, despair and nililism'. Richard Maltby has drawn attention to the contemporary attempts to view the series of tough post-war thrillers and melodramas as testimony to a general post-war malaise in America. But, as Maltby points out, the difficulties of viewing *film noir* as evidence of post-war national *zeitgeist* are many, and not least among them is the fact that such films represented only a small and unrepresentative sample of Hollywood's output in this period.[1]

Yet representative or not, *film noir* – and up to 13 per cent of American-produced films of the peak period 1946–51 can be placed in this category – still invites explanation.[2] Both social and existential issues were dealt with, and the films provided opportunities both for more realism – including more location shooting – and for aesthetic innovations that could be seen as the opposite of realism. As with *Crossfire*, expressionist techniques could be combined with efforts to engage with aspects of contemporary society. The series of films that French critics first classified in this way seemed to cut through much of the sentiment and affirmation that had been associated with American film since the early 1930s; early examples such as *The Maltese Falcon, Double Indemnity, Laura* and *Murder My Sweet* seemed to them to represent a significant departure from the normal content and style of Hollywood. The mood was one of cynicism and pessimism, and the darkness of tone was matched by an unusual tendency towards high contrast, low-key lighting. Thematically these films, and those that followed, were concerned with the underworld of crime and corruption, and with the individuals who struggled against fate and obsession. Frank Krutnik sees the series of 'tough' thrillers, based on the work of hard-boiled writers, as at the centre of *film noir* in the forties, although he points out that the crime film became more sociological towards the end of the decade. To Jon Tuska, who sees the form as a combination of sensibility, narrative structure and style, the *film noir* was a reaction to 'decades of forced optimism' in American film. To Susman *film noir* 'served to reduce the optimistic American vision to dust'.[3]

Thrillers and crime melodramas thus provided a training ground for a new generation of directors, including those discussed in the previous chapter, and others such as Robert Wise, Don Siegal, Mark Robson and Fred Zinnemann, who either began work or graduated to higher budget features in the immediate post-war period. In addition such films provided writers with some opportunity to deal with contemporary America. Yet the form covers quite widely different films, linked only, perhaps, by their tone and sensibility. Is *Boomerang*, for example, classifiable as a *film noir*? It has little of the visual style of the form, although one could see how it could have had such features – had, say, Edward Dmytryk directed it or John Alton photographed it. Nor does the film have a highly fragmented narrative structure. Not only does it use the semi-documentary technique that was being developed at the time, and which is often associated with *film noir*, but thematically the story, of civic corruption and of a man unjustly accused, has links with the core elements of many of these films. As Tuska suggests, however, the purest form of *film noir* precludes a happy ending – even a happy ending which arguably fails to resolve doubts provoked by, and contradictions in, what went before. *Boomerang* ends with a patriotic lesson drawn, while, for example, *Detour* or *Scarlet Street* end only with despair, and the inexorable logic of fate.[4]

In terms of the distinctive visual features of *film noir* the emphasis has been less on the new 'social' directors discussed in the previous chapter than on the émigré generation, including the German refugees Fritz Lang, Robert Siodmak, Max Ophuls and Edgar G. Ulmer. Ulmer, director of *Detour* (1945) – one of the most despairing of such films – shared with Lang a fascination with the notions of destiny and fate. Neither director was a stranger to social filmmaking – Lang with his early American films and with *Hangmen Also Die*, and Ulmer with his union-financed films about ethnic groups and traditions. In addition the crime genre of the 1940s was perhaps the last to benefit from the disciplined craft departments of the major studios. David Thomson has pointed to *Criss Cross* as an example of post-war *film noir* that draws on the crafts of the studio, in terms of the precise sets and lighting, while also allowing some rein to director and writer. Robert Siodmak brings something of the expressionistic heritage to the film, while, as Thomson suggests, Daniel Fuchs, the radical novelist, comes nearest to giving the film a consistant theme. The front office get an unusual product, while the artists enjoy a greater freedom, and more of an opportunity to see themselves as artists.[5]

A number of writers, including Thom Andersen, Carlos Clarens and Mike Davis, have pointed to the contribution of liberal-left writers and directors to the *film noir* form. Andersen chooses to concentrate on the contribution of a number of socially aware directors to what he sees as a sub-genre within *film noir*. In particular he calls attention to the work of Losey, Polonsky, Dassin, Rossen, Berry and Endfield, in the period 1947–51. Andersen sees this work as characterised by 'greater psychological and social realism', by a scepticism about the American dream and by pointed reference to the 'psychological injuries of class'. The vogue for contemporary urban dramas, of low or high life, and the related interest in low-key lighting and visual differentiation, provided opportunities for writers and directors with both a commitment to social analysis and a desire to satisfy their artistic peers as much as their employers. Since such films were seen generally as of low status, the creative workers were given more autonomy from the front office, from pressure groups, and – arguably – from the Breen Office. Even when political controversy made explicit social content a liability, *films noirs* generally evaded scrutiny. *Crossfire* received some critical consideration because its makers drew attention to their social objectives, but *Force of Evil*, slipped out into the world in a double bill, did not trouble the politicians.

To Clarens, *film noir*, more so than the more prestigious social dramas, 'reeked of the facts of life', while Mike Davis discusses the degree to which the films reflected the tension between the hard working, productive middle class and the idle rich, an opposition that he sees as important to the work of Raymond Chandler and James Cain. Certainly *film noir* seems to emphasise money as the crucial social dynamic, a perspective attractive to those who were critical of post-war social trends. James Agee, reviewing *Double Indemnity*, saw the story as 'soaked in and shot through with money and the coolly intricate amorality of money'.[6] Porfirio, while stressing the existential element in *noir*, draws attention to the role of writers such as Albert Maltz, B. Traven and Daniel Fuchs, and suggests that their post-war film work owed something to disappointed political – and perhaps also literary – hopes; he argues that any 'real social analysis was displaced into a negative view of existing options'. To Porfirio the vision of *film noir* is existential in the sense that, visually and thematically, the films reflect what was then a modern view of a disoriented individual and a confused world. Even in the more social and 'realistic' of late 1940s *noir* films, there is something of this sensibility, for example in the tired detectives played by Lee J. Cobb in *Boomerang* and *Johnny O'Clock*, and in Robert Young's detective in *Crossfire*. All seem to suffer from alienation as, it is implied, they fight a battle that is less successful, and less clearcut, than that of wartime.[7]

While the problems of returning GIs provided a rationale for the psychological concerns of some post-war *noirs*, as well as other films such as *The Best Years of Our Lives* and *Till the End of Time*, the *noir* cycle of the post-war decade exhibits a consistent interest in issues of maladjustment and psychosis. The problems of transition for men at the time are suggested by the remark by Al (Frederic March), in *The Best Years of Our Lives*: 'Last year it was "Kill Japs" and this year it's "make money."' Psychological concern post-dates the interest in the fascist personality exhibited in films such as *Crossfire*, *The Stranger* and *Brute Force*, where the high-contrast lighting and unusual camera angles are a form of visual metaphor for the mental and political distortions of fascism. In much of the *film noir* cycle this visual style reflects the sexual obsession of the central characters, and commentators have seen in the absence of stable family relationships in these films another subversive element. Yet feminist critics have generally found few positive role models for women among the recurring *femmes fatales* of *film noir*. To Deborah Thomas these films almost exclusively focus on male problems of adaptation at the time – from peace to war, and from bachelorhood to marriage. A psychological study of American films of the period 1945–8, including many *films noirs*, found that 'The image, and the actuality, of the 'bad' woman arises to satisfy sexual impulses which men feel to be disturbing.'[8]

While some of the better known *films noirs* were made with relatively high budgets, others were answering a need for B pictures to maintain the traditional double bills of the time. The divorcement by the studios of their exhibition wings, a process begun by the successful antitrust suit in 1948, meant the beginning of the end for the double bill, and for the heyday of the B *noir*. To Bordwell and others the conventions of *film noir* were either adaptations of previous genres, or were cinematic equivalents of well-established devices of American hard-boiled detective fiction since the early 1930s. But while some have played down the challenge that *film noir* posed to the conventions of classical Hollywood cinema – a cinema of seamless storytelling and happy endings – others have seen the B *noir*, in particular, as marking out an alternative practice in opposition to the predominant 'realism' of the A film and, increasingly, of colour cinematography. (By 1952 well over 75 per cent of features in production were shooting in colour.) To J.P. Telotte, the technical innovations of the late 1940s, from subjective camera to voice-overs and flashbacks, and the documentary style, were all relatively short lived, but for a time they undermined the traditional coherence, and omniscience, of classical narrative cinema.[9]

Other technical factors had an impact on *film noir*, not least the faster film stock that allowed a decrease in lighting levels, the attractiveness of 'night for night' shooting to financially constrained independent companies, and the competition for studio space that encouraged location shooting. It was also probable that the wider debate about the realism and adultness of American films had some effect on the move to location shooting; the physical detachment from studio sound stages not only added an element of documentary to films, but away from line and executive producers, directors could in some circumstances exercise greater autonomy. Mark Hellinger, an independent producer at Univeral-International, still regarded a proposal to shoot *The Naked City* on the streets of New York as risky and 'experimental' in early 1947.[10]

Some directors saw in the murder or crime melodrama a greater freedom. (The makers of *Crossfire*, for example, were less constrained than those of the A budget *Gentleman's Agreement*.) Abraham Polonsky has testified to the freedom that thrillers and crime pictures of the time gave to political expression, because in that area 'the intellectual content is absorbed into what people think is a dark, criminal type of picture anyhow and so there's an acceptance of it'. Edward Dmytryk and Richard Fleischer remember that one of the attractions of low budget crime melodrama was the opportunity to approach more realistically a neglected stratum of American society. Fleischer has talked of this post-war interest in the 'underbelly of society', and in the forties he and Anthony Mann made a number of low-budget films, predominantly at RKO – with its tradition of a style forged by its strong technical departments – and Eagle Lion, where style and visual invention were in part prompted by financial constraints.[11]

Classical *noir* themes involved either an investigation, following Chandler, down 'mean streets', or a descent into a criminal or social underworld by a middle class hero struck down by fate or passion or some combination of both. Dmytryk and Scott's *Murder My Sweet* is an example of the first form, while Fritz Lang's *Woman in the Window* and *Scarlet Street*, and Edgar Ulmer's ultra-low-budget *Detour*, represent the second theme. To Paul Schrader the most realistic phase of the *film noir* cycle was in the post-war forties; before that period the emphasis was on the private eye, while later, in the early 1950s, came a climax of 'psychotic action and suicidal impulse'. In this period a number of producers, either new to Hollywood or enjoying a greater autonomy than before, latched on to variants of the black and white crime drama or melodrama. Hal Wallis, Jerry Wald and Mark Hellinger, all with experience of the Warners system, exercised more personal control in the immediately post-war period. Wald was quick to see the implications of the success of *Double Indemnity*, while Wallis later recalled that he encouraged his writers to show 'how frustration, poverty, and a desperate need for money could drive people to psychotic extremes'. At RKO, and to some extent later at MGM, Dore Schary encouraged some innovation within the format of the limited budget crime film, and for a time Adrian Scott did the same. Finally, at Twentieth Century-Fox, de Rochemont was particularly associated with what was a wider vogue for semi-documentary features.[12]

George Lipsitz argues that *film noir* addressed, if inadvertently, some of the key post-war issues which related to the collapse of the wartime sense of unity. With the end of wartime life, with its stress on the collective interest, came also the death of Roosevelt and the beginning of a new ideological conflict. The period of the late 1940s was, looking back, a period of conflict between, on the one hand, the dominant ideology of the war years, and of Popular Front and New Deal liberalism, and on the other, the emerging notions of the Cold War, and of a more individualistic, materialistic ethos. Homages to the communitarian or family spirit – *Since You Went Away, A Tree Grows in Brooklyn, Meet Me in St Louis* – coincide with the absence of family in much of *film noir*. To Whittaker Chambers, whose own role in the melodrama of the politics of anti-communism may have contributed to the importance of paranoia in Hollywood fictions, the 'Popular Front mind' had dominated American life, at least from 1938 to 1948. Eric Johnston and other industry leaders were now encouraging an affirmation of the American system, and with the beginning of the cold war and the politics of anti-communism, the fight to define the ideological nature of that Americanism became more than usually contested. Irving Pichel, who directed *They Won't Believe Me* as a contribution to the *film noir* cycle, also wrote at the time of what he saw as a change in values in America. He referred to the 'unified morality' of America in the war years, but, writing in 1947 in *Hollywood Quarterly*, he felt that ethical principles that had until recently been beyond debate were now being questioned.[13]

The death of Roosevelt in 1945 has also been linked to post-war uncertainty and the decline of the dominant consensus of the war years. Roosevelt presided over and symbolised a sense of common purpose, and to Polan the President's death meant 'a sudden lessening of the power of these narrative forces of continuity and enunciating authority'. For screenwriters especially, the post-war period was a period of uncertainty. At a time of general affluence, writers in Hollywood faced the threat of unemployment as 1,500 writers competed for just over 400 jobs. The paranoia exhibited by the right concerning communist plots was sometimes matched by blacklist victims. Albert Maltz, for example, asked Abraham Polonsky to finish his novel for him, when he prepared to serve his prison term in 1950, on the grounds that fascism was overtaking the country and he would never be released. For others, from long term members of the party to the most uncommitted of fellow travellers, the era of investigations, loyalty oaths and blacklists meant facing an unwanted accountability for past associations. Something of this fear, and even the narrative motif of the past catching up with the protagonist – as in *Out of the Past* – may have been transposed into the *film noir* cycle. A writer, quoted in 1948, could have been the subject of such a film, when he testified that he was 'all loused up'; he continued, 'I'm scared to death and nobody can tell me it isn't because I'm afraid of being investigated'.[14]

While it would be dangerous to draw too many general conclusions from such an observation, it is at least interesting to relate such motifs to the concerns of those writers and directors for whom the Hollywood system seemed as much a trap as a source of opportunity. David Thomson has speculated, for example, that *film noir* may in part have reflected 'the collective resignation of the filmmakers at their subservience'.[15] Despite much discussion, and some superstructural change, the key economic parameters of film production were relatively unchanged, and well-educated writers with literary aspirations – or even delusions – may have expressed some of their frustrations in, and on, those smaller budget crime films to which they were asked to contribute. Political frustrations may also have had some influence, as liberals and especially radicals despaired of post-war developments, and as the breakup of the Popular Front alliance weakened both tendencies.

Warren Susman and Philip Kemp argue that *film noir* represented a kind of re-emergence of a suppressed element of American culture. Susman sees *film noir* as an indication of the doubts and uncertainties that began to arise in the post-war decade despite or because of the apparent successes. He sees the post-war years as a self-conscious 'age of anxiety' with new fears arising just as Truman completed the welfare state with his Employment Act, and as the economy provided new opportunities: 'It is specifically the noir movie that shows the audience that its desires, which they can now fulfil in the modern world of abundance, social welfare and security, are fundamentally dangerous and filled with evil possibilities.' To Kemp it is the repressed New Deal and Popular Front culture which somehow bubbled up in these films. He reads a number of *noir* films – often the work of those without left affiliations – in terms of their depiction of a class-riven society that was without any 'communal sense', and which was 'deformed and corrupted by the lust for cash'.

It is easier to find these recurring meanings – and they are further discussed later in this chapter – than to explain them. But any explanation is likely to relate to the political changes of this post-war decade, changes that led to the increasing ideological isolation of the creative Hollywood community. (The Washington hearings, of course, and the blacklist, were to have a significant effect on the political complexion of that community.) While the Truman years have been seen as a culmination of the New Deal vision, with the assertion of further state responsibilities for employment and housing, others see social reform as a victim of the early post-war development of the politics and rhetoric of anti-communism. The new President gave early signs, in his appointments, of his greater dependence on military and business elites, and seized the leadership of the anti-communist movement after the elections of November 1946. In 1947, a year in which the United States produced about one-half of the world's manufactures, came Truman's announcement of his 'containment' and Marshall Plan policies, and the HUAC hearings on Hollywood.[16]

Observers of American society at the end of the 1940s found evidence of crisis and anxiety. Post-war popular literature had emphasised the home as the rightful place for women now that war was over, and by 1950 Clyde Kluckhorn found the American family to be in transition as these increasingly dominant notions about the role of women – what would later be called the 'feminine mystique' – conflicted with a reality of more and more women trained for professional careers. The radical scholar C. Wright Mills found evidence that the American middle class were increasingly estranged from the wider community and alienated from their true selves, while David Riesman, writing in 1948/9, found that the inner-directed American was nearly extinct, and that society was increasingly characterised by the notions of conformity, uniformity and security. It is again easy to speculate – and less easy to demonstrate – that desires that were increasingly unacceptable in post-war society were displaced on to the world of the movie screen. The process by which a minority of post-war films recorded such anxieties – what Susman calls a 'return of the repressed' – is by no means clear, although Kemp's notion seems to depend in part on the lagged influence, given changing attitudes after the war, of Popular Front opinion, particularly as articulated by screenwriters.[17]

The dangers of reading film as revealing a national *zeitgeist* have been mentioned; an account of the social significance of post-war American film would also have to explain the success of *The Jolson Story*, *The Yearling* and *The Egg and I*, all of them bestselling films of 1947. Carol Traynor Williams has discussed the way in which the films of the 1940s have been contrastingly mythologised, with different films being cited to support a notion of the era either as 'age of anxiety' or as the original age of innocence and 'pure entertainment'. While *film noir* does seem to reflect – from somewhere – a cynicism about the family relationships held in such esteem in polite society, a pessimism more appropriate to a self-conscious 'age of anxiety', and even a visual style more in keeping with a modernism spread by the new commercial culture, it is still difficult to account for the tendency in precise terms. *Film noir* may have kept to the expressionistic and other devices of crime fiction, but this does not necessarily prevent popular art from playing a subversive role; Geoffrey O'Brien has argued that the paperbacks that distributed the hardboiled tradition of fiction to a new audience in the war years and the post-war decade, laying bare the 'sordid underside in American life', played very much this role. O'Brien sees the paperbacks of this period as a response to the 'arsenal of media (that) had been assembled to project the image of a nation prosperous and secure, of citizens steeped in home grown virtues and showered with material blessings'.

Contemporary observers of the period of McCarthyism of the early 1950s also pointed to the underlying 'status anxieties' of a post-war America enjoying renewed economic growth, and this interpretation also seems consistent with some of the recurring themes of *film noir*. Yet few would now have the confidence that Siegfried Kracauer showed in 1947 – in his study of pre-Nazi German cinema as revealing the national *zeitgeist* – in connecting a reading of films and underlying 'psychological dispositions'. *Film noir* also explored the city – including the city of the mind – as never before, and the city's place as the source of darkness in the traditional American polarity between city and country was reinforced.[18]

The *Motion Picture Herald* is quoted, referring to *Criss Cross*, as warning exhibitors that the film 'certainly is not the kind of entertainment for small town theatres'. In retrospect *film noir*, with its habitual pessimism, can be seen as running up against the pressure in the early 1950s for greater affirmation of America and its system, including key institutions such as the family. The culture of the increasingly dominant, provincial Republican elites of the early 1950s was one that was hostile to what Michael W. Miles has called 'the heterogeneous culture of the metropolis'. Instead mainstream Republican culture favoured the norms of 'free enterprise and small town life'. The political culture of the creative Hollywood community was by contrast cosmopolitan, and could still be associated with the culture of the left. E. Merrill Root, quoted by Miles, wrote in 1953 of the culture of the left as one of 'negation, despair, mockery, nihilism, a culture full of the virus of spiritual polio'. Officially approved culture in the 1950s was to wear its Americanism on its sleeve, leaving *film noir* as a marginal, low-budget ghetto. Both the expressionist and realist elements of *film noir* became less attractive as Hollywood repositioned itself to resist the threat of television. Modern art had become ideologically suspect, given the dominance of Cold War politics, while the rather desperate underside of American life was similarly avoided. To Susman the opening of Disneyland, in 1955, indicated the triumph of national hypocrisy, the assertion of super-ego over id, and of the myth of America in the name of commerce and foreign policy.[19]

APPLICATIONS

In the small number of wartime films that did much to establish the *film noir* form that was later recognised and established by

French critics, crime was observed without undue moralising – apart from the normal Breen Office rules – and it was viewed as part of a middle-class milieu in which greed and envy were particularly evident. The commercial success of *Double Indemnity* (1944) and *Murder My Sweet* (1944) encouraged producers to look for similar properties, while helping to legitimise, in the eyes of such producers, more personal, at times expressionistic, styles of filmmaking. Leff and Simmons suggest that the acceptability of *The Postman Always Rings Twice* (1946) to both MGM and the Breen Office indicated the beginning of the end of the era of strict code enforcement. The administrators of the code seemed to have only a limited effect on the preparation of a number of films in this category, even when Breen had expressed thorough opposition to early versions of scripts. Writing to RKO in 1946, Breen complained of the 'objectionably sordid flavour' of the characters in one story, which would be filmed as *Out of the Past*, and urged that it be shelved. He also pointed out that he had similar views on several other projects under consideration at the studio, feeling that they 'will do a definite disservice to this industry'.[20]

The pessimistic tone of the early *film noir*, and the working of fate, is most clearly seen in *Detour*, directed by Edgar G. Ulmer and released in November 1945. At a time when the boundary between a B and an A picture was around $400,000, *Detour* was apparently made for $20,000. Ulmer had come to America from Austria in 1934 and had made a number of films, financed by union and public funds, on the cultures of ethnic minorities. Lipsitz argues that the fact that he made such a despairing film as *Detour* in 1945 can be taken as evidence of Ulmer's perceptions of the decline of the sense of community of the Roosevelt era. In the film, totally without the romanticism of A-budget *noirs*, fate is totally victorious over the American dream, as the central character's journey from New York to Hollywood ends in hopelessness and murder.[21]

More typical of A-budget *noirs* is the Warners production, *Mildred Pierce* (1945). Although the film contains elements of the Warners tradition of social concern, the more realistic and socially conscious parts of the film, suggested in the early scripts of Catherine Turney and the written comments of Albert Maltz, were played down by Jerry Wald, who, influenced by the success of *Double Indemnity*, insisted on the flashback structure and the opening murder. These changes moved the film away from woman's picture and social realism towards *film noir*. (The changes also arguably reduced the emphasis of the central story of Mildred's success, which some have seen as reflecting a wartime 'nascent feminism', and strengthened those opening and closing frames that undercut her independence.) The contradictions implicit in the production history emerge in the film, which is often seen as reflecting post-war male disapproval of the independent woman.[22]

While most of the plots revolve around murder, the early films also show an interest in abnormal psychology that seems in part a legacy of the wartime struggle, both in terms of notions of superman, and of the emotional strains on the lives of veterans. In *Phantom Lady* (1944) the falsely convicted hero is an engineer who wants to build model cities, while the murderer justifies his attempt to frame his apparent friend by depreciating his life, referring to him as 'a mediocre engineer working in sewers, drainpipes and faucets'. In *Conflict* (1945), the drama is also predicated on a sham marriage, and on a central 'man of violent mind' whose perfect murder is revealed by his own conscience. The liberal screenwriter John Paxton, who worked on *Murder My Sweet*, *Crossfire* and *Cornered* with Adrian Scott and Edward Dmytryk, also contributed to *Crack-Up*, released by RKO in 1946. The story concerns an art forgery, and an attempt by the criminals to cover up their crime by discrediting a populist art expert at a museum. George Steele (Pat O'Brien), who is seen lecturing admiringly on a painting by Millet while disparaging a work of 'modern art', argues with the museum director over the function of the museum – whether it is a public institution or an 'exclusive tea party'. Again there is a sadistic criminal who, like the Nazis, wants to hoard art works, and who is finally unmasked as Steele is vindicated.

Several other films combine *film noir* effects with a continuation of wartime anti-fascism. *Crossfire* also includes a metaphor which is suggestive of some of the formative elements of the type of film under discussion. Samuels, the Jewish victim of the opening murder, is seen in flashback at a bar, explaining how he feels about the tension of the time. He says that 'it's suddenly not having a lot of enemies to fight anymore'; he picks up a peanut – the 'win the war peanut' – and then eats it to suggest the sudden loss of a focus and target for all the aggression

stoked up by war. After the 'all pulling together' notion of
wartime, individual desires are liberated at a time when the
recognised enemy has disappeared. Writing of it as a social
problem film in *Commentary*, Elliot E. Cohen praised its intentions, including what he saw as the use of the form of 'murder
melodrama' in order to reach a wide audience; but he argued
that the filmmakers would have done better to have studied
the literature on communications and persuasion, and that
Hollywood still generally shirked the complexity of life. More
specifically, Cohen is concerned that some anti-Semites might
actually identify with Montgomery, the murderer (although
such evidence as exists on the 'effects' of the film suggests that
this was not the case). Yet the dark and pessimistic tone of
Crossfire, its sense of the unreliability of evidence and of the
strange anomie that plagued men who were in a limbo between
the roles and identities of war and those of peace, is perhaps
more striking than the film's ostensible liberal message – a
message that is in any case undercut by the summary gunning
down of Montgomery without benefit of trial.[23]

A more obvious and conventional discussion of fascism in
America – in the form of a Nazi who has hidden himself in a
small Connecticut town – is found in *The Stranger* (1946), a film
directed by Orson Welles in part to rehabilitate himself as a
reliable studio director. Welles' own worries about 'renascent
Fascism', articulated in the director's column in the *New York
Post*, were not central to the film. Again in *The Big Clock* (1948),
directed by John Farrow from a screenplay by Jonathan Latimer,
another variation on the anti-fascist theme emerges in the
portrait of the dictatorial head of Janoth Enterprises, a concern
which Kenneth Fearing, the author of the novel, had based on
his experiences at Time Magazine. The tycoon, Earl Janoth
(Charles Laughton), moves around the monolithic modernist
architecture of his headquarters as the human equivalent to the
clock that sets the obsessive time for the imperial enterprise.
(The mistress whom he murders describes his office as the
'Berchtesgaden of the publishing world'). While the tone of the
film is lightened by comedy, and the emphasis is on the murder
mystery and the predicament of George Stroud (Ray Milland)
as both investigator and potential suspect, residues remain that
are critical of both dictatorship and the subservience required
of the modern 'organisation man'. While visually *noir*ish only in

the opening minutes, *The Big Clock* also follows the form of such films with its flashback structure, and its quality of middle-class nightmare; 'thirty-six hours ago', says Stroud during the prologue, 'I was a decent, respectable, law abiding citizen with a wife and a kid and a big job'.

The Spiral Staircase (1946), a film which has a period setting but which certainly looks and feels like a *film noir*, can be read as a political allegory, and illustrates the relationship – particularly evident in the work of some émigré directors – between the anti-Nazi film and the post-war *film noir*. The director, Robert Siodmak, was a Jew who escaped to America when the Nazis took over in Germany, while the producer was Dore Schary. The reference to racial purity – as we identify with the young deaf and dumb girl who is threatened – is absent from the original novel.[24]

Two further films released in 1947 extended the use of expressionistic point of view shots found in *Murder My Sweet*. In *Lady in the Lake* the audience only sees Philip Marlowe (played by the film's director, Robert Montgomery) as an occasional narrator, and on those occasions when he strays in front of a mirror. As has been pointed out, the use of this device at first encourages the viewer to question the complex reality of the film, but increasingly it underwrites a conventional and conservative narrative. At the end of the film there is a conventional rescue of the investigator by the authorities, while the mysterious self-made woman of the opening scenes is suddenly domesticated. The Warners film *Dark Passage* combines the pessimism of its original source, the novel by David Goodis, with a romantic liberalism and optimism associated with the producer and director, Jerry Wald and Delmer Daves, and with the central protagonists, played by Humphrey Bogart and Lauren Bacall. Bogart is the escaped convict whose viewpoint the audience shares until plastic surgery gives him a new identity; Bacall plays a children's teacher at a settlement house, and her help, in an otherwise bitter and threatening world – a world without community – eventually leads to salvation.[25]

While corruption in this period is often associated with wealth – for example, in *The Lady from Shanghai* – business and finance are relatively rare as settings. Apart from *The Strange Love of Martha Ivers* and *The Big Clock*, *The Web* also deals with corruption in the context of a major corporation. *The Web* was produced by Jerry Bresler and directed by Michael Gordon at Universal-International, from a script by William Bowers and Bertram Millhauser, and a story by Harry Kurnitz. While the film is perhaps only marginally in the *film noir* category, it invites examination in the context of Kemp's perspective, discussed earlier. Such discussion also allows consideration of a director who had been at the Yale Drama School with Elia Kazan, had directed a production of Albert Maltz's *The Black Pit*, and had worked with the Group Theatre and on Broadway. Gordon took the fifth amendment before the committee in 1951, and was blacklisted until he testified more co-operatively in 1958, and returned to filmmaking with *Pillow Talk*. (His last film before the blacklist was *Cyrano de Bergerac*, a film that allowed screenwriter Carl Foreman to make some barely noticeable allusions to contemporary pressures on writers.)[26]

The central figure in *The Web* (1947) is Andrew Colby (Vincent Price), an international financier and the head of several corporations, including Andrew Colby Enterprises. As in *The Strange Love of Martha Ivers* the business executive villain is countered by a protagonist from the other side of the tracks, Bob Regan (Edmond O'Brien) from Public School 45. Regan is an unsuccessful lawyer who is first seen championing the minor claim for damages of an immigrant client whose pushcart was damaged because of Colby's negligence. Colby talks of 'Dutch oil leases' and buys 'oilfields, steamships and headwaiters', and he is protected in his offices by a personal secretary, Noel Faraday (Ella Raines), who he appears to 'own'. In this web of corruption the relationships are governed by, and alienated by, money. Colby tells Faraday: 'All my life I've worked for only one thing – money, and the power that goes with it.' In this context, in which Regan goes to work for Colby as a bodyguard and immediately kills an apparent intruder in self-defence, a plot develops in which Colby attempts to kill, frame or control all the other characters. The inevitable ending, in which Colby's villainy is discovered, is only achieved by a theatrical trick – performed by the detective – which owes more to Drury Lane than *film noir*. But the acting, particularly of O'Brien, and of William Bendix as Lt. Damico, has a social depth, and if the film can be seen as a problem film in which the problem is an evil man, the context of the film, and the obvious alienation of relationships governed by ownership, seems more than local colour. It seems at least possible that those with the right prejudices, and some without them, may have made this reading. At the very least one can surmise why Gordon was attracted by the assignment, and why he tackled the project with such evident enthusiasm.

If some directors were happy to take up some of the social issues raised by criminal locales, to others they were incidental. But the degree of sympathy accorded the criminals in *The Asphalt Jungle* (1950), for example, and the relative complexity of the analysis linking crime to social and financial power, is probably related to the social concerns exhibited at the time by John Huston and the writer Ben Maddow. (Dore Schary purchased W.R. Burnett's novel of the same name for MGM during his first year at the studio as head of production.) As Maddow has pointed out, Burnett wrote the original novel from the perspective of the police. The original novel, as it appears in the MGM collection of script materials, begins by characteris-ing the story as one of 'the jungle that is a city without law', and of 'the battle waged by the one honest official in an otherwise corrupt city against the members of an underground faction'. Maddow, a left-wing documentary film writer and poet, depre-cates the idea that the shift of sympathy to the criminals, and the notion that crime was another form of business endeavour, was his intention.[27]

The literature and mythology relating to eastern novelists and playwrights who apparently lost their way in Hollywood, cor-rupted by its values and money, may underestimate the contri-bution made by such writers to American film. Clifford Odets is often cited as a classic archetype of this phenomenon, as a playwright whose visits to the film capital became longer and less productive. Odets put into the low-budget *Deadline at Dawn* (1946) – produced by Adrian Scott and directed by Harold Clurman at RKO – much of his talent for combining poetic dialogue and social philosophy. (Odets worked from a novel by Cornell Woolrich.) Set in a studio New York on one hot night, the desperate, ordinary characters are given Odets' own vision, somewhere between despair and exhilaration. A sailor is falsely suspected of murder, and he seeks help first from a young woman, June (Susan Hayward), and then from an unhappy, philosophical taxi driver, Gus (Paul Lukas). Gus, whose efforts to aid the young couple only lead to the revelation that he is the murderer, is a characteristic Odetsian figure. He tells June: 'The logic you are looking for, the logic is there is no logic; the horror and peril you feel, my dear, come from being alive. Die and there is no trouble – live, and you struggle. At your age I think it's beautiful to struggle for the human possibilities.' Odets had abundant sympathy for his characters – demonstrated in his other credits in this period, *None But the Lonely Heart* (1944), which he directed, and *Humoresque* (1946). In *None But the Lonely Heart* Ernie Verdun Mott (Cary Grant) asks 'When's the world coming out of its midnight?', a line that is echoed, probably unconsciously, by Abraham Polonsky in *Force of Evil*. While Polonsky gives Garfield an existential line at the end of *Body and Soul*, Polonsky's characters – compared to those of Odets – work towards attaining a more positive existential vision, involving the freedom of self-knowledge and responsibility.

It might not be too great a leap from *Deadline at Dawn* (1946) to *Lady from Shanghai* (1948). Odets' credits were to be few and far between, while for Welles, the low-budget *Macbeth*, filmed in 1947, a year after *Lady from Shanghai*, was to be his last American film for a decade. *Citizen Kane* has been seen as a key influence on *film noir* – particularly within RKO – in terms of its visual effects, fragmented structure and ambiguous perspective. After *The Stranger*, *Lady from Shanghai* was a more ambitious and personal film, and with Welles both narrating and playing the central character, it is difficult not to interpret the story as reflecting something of Welles' feelings at the time. The complex plot revolves around the adventure of Michael O'Hara (Welles), as his attraction for a married woman, Elsa Bannister (Rita Hayworth – Welles' estranged wife at the time), leads him to an exotic voyage on her husband's yacht, and to an intrigue of sex and money which only he, of the four major characters, survives.[28]

Harry Cohn hated the film, both for the complexity of the plot and the portrayal of Rita Hayworth, who was contracted to Columbia Pictures; the film died a death in a double bill, when belatedly released in 1948, and the experience further increased the director's alienation from the Hollywood system. Given Welles' committed liberalism, it is of some significance that Michael O'Hara describes himself in the film as having killed a Franco spy in 1939, while the character is later described on the radio as a 'notorious waterfront agitator'. By contrast, Grisby, Arthur Bannister's business associate, was on a pro-Franco committee during the Spanish Civil War. Such signifiers may not have much weight, but they give spectators the option of seeing the story as a kind of liberal romance, in which O'Hara, the innocent abroad, encounters and walks away from – with some increased wisdom – a web of corruption involving money, contracts and dependent relationships. Certainly Welles' view of Hollywood at the time, as he prepared to walk away, was no more charitable than his portrait of the reptilian inhabitants of the *Circe*. While Welles was also apparently able to make some jokes at the expense of Nelson Rockefeller, whose scheme for Welles to shoot a documentary film in Brazil had been so disastrous, the 'bright, guilty world' of *The Lady from Shanghai* is characteristic of *film noir*, albeit that much of the trial scene is played for comedy. Elsa Bannister warns O'Hara, even as she traps him: 'Everything's bad Michael, everything. You can't escape it or fight it, you've got to get along with it, deal with it, make terms.'[29]

Richard Fleischer, who has referred directly to the opportunities that *film noir* provided for social observation, made a series of low-budget films at RKO in the late 1940s, and most of them fit into this category, although a major feature of these films is the amount of location shooting, particularly in Los Angeles – for example in *The Clay Pigeon* (1949) and in the heist story, *Armored Car Robbery* (1950). In addition the films are distinguished by modest expressionist effects. In *Follow Me Quietly* (1949), a detective on the track of a murderer who kills at night uses a dummy of the murderer which at one point, with no one in the room, 'comes to life'. *Bodyguard*, released the previous year, also combines night and day location shooting and a number of inventive visual tricks to sustain interest. The plot concerns a 'profitable little enterprise' involving the watering of meat by a tacky meat-packing company, which leads to murder, and which supports a rather grand country-house lifestyle. The last, and in later years most celebrated, of Fleischer's films at RKO was *The Narrow Margin*, released in 1952. This last film has been admired for its visual inventiveness, as most of the story takes place in the narrow confines of a train on which a detective is escorting a key witness to a grand jury trial. Also interesting is the sense of class differences in the film, and the questioning of the detective's, and the spectator's, moral and social stereotyping. The dialogue also blurs usual distinctions: a racketeer makes reference to his role in 'a big company' with 'branches all over'.

Anthony Mann's career ran along similar lines in this period, and in *Raw Deal* (1948), made for Eagle Lion, he directed a film which combines a number of what came to be seen as central *film noir* themes and styles. As well as location shots of bleak open roads and gas stations, there is striking night-for-night shooting, fog effects, and high contrast interior lighting. In terms of theme, the film concerns a prisoner, Joe Sullivan (Dennis O'Keefe) – unjustly framed by a fellow gang member – who breaks out of jail with the help of his faithful girl friend, Pat (Claire Trevor). The couple on the run – Joe intends to collect money owed to him by the gang leader – are joined by Sullivan's parole officer, Ann Martin (Marsha Hunt). The drama is thus provided by two quests – of the police for the escaped prisoner, and of Joe Sullivan for his money. But in addition the characters are socially 'placed'. Sullivan grew up in an orphanage, while Ann Martin's father died in the 'war of the depression'; Pat comes from the other side of the tracks, from Corkscrew Alley in San Francisco. When Ann is kidnapped, Pat, about to depart with Joe in a ship for South America and a new life, does the right thing, rather in the manner of *Casablanca*. She tells Joe of Ann's plight, and he returns to Corkscrew Alley, to the rescue. Leopold Atlas, who wrote the script with John C. Higgins, later provided friendly testimony to the House Committee, after suffering three heart attacks.[30]

There are echoes of the Faust legend in several *films noirs*. The myth was filmed twice in the 1940s – in 1941 by RKO, as *The Devil and Daniel Webster*, and in 1949, by Paramount, as *Alias Nick Beal*. The classic story relates to the emphasis in *film noir* on contractual relationships, governed by money. In the Hal Wallis production at Paramount, *Sorry, Wrong Number* (directed by Anatole Litvak, 1948) the seeds of violence – the plan by Henry Stevenson (Burt Lancaster) to have his wife Leona murdered – lie in the contractual nature of a marriage, and in the power of wealth to determine the terms. As Henry earlier tells her: 'I work in a drug store, and your father owns hundreds of them.' Leona (Barbara Stanwyck) and her father are identified with the major drug company that they own; Henry is held to an implicit marriage contract which provides money and lifestyle, but not independence. *Film noir*, as Kemp suggests, can frequently be read as suggesting a society alienated by money, and class plays a significant, if unannounced role as the catalyst of the conflict. Differences in class also form the basis for the Enterprise film *Caught* (1948), written by the playwright Arthur Laurents – who later claimed to have been blacklisted – and directed by Max Ophuls. For an ordinary young woman, dreaming of the 'good life', going to a party for the rich is seen as an 'investment'. Again the rich man – apparently based on the RKO boss Howard Hughes – is paranoid and dictatorial, and is contrasted with a caring, altruistic character, a doctor working in a tenement district.

In *Night and the City* (1950), semi-documentary turns into expressionism, as London becomes a frightening underworld in which Harry Fabian (Richard Widmark) struggles for survival; to realise his dream of success Fabian hustles to create his own wrestling promotions, but steps on too many toes. Again, money provides much of the narrative and thematic drive, and the Twentieth Century-Fox film, directed by Jules Dassin in London, also captures something of the *Brighton Rock* spiv world of post-war Britain. But the energy and desperation, the emphasis on money changing hands in shady clubs and bars, and the milieu – on the uncertain boundary between business and gangsterdom – is part of the American world of *film noir*. There is talk of 'investment', of contracts, and of people being owned – the club owner Phil Nosseross (Francis L. Sullivan) tells Fabian that Helen is 'something that I've bought and paid for'. Later Helen says of her proposed business partner, Harry Fabian, who double-crosses her: 'I know Fabian, and I'll control him.'

The climax involves a chase through a Dickensian underworld as gang leaders offer £1,000 to anyone who can deliver Fabian. The police are notable by their absence, or ineffectuality, and everyone has their price. There is even, as the hunted and doomed Fabian rests briefly before breaking cover and meeting his death, an attempt to project this world back to Fabian's roots, running from 'welfare officers, thugs, my father'. A hunted animal near to death, Fabian confides in an old woman, 'I was so close to being on top, Hanna, so close.' (Given the film's box office failure in Britain, following the success of previous spiv films, it is interesting to suggest that ideological forces similar to those in America may have been pushing the British crime film towards the model represented by the hugely successful *The Blue*

Lamp (1949), a model that was visually more conventional and more supportive of the efforts of authority.) *Night and the City* was Dassin's last American-financed film before the blacklist led him to leave America for Europe in the early 1950s.[31]

THE CASE OF RKO

Of the 296 feature films released by RKO inclusively from 1944 to 1952 only 35 appear on one frequently used survey of *films noirs*. During the same period Twentieth Century-Fox, Warners, Columbia, MGM and Paramount each released between twenty and twenty-two such films. RKO was a significant source of films in this category, although RKO had a rather eccentric history in the years following Howard Hughes' purchase of the studio in 1948. Although Fritz Lang made three films for RKO release, one in 1945 and two in 1956, and John Brahm made *The Locket* at the studio in 1947, few of the émigré directors, who made such a striking visual contribution to the cycle, worked there. Instead the emphasis has been on the influential collaboration of Edward Dmytryk and Adrian Scott, and on the possible influence of Orson Welles – and particularly *Citizen Kane* – and of the wartime B unit at the studio presided over by Val Lewton. Robert Wise and Mark Robson, who would both direct films in the *film noir* style in the later forties, had both worked with Welles as film editors, and then for Lewton. *Murder My Sweet* and *Crossfire* were particularly influential with their use of what came to be recurring visual motifs of *film noir* – semi-expressionistic point of view shots, voice-over narration and the use of complex flashback structures.[32]

They Won't Believe Me (1947) was directed by Irving Pichel, a non-communist member of the Hollywood Nineteen, from a script by Jonathan Latimer. The story, again told in flashback, is framed by the defence summing up in a court case in which the narrator, Larry Ballantine (Robert Young) is accused of murder. The defence attorney warns jury and audience that they should decide the case on the murder issue, and not on the basis of the defendant's unsavoury lifestyle. Since the story reveals Ballantine to be compulsively unfaithful to women in general and to his wife in particular – but not a murderer – the film seems to offer a conventional moral tale. Before the 'not guilty' verdict is read Ballantine announces that he has reached his own judgement, and he is shot as he attempts to commit suicide by throwing himself from the courtroom window.

The accused man, Larry Ballantine, begins his story by explaining his 'contractual' relationship with his wife; to Greta 'I was private property, covered with signs marked "No Trespassing"'. Greta puts a stop to his interest in other women by buying him a 25 per cent share in a firm of investment brokers, and for a time, understanding the contract, he becomes the 'model young businessman'. Soon, however, he falls into familiar ways as a secretary whose obsession with money rivals his own makes herself indispensable to him. Ballantine takes over the 'franchise' to drive her home, and she quickly tabulates his 'value' – his '$3,000 jaloppy', a 'two story Monterey house with a swimming pool and a tennis court', '$500 a month rent' and 'two servants'. For a time Ballantine's contract with his wife still holds: when the secretary, Verna Carlson (Susan Hayward) suggests that he buy her lunch he resists by telling her that she has made a bad 'investment'. But he soon succumbs, only for Greta – happiest when chatting about stocks and bonds – to sell Larry's financial interest and take him to an isolated ranch house without a telephone. To Verna, who for a moment is prepared to take him without his money, Larry explains that 'The dough goes with Greta.'

As the plot unfolds Larry and Verna finally do go off together, only for fate to intervene just at the moment when, after a symbolic swim in a country lake, the lovers have destroyed the contractual nature of their own relationship by tearing up a $25,000 cheque that Verna at first demanded. Driving to Reno, their car crashes, and when Verna is killed Larry testifies that it is Greta who has died so that he can then murder his wife and inherit her money. In fact Greta has committed suicide on hearing of Larry's desertion, and only later does the past resurface (along with Greta's body) to set up the return to the courtroom.

Kemp's notion of a cash nexus, driving the characters and the narrative, seems evident in the film; all the rest, in Polonsky's phrase, is conversation. The events of Ballantine's story are constantly measured in terms of profit and loss, investment and contract; only briefly, and uncertainly, are other motives present. A post-war world of personal gratification is suggested, a world of false ideals. Jonathan Latimer, a 1930s hardboiled crime writer, had written the screenplay of *The Glass Key*, and he was also to adapt Kenneth Fearing's novel *The Big Clock*. *They Won't Believe Me* may be about a heel, but its script also exhibits a fascination with the impact of money on personality that seems a frequent motif in RKO *film noir* of this time.[33] While director Irving Pichel was a leftist – although not in the Communist Party – and the producer Joan Harrison was an experienced collaborator with Hitchcock, the obsessional concern with money seems difficult to explain only in terms of the intentions of the filmmakers.

Born to Kill or *Lady of Deceit* (1947), made the same year by Robert Wise with a screenplay by Eve Greene and Richard Macaulay from a James Gunn novel, can be read in a similar way. As in *Murder My Sweet* the course of the convoluted plot reveals wide disparities of wealth, and out of this skewed social structure come two driven – in one case psychopathic – characters. Sam Wild is clearly deranged and is nursed and humoured between bursts of violence by his friend Marty; in an opening scene in an sleazy apartment house in Reno Sam murders his girl friend and a man who he suspects of 'cutting in'. The bodies are discovered by Helen Trent, an independent woman who is in Reno to secure a divorce, but she decides not to inform the police so as not to embarrass the rich industrialist to whom she is engaged in San Francisco. When Sam and Helen meet on the train out of Reno they find that they have much in common. Both exhibit the attitude to ordinary people – Helen sees most men as 'turnips' – that recurs in films of this period, and is exemplified by Harry Limes's lines to his friend Holly Martins – in *The Third Man* (1949) – as they look down on common humanity from the Vienna ferris wheel.

But the logic of the film, written in the year following the end of the war, goes beyond these residues of wartime thinking. In San Francisco Sam calls on Helen at the mansion of her foster sister Georgia, who is the heir of a newspaper baron; when Sam discovers where the money lies he turns his attentions to Georgia, and they are soon married. Sam tells Helen that 'your roots are down where mine are', and the rest of the film deals with the efforts of both 'climbers' to reconcile their own relationship, an attraction of like to like, with the relationships that offer them economic security. As this intrigue continues a detective, Albert Arnett, tries to solve the original murders, but even he is open to offers, and his willingness to obstruct the process of justice for $15,000 from Helen does not prevent him from acting as a kind of chorus to the film, commenting from time to time on the way of the world.

The end comes with Sam killing Helen and being killed by the police, but the last words are spoken by Arnett. There is no surviving voice of authority, no campaigning DA of the 1930s, and no representative of the American way of the 1950s. The film seems to fit Polan's notion of a period of post-war flux in which Roosevelt's death lessened the role of forces of authority in the narratives of contemporary dramas. Instead such films, as Kemp suggests in his analysis of *Where Danger Lives*, often seem to reveal a bleak world of class envy and alienation; the conditions that led to the making of medium- and small-budget crime features seemed to allow writers, in particular, to express their disdain for what they saw as materialistic tendencies in post-war America. Abraham Polonsky was explicitly saying in *Force of Evil* that 'in America crime is part of the system', but some low-budget *films noirs*, unconsidered trifles, seem also to create a world that was hardly less bleak. Even in *The Locket*, directed by émigré John Brahm, and structured around a seemingly infinite regress of flashbacks, there is a social core to the psychological theme. A variation on *Citizen Kane*, the film recounts the story of a servant's daughter who – denied love as a child – carries this anger through her adult life.[34]

During the Dore Schary era other projects were instigated, although a number were cancelled or took years to realise under Howard Hughes' dynasty at the studio. Schary had suggested that Robert Wise direct a boxing picture, for example, and this was finally completed as *The Set-Up* (1949) with Robert Ryan. Described by Wise as a 'labour of love', the film records the last days as a boxer of a 35-year-old on a losing streak. The bleak and grubby world of 'Paradise City' is told with economy in dark and shadow. The film draws on the Warners boxing tradition, but it is a more pessimistic vision, and the triumph, such as it is, is shared with his younger wife. *The Window* (1949) was also instigated by Schary, and it was heralded in Britain as 'one of the few American post-war films to portray working class life in the city with authenticity'. There are neo-realist type shots of real New York tenements and streets, as the young boy walks vainly to the police station to tell a story that no one believes, and the confined family life is well caught.[35]

In *Where Danger Lives* (1950) there is again a representative of the public sector and the public interest, whose role is set against a society dominated by transactions of private interest. Into the public hospital where a concerned doctor, Jeff Cameron (Robert Mitchum), is working long hours, fate brings an emergency case of attempted suicide. The patient is Margo Lannington (Faith Domergue), who believes that 'poverty's sordid', and whose mental illness is associated throughout with an obsession with money. The marriage of Margo and her millionaire husband (Claude Rains) is reducible to a contract between youth and money; the husband explains that 'Margo married me for my money, I married her for her youth; we both got what we wanted, after a fashion.' *Film noir*, and particularly the films that root their narratives in broadly realistic American social settings, is full of such figures, including doctors in *Where Danger Lives* and *Caught*, an art expert in *Crack-Up*, the head of a city's public health service – an obvious Rooseveltian metaphor – in Kazan's *Panic in the Streets*, a parole officer in *Raw Deal* and a children's teacher in *Dark Passage*. Writers and directors with some record of social or political interest recur in the credits of these films: the writers Arthur Laurents (*Caught*), Leopold Atlas (*Raw Deal*), John Paxton (*Crack-Up*), and Daniel Fuchs (*Panic in the Streets*). Modestly budgeted crime films of the era were able to tell some home truths, as well as allowing some filmmakers on the left – in films such as *Force of Evil*, *The Prowler*, *Night and the City* and *The Sound of Fury* – cover to attempt more pointed comments on what Andersen calls the 'injuries of class'.[36]

Chapter 7

Into the fifties

ANTI-COMMUNISM AND THE BLACKLIST

By the time that the House Committee on Un-American Activities had relaunched its hearings on Hollywood, in March 1951, the country was in the grip of something like a national panic over the international and domestic threat of communism. In February 1950 Senator Joseph McCarthy's speech at Wheeling, West Virginia – in which he began his campaign against communists in the State Department – came in the immediate wake of the conviction of Alger Hiss and the arrest of Klaus Fuchs. Hiss, the former State Department official who had been accused by HUAC in 1948 of passing secrets to a communist spy ring, had lost his appeal and was beginning a five year sentence for perjury. To Pells, the conviction of Hiss lent credence to 'the theory that all communists should be regarded as potential foreign agents'. Fuchs, the former Manhattan Project physicist, confessed to having been a Soviet spy; later the same year the war in Korea began, and Ethel and Julius Rosenberg were arrested on a charge of conspiracy to commit espionage.

In April 1950 the Supreme Court declined to review the cases of Dalton Trumbo and John Howard Lawson, who had appealed on behalf of the Hollywood Ten; all ten began jail sentences of between six and twelve months. The overwhelming majority of those summoned to appear before the House Committee between 1951 and 1953 either admitted that they had been party members in the past and named names of party members they had known, or pleaded the fifth amendment. The latter course led to blacklisting, and in March 1952 the studios, under pressure from the American Legion, explicitly agreed not to employ those who took the fifth amendment. Over 200

Hollywood artists were in practice denied employment – until the blacklist tended to crumble at the end of the 1950s – by those studios that were members of the Association of Motion Picture Producers. Private organisations widened the blacklist to radio and television; in 1950 American Business Consultants published *Red Channels*, a list of 150 individuals, with details of past affiliations, memberships and petitions signed. Many who escaped the blacklist had difficulty finding employment – were 'greylisted' – because of these associations.[1]

Elia Kazan's testimony, which he went to some lengths to justify publicly, enabled him to work again in the American film industry, but caused widespread dismay among those who had worked with him in both theatre and films. Kazan's refusal to disown his particularly uncompromising testimony, and his relative success at the time, has made him a notorious figure in the debate about the period. While at times he has expressed a sense of regret he has always balanced this with the view that the testimony was justified as a symbolic act; in his autobiography he refers to the testimony as 'correct', but asks whether it was 'right'. Kazan's autobiography suggests that the crucial factor was that he was unwilling to sacrifice his film career for a cause in which he no longer believed. When this writer asked him about his testimony he replied that 'obviously you don't like naming names', but that he 'hated the Communists'. But Kazan also justified his decision on the grounds that the Communist Party was a conspiracy, and that he wanted 'to break open the secrecy'. Certainly this was his wife's view, and was reflected in the *New York Times* advertisement that she wrote for him. The view was shared by a number of anti-communist liberals in the early 1950s, including those whose views were represented by the American Committee for Cultural Freedom, which had been established in 1951, and which Kazan later joined. Arthur Schlesinger Jr, a member of ACCF, and whose 1949 book *The Vital Center* had been influential in the growth of non-communist liberal opinion, publicly supported Kazan's stance.[2]

But as I.F. Stone wrote at the time, this 'conspiracy' was 'so tenuous that even the top leaders of the Communist Party have been prosecuted for nothing more tangible than "conspiracy to advocate"'. Ceplair and Englund, despite their criticism of the party's 'inability to countenance debate and criticism', and its unquestioning acceptance of 'comintern directives', argue that all the informers knew that the Communist Party was no threat to the country, and only made public their feelings on the party, or its members, when appearances before the House Committee made this necessary for them to continue working. Yet, as Jeffrey C. Goldfarb has argued, referring to the wider 'purge' in unions, universities and elsewhere, 'silence and co-operation, even by those who were critical of the anti-communist hysteria, could be and was principled'. Much as Kazan could have found ways of publicising his views on American communism which did not enhance the legitimacy of a committee that caused so much pain and suffering, and probably contributed to some early deaths, it is difficult to see Kazan's motives as purely selfish. Rightly or wrongly, it seems that Kazan convinced himself, or his wife convinced him, that – as Pauly puts it – the 'reluctance to speak out on Communism increased its current threat'. Kazan's further decision to send a list of his credits to the committee and to Twentieth Century-Fox, presenting much of his work in terms of its 'Americanism', was the subject of additional, and understandable, anger. To Arthur Miller, who had tried to persuade Kazan not to name names, 'Who or what was now safer because this man in his human weakness had been forced to humiliate himself?'[3]

Jews and immigrants were particularly under pressure to affirm American values at the time, particularly if they had broken with the party some time before. Erik Erikson, himself an immigrant, describes the loyalty oath controversy that he faced in the McCarthy era as 'a test of my American identity'. Navasky's clear-eyed moral distinction between those who talked and those who didn't avoids the fact – attested to by many of his witnesses – that, when cruelly put on the spot, the politics of each individual had a significant impact on how they saw the choice before them, or whether they even saw a choice. As Gregory Black has argued, Navasky is 'more concerned with preaching about the morality of informing than in analyzing the forces which brought those people to that point'. Lillian Hellman, Navasky's 'moral exemplar', wrote of the special vulnerability of the 'children of timid immigrants' in this period, describing how, having achieved success, they were 'determined to keep it at any cost'. Hellman felt that Kazan's testimony was the price he paid to retain this success.

Navasky seems to give limited weight to the question of how significantly radicals of the 1930s and 1940s should bear some responsibility for denying what Lillian Hellman rather briefly referred to as the 'sins of Stalinism'. Budd Schulberg has, like Kazan, continued to justify his decision – whereas many others, following Sterling Hayden, have renounced their previous behaviour; Schulberg prefers to talk of the sins of Stalinism rather than the sins of – using the term broadly – McCarthyism; he told Navasky: 'they question our talking. I question their silence. They were premature anti-fascists but there were also premature anti-Stalinists.'[4]

Edward Dmytryk had, along with the other members of the Ten, eventually served his prison sentence for 'contempt of Congress' in the second half of 1950. (He claims to have joined the Communist Political Association at the end of the war, and to have left the party before the 1947 hearings: 'I was with them on the basis of freedom of speech.') Released from prison, Dmytryk decided that he was not going to become a martyr to a cause which, for whatever reason, he no longer espoused. In his testimony to the House Committee in April 1951, in which he identified 26 people as communists or former communists, Dmytryk discussed the case of *Cornered*, the Korean War and the various spy trials as influences on his decision to testify. In his book he refers to his wife's enthusiasm for his break with any association with the communist party, and to the large debts that he faced on leaving prison; he was willing to do whatever was necessary in order to make himself marketable, including the giving of the pound of flesh required by the 'Hollywood right wing'.[5]

Cy Endfield remembers Robert Rossen as personally ambitious, and at times ruthless, but as someone who also had a social conscience. Rossen had appeared before the committee in June 1951, but he refused to answer questions on other people. This did not satisfy the right, but the fact that he talked openly of his own experiences angered his friends on the left. Endfield remembers that Rossen was unable to obtain a passport, and was therefore unable to leave the country as Endfield and Losey were to do. Talking to Endfield in New York in October 1951, Rossen swore that those 'bastards aren't going to get me'. But he was in the position of being unable to work, and of having few friends. Foreman remembers him in this period, just before

Foreman left America, as 'sad, forlorn and sick': 'I had never liked him, but at the same time I could see his predicament.'

Rossen testified again in May 1953, and this time he fully co-operated with the committee, confirming the names of 57 individuals as party members. To Foreman, Rossen was a 'street fighter' who had destroyed 'his image of himself as a tough guy'. Endfield remembers meeting Rossen again in England in 1956, when Endfield was beginning to work under false names: 'I had met this very assured guy with the iron jaw and his great personal determination, and he was a shadow of that guy. He had lost his feeling for himself. He had said "They won't get me", and they got him.' Rossen worked again after his co-operative testimony in 1953, but he never returned to Hollywood, and only with *The Hustler* in 1961 did he achieve commercial and critical success. Rossen seemed diminished in his own eyes by his decision, along with Clifford Odets and others.[6]

While most writers could and did go underground – continuing to work, albeit anonymously and usually with poor material – directors could only change countries to continue working, if they were not prepared to co-operate with the committee. Jules Dassin (whose summons to attend the Committee was put off indefinitely, but who was nonetheless blacklisted) felt that the co-operative witnesses had 'placed career before honour', and he moved to France with his family in 1953. Fellow directors Bernard Vorhaus, Cy Endfield and Joseph Losey all set up home in London in the early 1950s, rather than face the blacklist or name names. John Berry, who later remarked that he was lucky to have a passport, settled in France in 1951. Michael Gordon was blacklisted, following his appearance before the committee in September 1951, at which he took the fifth amendment, but he began working again following his decision to clear himself – become an informer in Navasky's terms – in 1958. Lewis Milestone was greylisted, and lived in Europe in the period 1950–5. Politics contributed to a diaspora of writers and directors in the fifties but other factors played a part, including the increasing number of American-financed films being made in Europe. John Huston chose to live in Ireland from 1953, while in 1952 Charles Chaplin had his re-entry permit, necessary for a resident alien who travelled abroad, withdrawn while he was in Switzerland. Orson Welles continued to work in Europe, while he returned to Hollywood in 1956 to act in several films, and to make *Touch of Evil* (1958) for Harry Cohn.

Michael Wilson took the fifth amendment in 1951, and went to live in France following his work on *Salt of the Earth*. Other victims of the blacklist of the same period included Donald Ogden Stewart, Ben Barzman, Carl Foreman, Paul Jarrico and Sidney Buchman, who all went to Europe, and Albert Maltz, Dalton Trumbo, Hugo Butler and others, who lived in Mexico for some or all of the 1950s. Jarrico, who left the party in early 1958, has emphasised the 'logic to the reactionary position' during the early Cold War period: 'If you're going to call on people to give their lives in a fight against Communism internationally, you can certainly raise logically the question of why we should allow Communists or Communist sympathizers to express themselves domestically.' Howard Koch was one of a number of non-communists to be blacklisted, and he also spent time in England in the fifties. Among blacklisted actors and actresses were Howard Da Silva, Karen Morley, Jeff Corey, Will Geer and Art Smith.

In Britain in the later 1950s, the British television and film industry benefited from the availability of experienced writers and directors who were blacklisted in their own country. Hannah Weinstein, an American producer, had been a left-wing publicist and political organiser, and had worked for Henry Wallace in his 1948 presidential campaign. She avoided congressional investigation by moving to Europe in 1952, and in London she later developed the idea of a film series for television that would provide work for blacklisted American writers. The most popular of several series which she independently produced for the new commercial television network in Britain was *The Adventures of Robin Hood*. Ring Lardner Jr and Ian McLellan Hunter wrote approximately forty scripts, under pseudonyms, from New York, while Gordon Kahn and Waldo Salt were also involved. The films, which were also shown in America, were popular with adults as well as children, and the subject of the series provided an opportunity for discussion of tyranny, privilege and betrayal.[7]

THE CASE OF CY ENDFIELD

Cy Endfield was, like others of his generation, to some degree radicalised by his experiences in the early 1930s. His father's business had collapsed and this had threatened and delayed his entry into Yale; only in 1933, aged 19, did he move to New Haven from his home in Scranton, Pennsylvania, where he was born. Endfield remembers himself as an 'incorrigible experimenter' at Yale and sees his political activities – for example, organising unemployment marches for the Garment Workers Union in New Haven – as 'episodes in a much wider aspect of activities'. (He remembers Yale Drama productions, 'heeling' for the *Yale News*, and numerous other interests including 'Girls, Sculpture, Conjuring on a high level, practising Silver smithing, reading books and books and books.') He developed an interest in the ideas and practice of progressive, particularly Russian theatre, and he later worked as an itinerant director in various forms of left-wing theatre in New York, and ran an amateur group in Montreal. His difficult early experiences in Hollywood, in the early 1940s, were discussed above. (He remembers first meeting Orson Welles in a magic shop on Hollywood Boulevard, and later – as an assistant to Jack Moss at RKO – sadly witnessing the recutting of Welles' 'beautiful' first version of *The Magnificent Ambersons*, while the director was in Brazil.)

In Hollywood, Endfield remembers that he went to a 'couple of dozen different meetings that were communist meetings', but that he never signed up: 'I just didn't have the personal discipline, nor, most important, the desire to part with dues.' When he was in the army during the war, and after the war, he 'began to develop a good deal of scepticism about Russia'. Apart from theatre and drama Endfield was interested in science, and he was concerned about the criticism of both Einstein and the geneticists in the Soviet Union. He began to disengage, but was aware that his attendance at meetings in the early 1940s, and earlier in New York, had left him vulnerable.

Endfield was finally named as a communist at a congressional hearing in 1951, just after his career had reached an important, transitional stage. After the war he had worked on 'very B pictures' at Monogram and elsewhere, including several in a series of Joe Palooka features which had eight-day shooting schedules; in poverty row, Endfield recalls, 'it was junk and it could only be junk', although he remembers *The Argyle Secrets* (1948) which he wrote and directed, with some warmth. Then, at the end of the 1940s, Endfield was given the opportunity to make what was called a 'nervous A' picture for producer Hal E.

Chester, for United Artists release. With a four-week shooting schedule and a budget of around $400,000, *The Underworld Story* (1950) provided Endfield with considerably more opportunity. The film had a social message that was obscured by the requirement of the distributors that a dark-skinned white woman be cast as a black woman. *The Underworld Story* led to the opportunity to direct *The Sound of Fury*, for producer Robert Stillman, a former partner of Stanley Kramer who had formed his own company after being associate producer for both *Champion* and *Home of the Brave*.

Stillman had arranged for the financing of both films through his father, John Stillman, the head of a chain of department stores in the Middle West. Despite the greater uncertainty shown by private investors and banks towards independent companies by 1950, Stillman established his own company with his profits from the earlier films, and *The Sound of Fury* was its first production. John Stillman urged that the lessons of his own business experience be applied to the motion picture market: first, that the product of competitors be examined, and second, that the company should 'make a new and different kind of product which could be manufactured at a price which would turn a profit'.

The Sound of Fury (1951) is a social problem film in the tradition of previous films about lynching and intolerance, while also reflecting the post-war interest in documentary realism, and the conventions that came to be associated with the *film noir* form. The product is differentiated, as an anti-lynching story, both by the fact that the victims are guilty, and by the lack of the Southern locale associated with the subject. Instead the study of yellow journalism and mob violence is set in a post-war, suburban California community; Howard Tyler (Frank Lovejoy) begins his descent into crime, and ultimate death, through his weak character, his lack of a job, and his anxiety about the trappings of material success. Led on by the psychopathic Jerry Slocum (Lloyd Bridges), Tyler moves from gas station hold-ups to a kidnapping plan which ends with Slocum brutally murdering a hostage, carefully selected as the richest young man in town. To Endfield one of the men was a brutal psychopath, while the other was brutalised by society. Tyler's remorse and desperation – his wife is pregnant – leads to his capture, and to a climax in which the townspeople, stirred up by sensational press stories of the murder and of a local 'crime wave', storm the prison where the men await trial and lynch them.

Scripted by Jo Pagano from his own novel, the film also explores the local middle-class community, including the editor and chief columnist of the community newspaper. Overtly liberal sentiments are voiced by a visiting European scientist, Dr Simone, who tells his host, the writer of the sensational stories, that if 'frightened people are the measure of newspaper sales, it must be a profitable business nowadays'. Endfield reports that he had vain arguments with Stillman over the 'preachy element' that the producer favoured, and that he wanted to stick to the story of a man who 'loses control of what his instincts are'. The night-for-night scenes, including the murder, are strikingly presented, while the film is most memorable for its climax of mass violence, filmed in and around a real jail in Phoenix, Arizona. (Endfield was to display the same ability to deal with crowds in directing his best-known film, *Zulu*, in 1964.) Thom Andersen has linked the film with Losey's *The Prowler*, and with a small group of post-war films that were critical of the American dream; he stresses the unusual emphasis on class as an influence on the lives of the two veterans, and the unrelieved bleakness of the conclusion.

The Sound of Fury had gained critical recognition, but it was not a commercial success. To Endfield the film came at the end of the post-war period of social analysis in films, and its commercial prospects were damaged by a new atmosphere associated with the onset of the Korean War. Endfield next worked for Sol Lesser, a wealthy producer who made Tarzan pictures, but who claimed to want to make better-class films. The director signed a contract for $1,000 a week, and it was soon after that, in 1951, that he learnt that he had been named as a communist. Through his agent, the Sam Jaffe agency, Endfield discovered that Lesser wanted to close out his contract.

Endfield recounts that up to this point he had privately decided that he would not sacrifice his career 'for associations that I didn't treasure, for people who I disagreed with, and for a system that I disagreed with'. If he had to, he had decided that he would talk, and would clear himself. But at this time he began to give more thought to the implications of clearing himself by naming names:

And I thought of the situation of being in Germany, and your best friend was a Jewish doctor who saved your life as a child.

And you were coming down the street, and he is being kicked to death by a bunch of SS and Nazi activists. Then if you don't put your own foot in they say: Well, what's wrong with you, you're under suspicion.'

Endfield, drawing parallels between the Nazi period and his own predicament, remembers asking himself, in the terms of this analogy, whether he should kick as well. His feeling was that he *would* do so to save his life, but he was much less certain of such an action to save his job. His agent explained the procedure for becoming a friendly witness, beginning with a visit to an FBI office in Pasadena to answer questions. To Endfield, as this was explained, the process of becoming an informer seemed so seedy, seemed so much a propaganda exercise, that he developed a sense of personal revulsion.

Neither did Endfield wish to plead the fifth amendment, as he felt that many of those who were taking this route were protecting themselves politically. So he decided that he would not appear before the committee, and would take his own 'escape route'. He was fortunate that, before he was named, he had applied for and received a passport; had he waited until he was named he doubts if one would have been issued. While in New York in late 1951, *en route* to Europe, Endfield met Robert Rossen, who could not get a passport and who therefore could not leave the country. In London, Endfield was able slowly to rebuild his film career. While their careers later diverged, Cy Endfield and Joseph Losey have both been seen as managing to 'inject the staid British cinema of the 1950s with some much-needed toughness and vigour'. *Hell Drivers* (1957) in particular is an example of the introduction of American genre concerns and techniques to British subject matter.

Endfield has discussed the questions raised by the 'naming names' issue. Firstly, on the House Committee:

> Their wickedness was that they had only a remit for investigation with the aim of creating legislation against suspected red subversion. They changed it into a tribunal of judgement against individuals. In effect the hearings became trials leading to real punishments (the loss of careers) for 'joining' with little or no evidence of 'doing', often years earlier . . . It was all headline mongering. But the price exacted for taking a moral stance by us 'named' culprits was one's career – one's means of earning a living.

But, speaking at the end of 1989, the year of the collapse of communism in Eastern Europe and the repression of the student movement in China, he also reassessed the morality of the victims of the blacklist, given subsequent history:

It was 'reds under the bed' self-publicity. But on the other hand the victims were people who were lured into another position by lies [that were] as evil or more evil than those things. We don't want to pay our debts. We as individuals. I don't, I confess that. I say no, in the thirties, in the forties, I was an idealist . . . I thought that capitalism should be ended because capitalism ended inevitably in fascism or war, or both, inevitably. That was the Leninist doctrine at the time. Well, that's not what's happened. After seventy years and the sacrifice of a great number of generations, we find that all the good things in these societies were taken over by the bureaucrats, by the apparatchiks . . . So if you're that wrong you can't go around saying 'Oh, I only did it for the best motivations.' You were a fool. You were a companion of evil. I was a companion of evil, to the extent that I believed those things. Sure, I was doing things that I thought were good, and probably were good in a more local context, but really in the final way it's hard to say who was more wrong.[8]

ANTI-COMMUNISM AND THE FILM AGENDA

In the early 1950s the post-war impetus towards social realism ran up against the new and pervasive ideological concerns of the period. Hofstadter wrote that by the election of 1952 Harry Truman's rhetoric, with its occasional criticism of 'Wall Street', seemed passé and rather embarrassing. Arthur Miller, commenting on those who renounced their previous convictions before congressional committees, referred to the ideological shift in terms of a change in the atmosphere; the 'oxygen', he recalled, 'went out of the air for these ideas'. It would seem likely that the decline in the social content of Hollywood films that Dorothy Jones finds for the period 1947 to 1954 reflects a number of factors. The blacklisting and exile of many of the writers and directors who were most interested in social issues may have had an effect, but probably more important were judgements made by those who produced and financed films.

Whether or not the studios were ever very affected by the danger of picketing by the American Legion, it became prudent to be wary of scripts that might attract the attention of the professional anti-communists. However, by the mid-1950s the relative prosperity was throwing up problems that seemed quite different from those of the 1930s.

Oblique references to the political events were more acceptable in the context of recognised film genres of science fiction and the Western; *It Came from Outer Space* (1953) and *High Noon* (1952) are two prominent examples. *Broken Arrow* (1950), discussed earlier, also foreshadowed the greater social significance of the 1950s Western. Social problem themes were more sensitive: Bernard Vorhaus remembers trying to interest two studios in a story set in a girls' reform school, and finding that such topics, unpolitical but 'critical of certain social conditions', were seen as 'suspect'. (The Danziger brothers, theatre and hotel owners, agreed to finance a low-budget, New York production, and the film was released as *So Young So Bad* by United Artists in 1950.) Also in the category of socially conscious melodrama was another low-budget production, *The Well* (1951). Coming at the end of the race cycle of the late forties, this film shows the potential in a small-town community for racial distrust and conflict – when a child goes missing – and then for harmonious co-operation to save the child, when she is found trapped down a well. This theme of potential hysteria, encouraged or not by the press, is also characteristic of the time. As well as *The Sound of Fury*, with its emphasis on class, Billy Wilder was arguably more broadly cynical about American society in *Ace in the Hole* (1951). There are no liberal sentiments in Wilder's film, reflecting his own perspective; one study of Wilder sees the film as viewing America as a 'vast hypocrisy'.

Joseph Mankiewicz wrote and directed the social comedy *People Will Talk* (1951) at Twentieth Century-Fox, as a comment on America at the time, including references both to McCarthy and to the dispute in the Screen Directors Guild – of which he was chairman – over loyalty oaths. An unconventional university hospital gynaecologist, Dr Noah Praetorius (Cary Grant), is brought before a faculty committee hearing by a small-minded and suspicious principal (Hume Cronyn). The comedy is linked to the recurring 'out of the past' theme of *film noir*, but Praetorius is guilty not of any crime, still less of political deviationism, but of an innocence and zanyness that is viewed suspiciously by the mean-spirited 'official' world. (There is an element of the feeling in *Holiday* here.)[9]

Warners had not contributed to the series of liberal films on race, and by the early 1950s they had lost much of their reputation as a liberal studio with a specialisation in working-class themes. Of the three individuals identified by Buscombe as symbolising the Warners attachment to politics and working-class life at the end of the 1930s, only Jerry Wald was still at the studio, and he was soon to leave. Wald had produced some of the studio's most innovative post-war films, such as *Mildred Pierce, Possessed* (1947) and *Key Largo*, and it was he who co-ordinated what seemed like a venture into familiar Warners territory at the end of the 1940s. He played an active part in the planning of a film, to be written by liberals Daniel Fuchs and Richard Brooks, on the Deep South and the Ku Klux Klan. Yet Wald was clear that this was not to be a 'message film', and instead he argued that the key point of the film was the question of 'who is more guilty – the people who belong to the Klan, or the people who just turn their backs and say, "it's none of my business"'. The main focus was not to be on the Klan, but on the issue of testifying against it.[10]

The film, *Storm Warning* (1951, directed by Heisler), opens with the arrival in a small Southern town, Rockpoint, of a woman, Marsha Mitchell, who, in her first moments in town, witnesses a brutal assault and murder of a man by a group of Klansmen. The man turns out to have been a journalist who had been investigating the Klan, and the issue becomes one of whether Mitchell should testify as to what she saw. This is an isolated Southern town in which everyone is scared to talk, but the county prosecutor – Bert Rainey, played by Ronald Reagan – is determined that the local community should clean up 'our own nests', rather than wait for 'New York or Washington to start poking their noses in'. The moral problem for Martha Mitchell is complicated by the fact that one of the murderers is the husband of her sister, who she had been visiting in Rockpoint. Called to the stand, Mitchell perjures herself to protect her sister, and she only changes her mind after the sister is assaulted by her husband and decides to leave him. Mitchell's 'standing up' leads to her death, as, in a melo-dramatic ending, she is kidnapped by the Klan, and she and the murderer are shot dead when the police arrive at a Klan rally. The tone of the film presages something of the isolation from liberal America demonstrated by Southern towns and cities in the later civil rights conflicts; after Rockpoint came Little Rock. Liberal films found corruption in particular communities. In *On the Waterfront* – basically a liberal film behind the self-serving references – the docks are 'not part of America', while in MGM's *Bad Day at Black Rock* (1954), it is the small western town which is pictured protecting its guilty secret. In *The Sound of Fury* the voice for humanism is contrasted with the appalling, demonic power of crowds, but the film also places blame on the institutional elites who stoke the flames.

A picture of Hollywood at the turn of the decade is provided by *In a Lonely Place* (1950). Screenwriter Dix Steele (Humphrey Bogart) is the vulnerable and violent hero of *film noir*, but his experiences mirror those of writers driven by official suspicions of their 'loyalty' into mental breakdown or paranoia. Nicholas Ray directed the film for Santana Productions, the company formed by Robert Lord and Humphrey Bogart, both of them late of Warners. Andrew Solt wrote a screenplay from a novel by Dorothy B. Hughes, but transformed the story from the original one of a young psychopathic killer, roaming the beaches of Santa Monica and murdering young girls. In the film Steele is a writer who is down on his luck, whose best credits were pre-war, and who is scathing about contemporary Hollywood and its pictures; he is 'blacklisted' for his attitudes, and for his drinking and bad temper. When he is falsely accused of murder the audience is first encouraged to identify with him, and later with the woman who suspects that he is the murderer, and who witnesses his bouts of paranoid violence. Nicholas Ray claimed to be greylisted after making the film, which, James W. Palmer argues, holds the mirror up to Hollywood, and thereby exposes 'that community's complicity in creating the conditions under which people betrayed their friends'. (Biskind sees the film as conservative, with its contrast between the brilliant but unpredictable Steele, and the average, conventional people – notably Steele's old war friend, now a policeman.)[11]

High Noon (1952) is the best known of the films that made oblique comment on the Hollywood investigations. At the end of 1950 the Stanley Kramer Co. Inc. – the company that, as Screen Plays Corporation, had been so successful in the late 1940s – became a semi-autonomous unit within Columbia

Pictures. To Kramer, economic considerations forced him to bring the company into the orbit of a major studio, thus sacrificing some independence. Carl Foreman opposed the change, and stayed at the original company while Kramer and the others moved to the Columbia lot. There he worked on a story which he saw as a comment on the way the Hollywood community was crumbling under the pressure of external political intervention. Foreman's experiences of the loyalty oath issue that came before the Screen Writers Guild in 1950 put him in mind of the parallels between the Hollywood of the time and the situation described in a two-page Western short story published in *Colliers* in 1947. In 1951 Foreman was waiting for his own subpoena to arrive, while he saw others name names before the House Committee, including George Glass, one of the participants in the Screen Plays company. Foreman disapproved of the Communist Party he had left in 1942, but he refused to inform, as he saw it, and took the fifth amendment before the House Committee in September 1951. To Foreman, Kramer's disavowal of him within a few days of his committee appearance indicated something of Kramer's movement towards the 'safely controversial'. (In 1951 Kramer signed the newly 'cleared' Edward Dmytryk to a four-picture deal at Columbia Pictures.)

The film, of course, can be viewed and enjoyed without any understanding of this subtext, and director Fred Zinnemann has played down the contemporary relevance of the film. John Wayne may have hated the symbolism of the end of the film, in which the victorious Marshal Kane (Gary Cooper) throws his badge to the ground before leaving town, but in retrospect the film seems consistent with a view that stresses romantic individualism (the famous crane shot), the use of violence by those in authority to confront evil, and even the rightness – personified by the use of the right-wing Cooper – of standing up to communism.[12]

Johnny Guitar (1954) is a more explicit and detailed comment on the McCarthy period, as the writer Philip Yordan has testified. Yordan apparently employed surrogates to write some of his assigned screenplays, a practice which was made easier by the blacklist. Yordan fronted for Ben Maddow and others in the 1950s, but he claims to have written, or rewritten, the *Johnny Guitar* script. Each faction in the Western plot can be associated with the various actors in the wider drama – friendly witnesses, communists, fellow travellers, witch-hunters, government and business. Motivated by a threat to their economic welfare a posse comprising the marshal and the townspeople help Emma in her assault on Vienna, who is in shaky alliance with Johnny Guitar and the gang who, after being falsely accused and threatened by the authorities, have robbed a bank. The film is better remembered for its sexual passions and exaggerated colour, but it does depict the misuse of legal procedure by the authorities and vigilantes. Despite this comment on contemporary events, Nicholas Ray was happy to use Ward Bond and Sterling Hayden in the film – respectively one of the most militant members of the Motion Picture Alliance, and an actor who had 'named names' to the committee in 1951.

There are other references to the purge of domestic communism in the films of the 1950s. In 1950 the writers Daniel Taradash and Elick Mull succeeded in interesting Stanley Kramer in a story about a librarian who lost her job when she refused to take a book on communism off the shelves. According to Taradash plans for the film were dropped when the proposed star, Mary Pickford, who had agreed to make a return to the screen, was intimidated by protests by members of the Motion Picture Alliance. Only in 1955, with Columbia having inherited the property, was Harry Cohn persuaded by Taradash and the liberal producer Julian Blaustein to finance the film. The film, *Storm Center* (1956) – functional rather than stylish, except in its Saul Bass titles – again shows how fickle small-town opinion can be mobilised against someone who dissents from the conventional view. The librarian (played by Bette Davis) is denounced not only for refusing to ban a book – *The Communist Dream* – but for her wartime memberships of groups such as the 'Council for Better Relations with the Soviet Union'. She is hounded despite the fact that she resigned when she discovered that such groups were communist fronts; as in other liberal films of this and later periods, there could be no question of supporting the civil liberties of a communist.

The 'naming names' trauma surfaces elsewhere. The Walter Wanger production for United Artists, *I Want to Live*, directed by Robert Wise and released in 1958, is a powerful film in opposition to capital punishment. Based on the real life and death of Barbara Graham, the film includes a scene in which the accused is offered complete immunity if she agrees to 'sign a full statement naming names'. Two years before, in *Invasion of the Body Snatchers* – again produced by Wanger, for Allied Artists – the writer Daniel Mainwaring, a man of leftist associations and the writer of Losey's *The Lawless*, arguably expressed his despair at podlike conformity in America. How much of this intention is readable, and was read at the time, is another question. The totalitarian mob that takes over can be read as both McCarthyite or communist.[13]

THE ANTI-COMMUNIST CYCLE

In a rare contribution to the inquiries of the House Committee on Un-American Activities into communism in the film industry, Richard Nixon asked Jack Warner, during the studio chief's testimony of October 1947, whether Warner Bros had made, or was making, any films that revealed the 'evils of totalitarian communism'. Nixon seemed to suggest that the Jewish studio owners were prepared to make anti-fascist films but were negligent in what he saw as their duty to counter 'totalitarian communism'. Nixon's point has to be considered along with his use of red-baiting as a tactic in seeking office at the time. While the cycle of anti-communist films that came from all the studios at the end of the 1940s and into the 1950s can in some cases be seen as an exploitation of a topical issue, in other cases there may have been an attempt to curry favour with the Committee, and with governmental authority in general.

Daniel J. Leab recounts the story of Darryl Zanuck's desire, with the film *The Iron Curtain* (1948), to be first in the queue to exploit the new issue of the Cold War, and of communist perfidy, just as *Gentleman's Agreement* had beaten *Crossfire* to release as the first film attacking anti-Semitism. To Leab the motive of the studios, certainly at the end of the 1940s, at the beginning of the cycle, was less fear of the House Committee than a more traditional fear of missing out on a box office dividend. Howard Hughes at RKO had taken a personal interest in the tortuous production of *Woman on Pier 13* (1949) – planned as *I Married a Communist* – on which the liberals John Cromwell and Nicholas Ray were required to work for a time. But it was during the period 1951–3 that the cycle peaked, with some 41 films being released in these three years. Three well-known and well-documented films of this cycle are *Big Jim McLain* (Warners,

1951), *My Son John* (Paramount, 1952) and *Walk East on Beacon* (Columbia Pictures, 1952).

Richard Nixon, in his 'chequers speech' during the 1952 election campaign, had called on viewers to help him drive the 'crooks and the communists' out of Washington, reminding his audience, and Dwight D. Eisenhower, of his role in the investigation of Alger Hiss. The equation of domestic communism with gangsterism is a feature of a number of the films that picture an 'enemy within', while most of them are explicitly or implicitly anti-intellectual. *Walk East on Beacon* was produced by Louis de Rochemont and the script was based on a article by J. Edgar Hoover; the semi-documentary form was used to dramatise the techniques employed by the FBI to uncover a ruthless Soviet agent. Related to this cycle were early 1950s science fiction films which, according to one commentator, taught the viewer 'to be wary of inept scientists and to have faith in the FBI and the military'.[14]

To a degree the anti-communist films drew on the services of the Hollywood right, just as the wartime anti-fascist films had made use of the Hollywood left. John Wayne, one of the founders of the Motion Picture Alliance for the Preservation of American Ideals, used his own production company to make *Big Jim McLain*, in which Wayne played a heroic agent for the House Committee. *My Son John*, which like *Walk East on Beacon* glorified the informer, reflected the politics of director Leo McCarey, another Motion Picture Alliance member, and writer – the self-described 'old rightist' John Lee Mahin. Yet the fear of internal communist subversion was not as widely held in the early 1950s as the wartime fears of fascism that the left reflected. While Cold War liberals interpreted the McCarthy phenomenon as reflecting a mass discontent that threatened the democratic system, later interpretations put less emphasis on popular (and populist) support, and more on the various institutional political and economic elites, notably the Republican right, who protected or encouraged the congressional 'investigations'. To Rogin, 'Hollywood, like Washington, was an arena of institutional, not mass power.'[15]

FIFTIES: KAZAN

To the critic Jim Kitses, Kazan's films of the 1950s reflect the changing times, from the 'socially conscious forties' to a period in which the emphasis was on 'greater personal freedom and introspection'. To Pauly, Kazan in the 1950s reformulated a central myth of the past for the 'new times' of the 1950s: the common man of 1930s Capra or Warners was less evident, while the hero 'turns inward and the social battle becomes psychological'. Others have seen Kazan's naming of names, in his second appearance before the House Committee, in April 1952, as a decisive influence on his film work. Abraham Polonsky, for example, has argued that Kazan's post-testimony films were marred by 'bad conscience'.[16]

Panic on the Streets (1950) was made in New Orleans, where Kazan enjoyed greater freedom from the studio than on *Boomerang*, while also, as with the previous film, working on location with scriptwriter Richard Murphy. With much night shooting, the film combines the studio's semi-documentary tradition with a *film noir* exploration of the New Orleans underworld. There are shades of *High Noon*, as a central authority figure fights for what he sees as the public interest. As with *Crossfire* the figure of authority is associated with the New Deal ethic – in this case a doctor attached to the Public Health Service who sees the social dangers of a local case of plague more clearly than the local press and notables.

The year 1950 was also when Kazan began to plan more ambitious productions; as he began work on a film version of Tennessee Williams' *A Streetcar Named Desire*, he was also awaiting film scripts from John Steinbeck and Arthur Miller. In 1947 Jack Warner had testified to the House Committee that Elia Kazan was 'one of the mob', but three years later Kazan renewed a long and generally harmonious relationship with Warner, one of the longest surviving of the old studio heads. From the mid-1950s Kazan was to combine independent, New York based filmmaking with the backing of the old Hollywood studio. While Charles Feldman received the producer credit when *A Streetcar Named Desire* was released by Warner Bros in 1951, Kazan in effect produced the film – and strongly defended the 'Elia Kazan Production' credit against pressure from the studio. Kazan was in constant touch with Warner on a range of issues from casting to advertising, and in the fight to protect as much of the meaning of the play from the Production Code officials. In response to persistent objections from the Breen Office to the rape scene, the director claimed to have set the crucial deal by insisting, at a meeting in Jack Warner's trophy room, that the rape of Blanche be retained, but that it could be compensated by some form of punishment for Stanley at the end. The seal was obtained, but the studio was then pressured by the Legion of Decency into further trimming of the film just before its opening in September 1951, an action which led Kazan to write a protesting article for the *New York Times*.

Referring to another of the circumlocutions imposed on the script by the Breen Office, Hollis Alpert, in his review, argues that it would take a 'singular obtuseness not to know what Blanche is referring to when she speaks of the unmanliness of the husband'. Some critics have accused Kazan of making Stanley's character too sympathetic, and even of identifying with the male character's 'new realist' contempt for Blanche's (and Williams') old illusions. But the film both indicated the widening of Hollywood's sexual horizons, and was also part of what Manny Farber saw as a wave of 'art or mood' films, including *A Place in the Sun, Sunset Boulevard, People Will Talk* and *Detective Story* (1951); to Farber these 'Freud-Marx epics' represented the social significance of the 1930s gone sour. Kazan's continuing social interests in 1950 are indicated by his brief partnership with Arthur Miller in an attempt to interest Columbia Pictures in 'The Hook', Miller's New York waterfront story. Indicating the sensitivity of direct social content in film at the time, Harry Cohn asked Roy Brewer to comment on the script. (Brewer, head of the International Alliance of Theatrical Stage Employees – IATSE – was a prominent anti-communist who played a key role in the blacklist, and in the procedures by which ex-communists could clear themselves.) While Kazan was prepared to continue negotiating, Miller saw the proposed changes as damaging the integrity of his script, and withdrew. It was only later, after his testimony, that Kazan began working on the same subject with Budd Schulberg.[17]

In 1948 Kazan and John Steinbeck had persuaded Zanuck to purchase the rights to a project on the Mexican revolutionary Emiliano Zapata from MGM. MGM had first become interested in the subject in the late 1930s, and in 1941 Fred Zinnemann had urged that the studio go ahead with a film that would 'stress and foster Pan American solidarity'. Zinnemann envisaged a 'tremendous final scene of Zapata lying in state while the people filed past his bier'. But MGM's interest only revived in 1947, and then quickly cooled when the proposed screenwriter, Lester Cole, was blacklisted as one of the Hollywood Ten.

John Steinbeck began researching and writing in 1948, but filming only took place in the summer of 1951, and followed a series of script conferences chaired by Darryl F. Zanuck. Paul Vanderwood, in his survey of the various treatments and scripts, argues that 'What began as an endorsement of revolution with determined leadership as a means to social change ended up as a rejection of power, strong leadership, and rebellion in favor of a grass-roots democracy which promises little, if any, change at all.' Yet while the political pressures of the time clearly led to changes in the script, the notion of a repudiation of power by Zapata can be found in early drafts. In an October 1949 treatment Kazan reflected this perspective: 'When Zapata left the Capital, or rather abandoned it, he was in effect committing suicide. I believe he knew it.'[18]

It is probably fair to say that the project would not have survived to be filmed at any studio at the time other than Twentieth Century-Fox. Zanuck's struggle to protect his invest-ment in the film can be viewed in the notes of script conferences held in 1950 and early 1951. Zanuck had been sold on the idea of the film's visual sweep and excitement, but he would also have been aware of the ambitions of both Steinbeck and Kazan to produce a distinctive product within the studio system. Zanuck wanted stirring heroism – in line with the 'big Western' notion he had in mind – but he was increasingly wary of the political interpretation that might be placed on the completed film. This concern would have been increased by his knowledge – Kazan told him – of his director's membership of the Communist Party in the mid-1930s. (Zanuck was similarly worried, at around the same time, that Humphrey Bogart's defence of newspaper freedom against the threat of monopoly, in *Deadline USA* (1952) – written and directed by Richard Brooks – would be seen as communist.) In conference notes of December 1950 Zanuck argued that he wanted 'something to get the audience rooting for Zapata', but was worried lest that something be seen as communism; he continued, 'I hope people don't get the impres-sion that we are advocating revolt or civil war as the only means to peace.' As well as this Zanuck also feared a 'down-beat picture of total frustration', and pointed to *The Grapes of Wrath*, in which the Joads 'were never frustrated'. The most noticeable of the changes demanded by Zanuck before shooting was the enlargement of the role of Fernando (Joseph Wiseman) – the ubiquitous and unprincipled professional revolutionary – in order to add a stronger anti-communist and anti-Stalinist element to the film.

The argument that the finished film unacceptably distorted the historical record, and that as a fable it was conservative in its implications for the possibility of successful popular revolt, was put most strongly by John Howard Lawson, writing after Kazan's 'friendly' testimony of April 1952. To Lawson, 'If power is an absolute source of corruption, if it must be renounced by every honest leader, the people are doomed to eternal submission.' Yet a notion of power and progress can be found in the film. This concept implies that change is more gradual, and that more crucial than the role of leaders is the on-going popular struggle. On returning to Morelos from the Presidential Palace – an action which does seem irresponsible – Zapata (Marlon Brando) warns his people, in a long and particularly emphasised speech, that 'a strong people is the only lasting strength'. As he embarks on his final and fatal mission, the leader also instructs his younger supporters on the need for further struggle; among them is the young man who spoke up to him when he was President, as Zapata had done earlier to Diaz. Finally, when Zapata is murdered, his white horse, symbolising his ideals and the continuing struggle, lives on. The ending is by no means as strong as earlier endings which linked Zapata's memory with the better life enjoyed by later generations, but it can still be read in terms of the importance of Zapata's life as inspiration and myth. Zanuck suggested the use of the horse, and summed up his own or his writers' ideas on the ending, in the phrase: 'He dies but his idea lives'.

The film has some strong defenders. John Womack Jr, author of a standard work on Zapata and the Mexican revolution, has testified that the film developed a 'portrayal of Zapata, the villagers, and the nature of their relations and movement' that he found 'still subtle, powerful and true'. In England a socialist writer pointed out that 'the Mexican peasantry had to wait another generation before the realisation of the Zapata programme under Cardenas'; he found the film – 'within the limits imposed by filmic convention' – to be 'an accurate picture of a great revolutionary leader'. Writing a quarter of a century later,

Dan Georgakis echoed this judgement, concluding that far from the film suggesting that 'revolutions inevitably corrupt their leadership', its 'strongest emotional statement' was 'that there are heroic human beings who are dedicated revolutionaries of absolute incorruptibility'.[19]

Kazan emphasised *Viva Zapata* (1952) as an 'anti-communist film' in the notes on his films that he supplied to the House Un-American Activities Committee, and in contemporary letters in the *Saturday Review*. But while the role of Fernando (earlier Bicho) had been strengthened in a script conference early in 1951, the idea of contrasting Zapata with a communist revolutionary had been present in early drafts. The distinction between natural leaders and professional revolutionaries can also be found in Steinbeck's pre-war work, and he was also critical of the Soviet Union in the post-war period. The evidence suggests that neither Steinbeck nor Kazan were opposed to the strengthening of the anti-communist angle, and in this sense Kazan's first public criticism of the Communist Party came before his April testimony, with the opening of *Viva Zapata!*[20]

Having said that, the visual strength of *Viva Zapata!* was beyond anything in Kazan's previous work, and a number of scenes, particularly in the first half of the film, dilute the overall anti-communist thrust of the film. (It seems difficult to sustain Biskind's view of the film as a 'sustained anti-Communist polemic', much as Kazan encouraged this partial view of the film at the time.) Charles Silver has commented that 'Steinbeck's over elaborate schematic, particularly the use to which Joseph Wiseman is put, eventually tends to overtax Kazan's visuals'. The apparent message gets in the way of something subtler, and few of Kazan's outraged friends or ex-colleagues looked further than the over-neat summary of the film which the director served up to the committee. The pressures of the time reinforced the views – and the interests – of the director, at a time when many writers and artists, even those not threatened with a blacklist, had come to see domestic communism as beyond the normal protection of the First Amendment. When Kazan decided to name names to the House Committee on Un-American Activities, a month after the new film opened, he was able to cite its anti-communism in support of his stance. But, especially as the years have passed, the film's attack on bureaucratic betrayal has not dimmed the sympathetic treatment of a leader identified – before and after his death – with the popular struggle for justice and progress.[21]

Zanuck was particularly struck by the poor box office returns of *Viva Zapata!*, and drew the conclusion that audiences were no longer interested in message pictures but were looking for more escape from 'the gloomy news of the moment'. Stressing the importance of foreign revenues, Zanuck ordered a move towards a policy of 'strictly entertainment films'. There was also a move to Technicolor for half of new productions, and Zanuck became particularly interested in the possibilities for CinemaScope. In a memo to staff of March 1953 Zanuck promised that after several standard films had been completed the studio would 'concentrate exclusively on subjects suitable for CinemaScope'. The era of Fox message pictures, and of 'talky' dramas such as Joseph Mankiewicz's *People Will Talk*, seemed to be in the past. In the midst of his obsession with the widescreen process, Zanuck was the first to turn down Elia Kazan, his former contract director, when he and Budd Schulberg offered him the *Waterfront* project.[22]

In the immediate aftermath of Kazan's testimony to the House Committee he went to Germany to make, at Zanuck's urging, a film about a small travelling circus that makes a dramatic escape to the 'west' from communist Czechoslovakia. *Man on a Tightrope* (1953) was commercially unsuccessful, like most of the films with an anti-communist theme, and Kazan was never satisfied with the Robert Sherwood script. Meanwhile Kazan's ties with Warners grew stronger, as he discussed a film to be made with Tennessee Williams – which eventually became *Baby Doll* (1956) – as early as February 1952. Early the next year Kazan signed a contract with the studio to produce and direct *East of Eden*, from part of John Steinbeck's novel. (The contract gave Kazan final cutting rights unless three previews indicated to Warner that changes were required.)

On the Waterfront was turned down by all the major studios in 1953. Only the maverick producer Sam Spiegel, no longer in partnership with John Huston, saved the project, and persuaded Marlon Brando, one of the Actors Studio graduates who had cooled to Kazan as a result of his testimony, to work for the director once more. Kazan sought out Budd Schulberg, who had made his own 'friendly' testimony to the House Committee in 1951, and who had also, like Miller, written a script based on events on the New York waterfront. (Schulberg was – and has remained – strongly unrepentant about his testimony, linking it to his concerns for the fate of Soviet writers who he had met on a visit to the Soviet Union in the mid-1930s.) In further researching the story Schulberg involved himself closely with those fighting the notorious corruption of the waterfront, including rank and file activists such as Anthony 'Tony Mike' de Vincenzo – the model for the Terry Malloy character – and the waterfront priests who advised them, notably the Rev. John M. Corridan. De Vincenzo testified to the New York Crime Commission in December 1951.

Despite the evidence of collective action, albeit by a minority, the film – reflecting the norms of the industry – concentrated on one individual. As Schulberg accepted: 'The film's concentration on a single dominating character brought close to the camera's eye made it aesthetically inconvenient – if not impossible – to set Terry's story in its social and historical perspective.' Thus fragmentary elements in the film suggest the broader, deep-seated structure of power – what Corridan called the 'triple alliance of business, politics and union racketeering' – while the climax seems to offer an emotional resolution. But the form of the film also suited what was, certainly to Kazan and probably to some extent to Schulberg, a clear subtext: that liberals could and should break the code of secrecy concerning the Communist Party, and testify openly about it, as they had done, to the public authorities. (The moral questions – discussed elsewhere – spring from the nature of the body to which the testimony was given, and the effects of the process on others.)[23]

Kazan originally talked, when he was allied with Arthur Miller, of filming the story in the manner of neo-realism, and certain scenes of the film still betray that intention. The early scenes of Terry's life on the roof, and the conversation in the park between Malloy and Edie Doyle, suggest this influence. *On the Waterfront* (1954) has echoes of 1930s film: from Warners comes the topical theme, working-class locale, and the priest as a key voice of moral authority, while from Capra comes the notion of a loser redeemed, and a central performance that stands in for the director's concerns. There are also links to the social drama of the Group Theatre, and in particular the Group production of Clifford Odets' *Golden Boy*, in which Kazan, Lee J. Cobb and Karl Malden acted. There is Terry Malloy's lack of fulfilment, and even something of the plea that life should not be written on dollar bills, albeit camouflaged in Father Barry's Christian rhetoric.

Malloy's character is deepened, broadened into a kind of fifties everyman, by his bitterness about lost opportunities. Marlon Brando's performance was characteristic of the 1950s Method actors who, as Leo Braudy argues, 'brought into films experiences and feelings that official culture either ignored or actively attacked'. The response to Brando's early 1950s films – and to those of James Dean – revealed something of the growing alienation of young people at the time, and the dawning of a 1960s youth culture. Peter Biskind sees Father Barry as the key manipulating figure, pushing Terry to exchange his old affiliations for a broader loyalty to a classless state, and although the priest does play this structural role, the emphasis on Terry's 'conscience', Brando's powerful performance, and the strong play given to the contrary advice that Terry have nothing to do with the investigators, all reduce the sense that he is merely a token in Kazan's overall scheme. (The seeds of Terry's decision are visible from the start, in his uneasiness about his role in Joey Doyle's killing.) There *is* a distortion of the reality of power on the waterfront, which reflects both Kazan's subtext and the broader inability of Hollywood drama to deal with collective action, but the emphasis on alienation and individual conscience nonetheless did connect with many people's experiences.[24]

The relationship between Charlie and Terry Malloy can be compared to that of Leo and Joe Morse in *Force of Evil*; but for a radical filmmaker the 'force of evil' (i.e. capitalism) is all-pervasive, and corrupts even the central character. The decision of Charley Davis (Garfield) to defy the mob at the end of *Body and Soul* is linked to a return to the values and community of his own people; the social significance of Malloy's rebellion is more debatable given his isolation, although some growth of social awareness among the suspicious longshoremen is suggested, particularly when Malloy takes Johnny Friendly on in person. Society in the later film is largely represented by the state, as Father Barry diverts Malloy's private anger (at his brother's murder, and at some broader resentment against his culture) towards testimony to the Crime Commission.

Kazan's next two films display contrary tendencies, while both move away from the political symbolism of *Viva Zapata!* and *On the Waterfront*. Kazan has seen *East of Eden* (1955) as 'the most autobiographical film I'd made until this time', with Cal (James Dean) rejecting, and being rejected by, his father, before finally coming to terms with him. With two commercial successes behind him, Kazan was then able to spend four months in Mississippi making *Baby Doll* (1956), a black comedy in which everyone has their reasons. The film is best remembered for the 'condemned' rating awarded by the Legion of Decency, following Cardinal Spellman's sight unseen remarks from the pulpit of St Patrick's Cathedral. Kazan, worried about censorship, suggested to Jack Warner: 'We've got to break our own taboos and strike out for increasingly unusual and daring material. Either that or just quit and sign up with the TV guys.' (By the mid-1950s the emphasis at Warners was in fact on production for television.)[25]

At the time *A Face in the Crowd* (1957) – a 'totally collaborative effort' between him and Budd Schulberg – was conceived as a 'warning to the American people'. The film begins with the 'discovery' by radio producer Marcia Jeffries (Patricia Neal) of Lonesome Rhodes (Andy Griffith), serving time in an Arkansas jail. Rhodes, as singer, raconteur and celebrity, becomes a national success on radio and television and in advertising, and finally becomes uncontrollable by everyone except a group of right-wing politicians and businessmen, who exploit his rural populist appeal. (In 1988 Kazan stressed what he saw as the film's 'secondary story', relating to his own relationship with his first wife.)[26]

A mixture early on of realism and satire, the film lacks most of the condescension towards mass culture that was characteristic of 1950s educated opinion, and which is found in Schulberg's short story. Kazan and Schulberg sat in on the work of Madison Avenue advertising agencies, and interviewed politicians Stuart Symington and Lyndon Johnson. They were also aware – in their conception of Lonesome Rhodes, of various real figures, including Will Rogers and Walter Winchell. The portrayal of the mixing of politics and entertainment, and the power in public life – itself increasingly an electronic territory – of what came to be known as celebrity and charisma, is striking. The emphasis on folksy, 'country boy' style perhaps allowed suburban and urban audiences to laugh at Rhodes' rise to power – not be as seduced as the masses in the film. In the first half

Rhodes is something of a hero, with some insight and self-knowledge, but at the height of his success he has become a monster, and the attempt to make him a tragic figure is less than successful. While the film is good on the new mechanisms of public influence, it lacks an overall critique, or even the dark, *film noir* surface of *Sweet Smell of Success* (1957). The filmmakers suggest, like Ed Murrow in one of his famous telecasts on McCarthy, that 'the fault, dear Brutus, lies not in our stars, but in ourselves'.

The rather unconvincing writer (played by Walter Matthau) concludes that the strength of the people is that 'they get wise' to demagogues. But it is only because of Marcia's action, allowing Rhodes' abusive post-broadcast remarks to go out on air, that the people see the light. The advertising-politics-industrial complex effortlessly finds a new man, while Rhodes, suddenly a non-person, abandoned also by Marcia, is left baying to the moon, and to his applause machine, in his top floor apartment.

RADICALS, THE BLACKLIST AND FILM

Rather as Abraham Polonsky talked of *Force of Evil*, Paul Jarrico, the producer of *Salt of the Earth*, saw this film, the only production of the Independent Production Corporation, as something of a 'crime' to fit the punishment of the blacklist. Jarrico and Herbert Biberman, together with Simon Lazarus, had founded the IPC in 1951 as a vehicle for blacklisted Hollywood personnel. (Some sources also cite Adrian Scott as being involved.) Writer Michael Wilson spent time in Hanover, New Mexico in late 1951, observing part of a bitter, fifteen-month-long strike at a mine owned by a subsidiary of New Jersey Zinc. The film was financed by the International Union of Mine, Mill and Smelter Workers, and completed, despite extensive attempts to hamper and sabotage the production, in 1953; the film opened in New York in 1954 but gained a very limited distribution.

The film is also unusual in that those who made it, unbeholden to any studio producers, shared a particular ideological view and were able to reflect this in the script. Writer and director saw the strike, which was real enough, from a perspective that emphasised the broad categories of Communist Party social analysis. Producer Paul Jarrico had, with Michael Wilson,

Plate 9: During production of *Salt of the Earth* (Independent Productions Corporation and the National Union of Mine, Mill and Smelter Workers, 1954) in New Mexico. Far left: Paul Jarrico; far right; Michael Wilson; in the centre are (crouching) Leo Hurwitz and (sitting) Herbert Biberman. Reproduced courtesy of BFI Stills, Posters and Designs.

become influential in the Hollywood Communist Party in the early fifties. Jarrico's most remembered screen credit had been for the story and screenplay of *Tom, Dick and Harry*, directed by Garson Kanin at RKO in 1941. This Ginger Rogers comedy does represent a mildly populist fantasy in which Rogers, choosing between three suitors, selects the man who is the poorest and least conforming. (Jarrico later commented that 'It's pure romanticism, but at the time I thought it was politics.') Michael Wilson and Jarrico were interested in the possibilities of social content in film, whether in terms of racism or broader problems of capitalism. Far from moving away from the party after the war Wilson was quick to embrace the implications of the Duclos letter, and he talked of the responsibility of the writer to 'preserve human values in all his work', despite the ultimate front office control. Never subpoenaed, he worked in the early 1950s on a series of low-budget blackmarket scripts with Dalton Trumbo, while contributing two biting surveys of the effect of the political mood on contemporary Hollywood output. In the second of these, published in 1954, he complained that not only had Mr Deeds vanished from the screen, but that the 'fascist personality' was replacing the romantic hero.[27]

Into the vacuum created by the collapse of the humanist strand in filmmaking, Scott argued, came an anti-communist cycle, and a series of films about World War II which glorified the services. Michael Wilson pointed to the impossibility of producing equivalent films in the 1950s to the biopics of 'great humanists' that Warners made in the 1930s, while he also compared the James Stewart persona in the Capra films with that in *The Naked Spur* (1953), and the John Wayne role in *Hondo* (1953) to that in *Stagecoach*. To Wilson the war films were stripped of the anti-fascism that characterised films made during the war, while a film dealing with the war in Korea, like *Fixed Bayonets* (1951), illustrated only one theme, the 'struggle of a frightened youngster to develop the killer instinct'.[28]

Herbert Biberman had been a long-standing radical and political crusader who had joined the Communist Party on his arrival in Hollywood in 1934. Biberman consistently argued for a more equalitarian society, although one study which draws on his unpublished writings emphasises that he tended to 'divide the world into good people and bad'. The emphasis in official party thinking after the war was on class and the ills of capitalism, and wartime feminist perspectives on the 'Woman Question' represented a minority view. But whatever Wilson's thoughts, he was faced, on arriving in Hanover, New Mexico in October 1951, with a strike in which women had played a significant role. It was Wilson who set the central structure of *Salt of the Earth*, and the pre-eminence of the character of Esperanza. There was widespread consultation with local miners and their families and this led to changes that included a 'cleaning up' of several unfavourable aspects of Ramon's character in the film. The end result was influenced by the technical constraints, the effect of the militant consciousness generated during the dispute, and the ideological and aesthetic assumptions of producer, director and writer. The film was certainly unique at the time in its view of class, ethnic and feminist issues, and it has become revered as an icon of the blacklist period.[29]

Pauline Kael attacked the film at the time, getting rather agitated by what she saw as its potential function as propaganda for Soviet efforts to discredit the United States in the eyes of 'colonial peoples'. More persuasive is her comment that the 'oppressed' seem to be curiously uncontaminated – ideologically – by their condition; she puts the same criticism by arguing that although Hollywood would glamorise their lives it would do 'justice to their dreams'. But this begs the question of the degree to which, in the Marxist perspective of the time, 'false consciousness' was powerfully present among Mexican Americans who were barely touched by the booming post-war capitalist economy. It is true that the film is more of a timeless fable than a documentary – still less of a 'fly on the wall' kind – and that this aspect of the film is enhanced by the 'correct' attitudes, the 'Madonna' role signified by Esperanza, and the black and white morality. (Leo Hurwitz withdrew as a 'consulting director', after a dispute with those making the film.) *Salt of the Earth* was a rare effort to beat the system, and its energy and morality play aspects helped it survive to a later age when the way in which it was ahead of its time, especially in its treatment of feminist issues, could be recognised.[30]

An interesting case in the 1950s is that of Abraham Polonsky, whose last credit before the blacklist was *I Can Get It For You Wholesale* (1951), a Twentieth Century-Fox production directed by Michael Gordon. Gordon was blacklisted following his appearance before the committee in September 1951, while

Polonsky took the fifth amendment when he appeared in April of that year, and was himself blacklisted when Zanuck, pressured by the trade press, felt obliged to fire him. Working from a treatment of a 1930s novel by Jerome Weidman, Polonsky had written a new and largely original script which raised a number of feminist themes, while also placing them within a story that owed something to his previous film fables.

Harriet Boyd (Susan Hayward) is an ambitious, independent dress designer who becomes ruthless when she sees the chance of greater individual success beyond the business partnership that she had formed with a salesman, Teddy Sherman (Dan Dailey), who is in love with her. Trying to persuade her mother to part with the insurance money she is saving up for her other daughter's marriage, Harriet promises that the success of her enterprise will make them all independent; when her mother is shocked by this view Harriet replies that it is the 'outlook men taught me'. In an early scene at a restaurant Sherman is shocked when Harriet adopts traditional male tactics by flirting with a male buyer to advance a sale; when Harriet's business partner proposes marriage she turns him down: 'I've worked and schemed to get a business started just so I could be free of men like you, so I could belong to myself.'

The film ends more conventionally, with Harriet forced to decide between her original business partnership – and her relationship with Sherman – and the big-league designer, Noble (George Sanders), who invites her to make original designs for his international fashion house. For a time Harriet betrays her original partner in favour of a partnership with Noble in which, as she tells him, 'our only pleasure is business'. There is a rather distant echo of Garfield 'coming home' at the end of Polonsky's earlier films, although Harriet's return to the less glamorous world of $10.95 dresses and to the man who loves her is equally consistent with the Hollywood preference for a romantic ending. Darryl Zanuck's contribution, commenting on the script, was to suggest that 'Harriet gets off too easily', and to insist that at the end she 'has learned that there is value in loyalty and integrity'. But since the latter notion is not completely at odds with Polonsky's intention it is not surprising that he remembers Zanuck at the script conference as co-operative and professional. For those with ears to hear, the ending of the film, complete with swelling music, will not have resolved all of the

previous contradictions. While the Communist Party encouraged its members to deal with social problems, Polonsky's scripts
reflected his belief that 'bad and good things happen together'.[31]

After Polonsky was dismissed he moved to New York and
began writing for film and television, using various pseudonyms
and fronts. Between 1953 and 1955 Polonsky wrote twenty
five episodes of the CBS network programme *You Are There*,
while other episodes in this series of dramatic recreations of
historical events, anchored by Walter Cronkite, were written by
two other blacklisted writers, Walter Bernstein and Arnold
Manhoff. The blacklist had spread from Hollywood to the
television industry in New York, and CBS, despite or perhaps
because of its involvement with the *See It Now* programmes on
Senator McCarthy in 1954, was very sensitive to pressures from
right wing groups. Despite this pressure, a number of the scripts
betray the events of America in the early 1950s as a clear
subtext. In 'The Vindication of Savonarola', for example, broadcast on December 13, 1953, Polonsky's script refers to the
burning of books in Florence in 1497 and to 'the influence of
a new prophet of piety, patriotism, doom and destruction'.
Polonsky has characterised the *You Are There* series as 'probably
the only place where any guerilla warfare was conducted against
McCarthy in a public medium'.[32]

Until it began to collapse in the wake of the Khrushchev
speech to the Soviet Party Congress in 1956 Polonsky still saw
the Communist Party as 'the best vehicle for bringing about a
socialist transformation of society'. In that year he wrote an essay
in the party cultural journal *Masses and Mainstream* in which he
addressed the crisis in Marxism and he defended intellectual
freedom against claims by communists to the 'infallibility of an
absolute science'; he made comparison between the House
Committee interrogation of Arthur Miller and the attack by
the party and *New Masses* on Albert Maltz in 1946. Polonsky
summed up his experience during this period by commenting
that 'To betray your friends is a moral crime; not to believe in
something you believed before is an act of liberation.' In his
novel *Season of Fear*, begun in the early 1950s and published in
1956, Polonsky also commented on the pressures of the time.
The novel traces the effect of suspicions of past associations,
and the requirement to sign a loyalty oath, on a group of
professionals. One response identified is that recommended by

an analyst who counsels that 'nowadays, a man has to learn how to live with his weakness and not wear himself out fighting it'. 'Such fights', the analyst continues, 'are useless and cause disease.' The central character in the novel sees a colleague lose his job when he refuses to sign an oath, and he drifts morally, seeking only survival, until a confrontation with a mountainous sea gives him some sense of the need to fight to maintain his (moral) position, as the sea – like life itself – threatens to sweep him away. Polonsky continued to work on the script black-market, but little of his work is known before he was able to use his own name again in the mid-1960s. Only his script for *Odds Against Tomorrow* (1959), from a novel by William P. McGivern and directed by Robert Wise for Harry Belafonte's production company, is public knowledge. Wise recreates something of the feeling of his *The Set-Up*, and Robert Ryan and Gloria Graham also suggest the mood of *film noir*, while Polonsky's script makes the black character, played by Belafonte, the most justified and positive of the doomed gang of robbers.[33]

TOWARDS A NEW LIBERALISM

The Cold War increased the influence of the military in society, a trend symbolised by General Eisenhower's elevation to the presidency, and marked by an increase in war films. Adrian Scott argued that the blacklist had hampered liberals, as well as those actually denied employment, and he compared the pre- and post-1947 films of writers and directors such as John Ford, William Dieterle, William Wyler, Dudley Nichols and Nunnally Johnson. To Scott few of the films on which these liberals had worked since 1947 'dramatised the humanist, democratic and anti-fascist values that illuminated their work in the Roosevelt era'. He cited several films as characteristic of the new mood brought on by the blacklist; he saw *The Wild One* (1951) and *The Blackboard Jungle* (1955) as two social films which lacked any social criticism or analysis, and *Executive Suite* (1954) as an example of the new glorification of business and of business heroes.[34]

Of the director-stockholders of Liberty Films, George Stevens had felt most strongly that the acceptance of the offer from Paramount for their company was a 'sellout of our artistic freedoms'. The new contracts gave Paramount the right of story approval, and Stevens and the studio found it difficult to agree on a suitable property. Paramount wanted a comedy, whereas Stevens, who had not really wanted to make *I Remember Mama* (1948), favoured a more serious subject. It was only in 1949, after Paramount had rejected the project for censorship reasons, that Stevens was finally given New York studio approval to produce and direct a film from Theodore Dreiser's 1925 classic, *An American Tragedy*. (The fact that Dreiser had joined the Communist Party just before his death in 1945 may have increased the nervousness of the studio.)

Stevens wanted the film, *A Place in the Sun* (1951), to deal with contemporary life, and felt that the film would be about 'young people trying to get somewhere in the world and running up against things they haven't always been taught too much about – love, sex, ambition – and so on'. Michael Wilson, one of the most politically committed of Hollywood screenwriters, produced a first draft script for Stevens in June 1949. Wilson was interested in the possibilities of, and constraints on, 'democratic film content', and later, in a speech celebrating John Howard Lawson, he talked of the struggle of the 'humanist writer' to 'preserve human values in all his work'. (Wilson was blacklisted in early 1951, at the same time as the film was released and before his uncompromisingly 'unfriendly' testimony to the committee in September.)

Full assessment of Wilson's work would involve consideration of his scripts, and of the additions and changes made by Harry Brown, who ultimately shared the writing credit with Wilson. Wilson felt that most of his work remained in *A Place in the Sun*, but that Stevens was afraid of the possible response if the film was overtly political. Stevens emphasised the relationship between George Eastman (Montgomery Clift) and Angela Vickers (Elizabeth Taylor), and perhaps sacrificed some of the distance between their two social worlds. Clift set out to play George as calculatingly ambitious for the place in the sun that marriage to Angela would secure, a place of horses, speedboats and fast cars. This reading reflected the initial script, which, according to Anne Revere, portrayed George as 'conniving' and Angela as a 'spoiled, mean bitch'. Yet in the completed film George appears as indecisive and confused, reflecting something of Clift's own persona. To the extent that Eastman is seen as guilty, if not of actual murder then of thinking and planning it – seduced by a materialistic culture – then the film is unusual in viewing him with some sympathy and understanding, right up until his final walk to the electric chair. (As Gavin Lambert commented at the time, 'Stevens does not appear to have made up his mind whether it was all socially significant or not.') To George Barbarow, Dreiser's 'indictment of a social and economic system' becomes an illustration of the familiar Hollywood cliché that 'Crime Does Not Pay'.[35]

The first script also contained more of George's mother, and the world from which George was escaping. (Anne Revere, who played the mother, was named by Larry Parks before the committee in March 1951 and she took the fifth amendment when called a month later.) Yet if the final result was more romantic, it was so in an unusually downbeat form. Stevens' film, with its slow dissolves and giant close-ups, represented – with Kazan's *A Streetcar Named Desire* – a move towards the Hollywood art film. Like the Kazan film it also reflected the beginning of the end for the system of self-regulation through the Production Code Administration. Because of the code there could be no mention of abortion in the scene in which Alice (Shelley Winters) goes to a doctor for help, and Stevens' dissolve from night to morning through Alice's window was the more effective in not being reinforced by any shot – prohibited under the PCA's requirements – of George leaving in the morning. Arguably such changes reflected the increasing weakness rather than the strength of the regulation system; already undermined by the 1948 antitrust decree, the code system was to be further weakened by the 1952 Supreme Court decision which in effect gave motion pictures the protection of the First Amendment.[36]

Domestic and international events meant that Hollywood had to treat military topics with considerable caution. Of his experience at Columbia in the early 1950s in making *From Here to Eternity* (1953), Fred Zinnemann stressed the automatic respect shown towards federal authority at the time. *The Caine Mutiny*, Herman Wouk's bestselling novel of 1951, had balanced the exciting story of a wartime 'mutiny' with a conclusion which stressed that the mutineers were themselves to blame for the events on board ship. Willie Keith, the young ensign whose personal story is followed in book and film, comments on his traumatic experiences on the *Caine* in a letter to the woman he wants to marry; he refers to his disloyalty and that of the other officers, and sums up his perspective, and that of Wouk, by suggesting that 'the idea is, once you get an incompetent ass of a skipper – it is a chance of war – there's nothing to do but serve him as though he were the wisest and the best, cover his mistakes, keep the ship going, and bear up'.

The script follows the plot and tone of Wouk's book, although cuts in Stanley Roberts' script were required in order to satisfy Harry Cohn's demands for a film of approximately two hours. The film follows events on board the *Caine*, as the increasingly arbitrary and dangerous behaviour of Captain Queeg (Humphrey Bogart) leads to disaffection in the ward room and, in a particularly violent typhoon, to the taking over of command by Lieutenant Steve Maryk. The natural climax of the film comes with the captain's appearance at the court-martial, and with Maryk's ultimate acquittal. Up until this point audiences are encouraged to identify with the opposition to Queeg's petty tyranny and incompetence, but in a scene that immediately follows the court-martial the blame for the previous events is clearly placed on the captain's senior officers, and the principle of authority is strongly reaffirmed.

Barney Greenwald, Maryk's defence counsel, walks drunkenly into the celebration party following the end of the court-martial. Greenwald, having successfully defended Maryk, now turns on the officers who opposed Queeg, accusing them of disloyalty and of failing to help their captain. Keefer, the equivocating novelist, welcomes his humiliation (earlier Keefer remarked that he was 'too smart to be brave'). Keith and Maryk, in their sudden silence in the face of Greenwald's tirade, confirm the defence counsel's 'navy' view of authority. The only rebellion endorsed in the film – in the much simplified rendering of Keith's romantic problems – is the private rebellion of the young ensign against his mother in his belated decision to get married.

Edward Dmytryk thus worked within the constraints implicit in the project – including the need for navy co-operation – to reproduce the plot and tone of the original book. The film, which ends with a prominent dedication to the United States Navy, provides its audiences with the thrill of complicity with mutiny, while also paying homage to the notion that authority was always deserving of respect and obedience. *The Caine Mutiny* (1953) was made for $2.4m and the receipts from rentals of the film in North America were $8.7m, more than any other Kramer-Columbia release. Dmytryk had taken the step to the large-budget international film making of his later career.[37]

Robert Aldrich directed three films in the early fifties which have also been seen as social commentaries. Aldrich had worked as assistant director on *The Stange Love of Martha Ivers*, *Body and Soul* and *The Prowler*. He and Losey at one point planned to form a production company together, before Losey left for England. Aldrich's first film as director was *The Big Leaguer*, at MGM in 1953, but it was *Apache* (1954), a film for Hecht-Lancaster productions, that did much to establish his career. Burt Lancaster played the dignified but doomed Apache warrior, but United Artists insisted on a 'happy' ending in which the supposedly independent spirit is persuaded of the 1950s virtues of domesticity.

For *Kiss Me Deadly* (1955) the writer A.I. Bezzerides changed much in the Mickey Spillane original. The film follows the form of private eye *films noirs*, as Mike Hammer investigates a murder, but the tone is bleak and sleazy, and the protagonist has none of the moral authority of Philip Marlowe or Sam Spade. The writer also invented the box of atomic, radioactive material – in the book the quest is for Mafia drugs – that represents the film's MacGuffin. Hammer's investigation leads to a succession of selfish characters, and finally to the discovery of the 'great whatsit', and to the apocalyptic ending. Aldrich has played down some of the more sweeping social interpretations of the film, and has argued that the political intentions that it did have were largely not seen or understood at the time, but to him his later career was 'due to the European reaction to *Kiss Me Deadly*'. As with Daniel Mainwaring's script for *Invasion of the Body Snatchers* (1956), and Orson Welles' final Hollywood film, *Touch of Evil* (1957), the film is less radical in any positive sense than reflective of the decline of their great liberal hopes.[38]

Aldrich's next film was *The Big Knife* (1955), made independently by Aldrich, and adapted by James Poe from the original play. The film reflects, as did the 1949 Broadway play, much of Odets' frustrations with the studios, and particularly with Columbia Pictures, in the late 1940s. Yet Hollywood had moved on since then, and in 1955 the film rather overstates the power of the old moguls and understates the options available to actors and agents. (John Garfield had left Warners at the end of his contract and gone into production himself, with Bob Roberts; the collapse of Garfield's career was the product of the House Committee's relentless campaign against him, a campaign that may have contributed to his fatal heart attack in 1952.) In an opening scene the gossip columnist Patty Benedict asks the frustrated actor Charlie Castle (Jack Palance) how long they had known each other; when Castle talks of nine or ten years Benedict comments that when they first met 'all you could talk about was the New Deal, or the Fair Deal, or some deal'. Castle tells her he now believes in 'health, hard work, rare roast beef – and good scripts'.

By the mid-1950s writers were becoming increasingly conscious that the depression politics, of economic crisis and class conflict, had given way to a new politics based on consensus and prosperity. The Gross National Product of the nation had doubled since the war, and prominent intellectuals embraced what they saw as a new politics of claims rather than causes, of pragmatism rather than ideology. With the bipartisan censure of Joseph McCarthy by the Senate in December 1954 anti-communism was ceasing to be a divisive issue in American politics and had become part of the common ground, at least that which was heard in public discourse. While the prosperity brought new fault lines in American society, not least that between older Americans conscious of depression and war, and children and teenagers whose tastes and fads were an emerging target for commerce, it also helped to dissolve memories of the 1930s. In particular the suspicions of business had been replaced by a culture that stressed business, including the new leisure industries, as central to the American way. The purges and investigations of the post-war decade had removed many on the left from public positions, while others had blown with the new winds; for old leftists who were still keeping the faith the revelations of Khrushchev's speech to the Soviet Party Congress in 1956 were the last straw. As Albert Maltz said much later, 'no one I knew in the CP would have stayed in the Party had they known then what they found out later'.[39]

The liberals of the mid- and later 1950s, and into the 1960s, were anti-communist, and the civil rights movement based its attack on the indefensible political and legal discrimination of the Southern states. Some intellectuals were happy to reject or question American materialism, but C. Wright Mills and others who saw a power elite, where most proclaimed elite pluralism, were lonely figures until the emergence of a more widely based 'new left' critique in the early 1960s.

Fewer and more individually made and marketed films were being produced, and with due regard to the international scope of the American film industry; 45 per cent of the industry's gross revenues came from abroad in the later 1950s. The success of *Marty* (1955) encouraged the increasing use of directors and writers whose early experience had been in New York television. While this generation was liberal, only Martin Ritt and Sidney Lumet, among the directors, were to be still strongly aware in their concerns of the social legacy of the 1930s. Ritt had been blacklisted while working as a director for CBS television in 1951. His first film, the labour drama *Edge of the City* (MGM, 1957), from a television play and script by Robert Alan Arthur, provided a dignified – even saintly – role for Sidney Poitier. To Peter Biskind, Lumet's first film, *Twelve Angry Men* (1957), was 'more interested in consensus than justice', and reflected a new ideology of pluralism – what Daniel Bell saw as a rejection of the old 'isms' – in which conservatives and 'corporate liberals' agreed. Within this consensus, the liberal agenda included films on capital punishment (*I Want to Live*, in 1958, and *Compulsion* in 1959), and a number of films in the late 1950s linked the older left perspective with the emerging civil rights movement.[40]

Chapter 8

The sixties

By the early 1960s the 'package' was central to the Hollywood production system; producers or talent agencies were able to draw on the whole industry – rather than one studio – in arranging particular deals for each film. The total number of films produced in the United States had fallen, from 391 in 1951 to 131 in 1961. The mass audience had gone by the later 1950s, and the object was increasingly to differentiate each film and to appeal to a particular section of the audience. An early example of such targeting had been the low budget films made for the teenage audience of the drive-in theatres that opened in great numbers in the 1950s. Michael Wood sees *Cleopatra* (1963) as the film which showed that the myths and assumptions of studio era filmmaking were out of touch with a new audience.[1]

In the late 1950s the cautious interest of the US Senate in civil rights, a belated response to the civil rights movement in the South and the Supreme Court's pioneering 1954 decision on school desegregation, had been reflected by the appearance of a number of films on the topic. Such films as *The Defiant Ones* (1958) (produced and directed by Stanley Kramer, and written by two blacklisted writers), *The World, the Flesh and the Devil* (1959) and *Odds Against Tomorrow* (1959) raised the increasingly salient racial question. The victory of John F. Kennedy in the presidential election of November 1960 encouraged producers to greater boldness in seeking support for films dealing with subjects on the liberal side of the late 1950s anti-communist consensus. While Kennedy's rhetoric primarily addressed the issue of the Cold War, and the rivalry with the post-Sputnik Soviet Union for technological and international influence, there was also a renewed interest in domestic issues that threatened international embarrassment. Further, Kennedy's appeal aided the rehabilitation of the New Deal tradition in American public life. Dore Schary, who had retired from filmmaking after being fired by MGM, seemed to suggest a parallel between Kennedy and Roosevelt in his production of *Sunrise at Campobello*, based on his own play; although the film, released during the 1960 campaign, had little impact, it has been seen as reflecting and encouraging a cautious move towards political involvement by some long dormant Hollywood liberals. Stanley Kramer also continued his commercially successful interest in social topics with his productions of *On the Beach* (1959), *Inherit the Wind* (1960) and *Judgement at Nuremberg* (1961) – all of which he also directed – and of *Pressure Point* (1962).[2]

The cautious opening to a new domestic agenda during the Kennedy years was reflected, and to some extent reinforced, by American film. A number of films, from *Spartacus* (1960) – Dalton Trumbo's first screen credit following the blacklist – to *West Side Story* (1961), seemed to suggest the opening to new, generally more liberal film topics.[3] Billy Wilder, who had directed *Ace in the Hole* in 1951, presented the Cold War as farce in *One, Two, Three* (1960), and ridiculed the new business culture in *The Apartment* (1961). Roger Corman risked a departure from his normal youth and drive-in oriented product by producing and directing *The Intruder* (1962), a study of Southern racism. At the same time a number of directors and writers who had worked in television drama in the 1950s, made their first films at the end of that decade or in the early 1960s. Such directors as Delbert Mann, Martin Ritt, Robert Mulligan, Sidney Lumet, John Frankenheimer, Arthur Penn and Franklin Schaffner contributed to the modest revival of social realism in American film, while some of them also reflected the first signs of an influence of the European art film.

The media excitement generated by Kennedy's presidency, and the reassessment provoked by the Cuban Missile Crisis in 1962, led to a renewed interest by filmmakers, and the studios that still primarily controlled financing, in public issues. Frankenheimer, with *The Manchurian Candidate* (1962) and *Seven Days in May* (1964), Schaffner with *The Best Man* (1964), Otto Preminger with *Advise and Consent* (1962), and Lumet with *Fail Safe* (1964), all dealt with issues of state, and occasionally raised substantive issues (nuclear war, McCarthyism) beyond their concern with the ethical problems of individuals. Herbert Gans, discussing the social filmmaking of this period, argues that 'the possibility that delinquency, corruption and even mental illness reside in the social system is not considered'. As indicated by Wilder's relative freedom, the most subversive films were arguably those that suggested laughter as an apt, and perhaps as the only response to contemporary problems. *Dr Strangelove*, directed by Stanley Kubrick from a script by Terry Southern, and released in 1963, reflected the new thinking and questioned the system as a whole, and the premises on which it operated.[4]

Of the older generation of directors, their 'negotiation' with Hollywood was still difficult. John Huston returned to an American theme after a number of unsuccessful international pictures; in *The Misfits* (1961) Huston and Arthur Miller suggested the damage that modern commerce was inflicting on the ideals of the American west. A decade later the revival in Huston's critical standing began with *Fat City* (1972), a realist study of a contemporary loser. Nicholas Ray, who lived in Europe for most of the 1960s, directed a socially conscious biblical epic, *King of Kings* (1961), but made no more commercial films following the traumas he experienced making a second epic for producer Samuel Bronston, *55 Days at Peking* (1963). Ray was offered further projects, but, he recalled, 'Nothing I was interested in, though.' Orson Welles directed *The Trial* (1963), from Kafka's novel, after being given a choice of classic properties by the producers Michael and Alexander Salkind. The result was, almost uniquely after *Citizen Kane*, a Welles film that was adequately financed and over which the director had reasonable control. K (Anthony Perkins) is less passive than in the novel, and Welles gives him a speech in which he protests to the Advocate of a conspiracy to 'persuade us all the whole world is crazy – formless, meaningless, absurd'. K is lost in the totalitarian maze, represented by Welles primarily by the rooms and corridors of the Gare d'Orsay. K's fate, when it comes, is accompanied by a reference to a contemporary nightmare, the nuclear holocaust. Welles' more personal and affirmative vision – favouring the 'good life' over affairs of state – was seen in his next film, *Chimes at Midnight*, shot in 1964–5, and released in 1966.[5]

The Vietnam war, which helped to politicise the baby boom generation of the 1960s, was not directly reflected on the screen in the decade, either during the period when there was a broad consensus in favour of the war, or later, when the lack of military success unsettled this broad support, and when the anti-war movement gained momentum. The only direct exception was John Wayne's *The Green Berets* (1968), although a number of films made tangential or metaphoric reference to the war. Just as in television the Tet offensive in early 1968 had a powerful influence on the frame of reference of television news, so at about the same time the powers-that-be in Hollywood began to recognise the social, and to some extent political concerns of the youthful counterculture. Ryan and Kellner see 1967 as the turning point, and the success of low budget films such as *Easy Rider* has often been cited as explaining Hollywood's sudden, and relatively short-lived, shift to the left. (What was more lasting, of course, was Hollywood's recognition that young people increasingly represented the bulk of their audience.) The doomed outlaw became a recurring motif in such box office successes as *Bonnie and Clyde* (1967) and *Butch Cassidy and the Sundance Kid* (1969), while the temper of the time allowed Martin Ritt to direct, and produce with writer Walter Bernstein, *The Molly Maguires* (1968), a grim study of failure and betrayal set against the conflict between brutal mine owners and a violent 'secret society' in the coal mines of Pennsylvania of the 1870s.[6]

Jules Dassin made a return to American filmmaking during this period, getting financial support from Paramount to make a film – *Uptight* (1969) – that was both an account of the black struggle in the country in the immediate wake of Martin Luther King's assassination, and a re-make of John Ford's 1935 version of Liam O'Flaherty's novel *The Informer*. Dassin felt that he should introduce two black collaborators who were in closer touch with events in America – Ruby Dee and Julian Mayfield – to work with him on the script. The final result was a film that provides a vivid snapshot of the ideological debates within the black movement at the time, but which suffers dramatically from the uneasy relationship between a story derived from a literary and film classic – presumably a key factor in Paramount's decision to provide finance – and a quite different social and historical context.

Uptight begins with shots of King's funeral in Atlanta, Georgia; in Cleveland, Ohio younger blacks watch on television, and listen as the dead man's 'I have a Dream' speech, symbolising

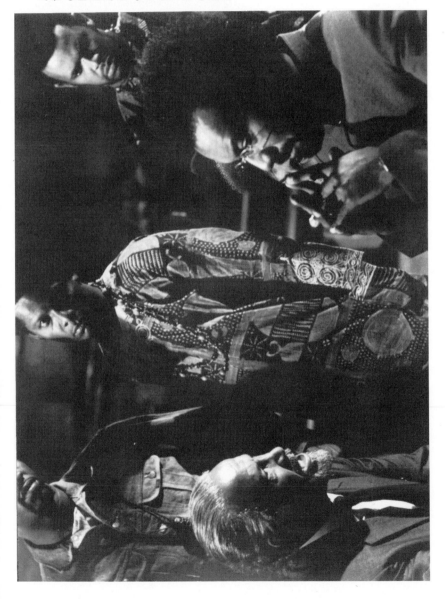

Plate 10: In the foreground, the confrontation between Kyle (Frank Silvera) and B. G. (Raymond St Jacques) in *Uptight* (Paramount, 1968). Reproduced courtesy of BFI Stills, Posters and Designs.

the integrated civil rights campaign that reached its climax in Washington DC in 1963, is relayed to the streets by loudspeaker. Official leaders urge peace, but the central figures in the film are blacks who feel that the answer now lies in 'Guns, more guns'. A key scene in a bowling alley depicts a fierce and protracted debate between two groups. An older man, Kyle (Frank Silvera), wants 'constructive' action, including work to organise the poor across racial barriers; he does not see anything wrong with the idea of running for Congress as a way of advancing black interests. He argues that violent action will not succeed, will 'be the excuse for fascism in this country', and will 'bring on the camps'. However, to B.G. (Raymond St Jacques), who heads the separatist committee that sees 'Black Power' in more militant terms, there is no going back – he tells Kyle: 'Selma, lunch counters, Birmingham – Yesterday.'

The debate is carefully balanced, and Dassin clearly felt it difficult, as a white, and also as an old leftist who favoured racially co-operative action for progressive change, to express a point of view. Arguably the violent tactics illustrated in the film – a raid on an arms store in which a guard is shot and killed – in reality only contributed to the white backlash that helped to elect Richard Nixon, and underscore his policy in the 1970s of 'benign neglect' on the racial issue. But the film does capture the end of the integrationist phase of the civil rights struggle; as Stokely Carmichael and Charles Hamilton wrote in 1967, 'Before a group can enter the open society, it must first close ranks.'[7]

The later scenes of the film are much less effective, as they trace the decision of Tank, a drunken ex-union organiser who has been excluded from the militant committee as unreliable, to inform on his friend – who killed the guard – for $1,000. It is difficult to take him seriously enough for his tragedy – he is eventually killed on the orders of the committee after a trial at which the broader debate about strategy is renewed – to carry much weight. As Donald Bogle points out, 'if *Uptight* made any statement at all, it was that blacks were effectual only at wiping out one of their own'. (And the real police informer – also gay and a drug addict – is somewhat surprisingly left untouched by the militants.)[8]

It was through the Western that filmmakers made oblique and metaphoric reference to the Vietnam war, in a series of films including *The Wild Bunch* (1969), *The Professionals* (1966), *Little Big Man* (1970), *Ulzana's Raid* (1972) and *Two Mules for Sister Sara* (1970). The last-named film, with a script from Albert Maltz, suggested a parallel between France and 1790s Mexico on the one hand, and America and Vietnam on the other. There were also post-blacklist American credits for screenwriters Ring Lardner Jr (*M*A*S*H*, 1970) and Michael Wilson (*Planet of the Apes*, 1968), and for directors Herbert Biberman (*Slaves*, 1969) and John Berry (*Claudine*, 1974). In *Medium Cool* (1969, directed by Haskell Wexler), there was some attempt to provoke questions about the role of the media, in the context of the turbulent events surrounding the 1968 Democratic Convention. But elsewhere there were reflections of middle-class male *angst*, and of the influence of European art cinema, and the theme of the search for personal identity. As well as Kazan, Billy Wilder, in his more distanced and comic film *Avanti* (1973), raised questions about American identity; Wilder's executive hero is humanised, and comes to terms with his father and himself, on his European trip. Other attempts to question American lives and values are found in *The Swimmer* (1968), *Seconds* (1966), *The Hospital* (1971), *Bye Bye Braverman* (1968) and *Save the Tiger* (1973). The dialectic that produced the shift away from the politics of liberalism and the left, and which led eventually – and in the wake of defeat in Vietnam – to the success of the New Right and of Ronald Reagan, was soon reflected in film. Political film, like political America, became polarised, with liberal concern 'balanced' by films of the right from *Dirty Harry* (1971) to the Rambo cycle.[9]

ROBERT ROSSEN

With *The Hustler* (1961) Robert Rossen returned to a world he knew well. Rossen remembered spending much of his adolescence in billiard rooms, and in 1936 he had written an unproduced play, 'Corner Pocket', about unemployed young men who hang out in a down-at-heel pool hall. In Hollywood Rossen transferred this Depression education to several Warner Bros characters. In *Out of the Fog* the petty gangster, Goff (John Garfield), refers to the formative influence on him of 'the brakerods and the bread lines and the pool rooms and the beer parlours of the big cities'. While Twentieth Century-Fox was initially unenthusiastic about Rossen's desire to adapt Walter

Tevis's novel for the screen, the completed film, which Rossen also produced, and co-adapted with Sidney Carrol, marked a return to critical and commercial success for the director after a decade in the wilderness.[10]

Both novel and film are crucially structured around two pool games between the master, Minnesota Fats, and the ambitious young hustler, Eddie Felton. Defeat in the first game, after Felton led by $18,000, convinces the gambler and entrepreneur Bert Gordon that Felton has the talent but not the character to become a 'winner'. In the novel Felton's affair with the lonely and drunken would-be writer Sarah Packard ends when Eddie agrees to be managed by Gordon, and to pay him 75 per cent of his earnings. Rossen develops the relationship, and gives it a warmer dimension, thus making it central to the humanistic theme of the film; the relationship comes to an end when Gordon's advances to Sarah – in Louisville – lead directly to her suicide. Following Eddie's final victory over Minnesota Fats the victor asserts himself over Bert Gordon in book and film, but Rossen's Eddie refers to their joint responsibility for Sarah's death in more conclusively rejecting Gordon's managership, and accepting a ban from the major pool halls as a result.

The film thus becomes much more a story of emerging personal identity and awareness, and the notion of 'winning' is stretched from the sporting arena to the game of life. In retrospect Eddie (Paul Newman) sees that he has lost something more valuable than success on Gordon's terms, and perhaps on his own terms as well. To Rossen the drama, in 'this story of two cripples', is that 'she needs a cane and that he can give her only a billiard cue'.[11] Only after Sarah's suicide, and after his victory over Minnesota Fats (Jackie Gleason), does he tell Bert Gordon (George C. Scott) that he loved Sarah Packard (Piper Laurie), but that he had 'traded her in on a pool game'. Given that Gordon reacts by placing a ban on Felton playing in the major halls, the end of the film sees Eddie Felton having grown in moral stature, but having lost both the relationship with Sarah and the stage on which he is most fulfilled.

The film not only draws on the wider American mythology of success, but there are also references to *Body and Soul*, and to the work of Clifford Odets. In this tradition the sensitivity of the 'artist' or sportsman is corrupted by the 'system', and Rossen linked *The Hustler* to this work by seeing the film as 'about the artist in society' and about 'what he had to do to be a success'. Rossen saw the film in terms of an individual's efforts to preserve his dignity against the 'competitive objectives' created by modern industrial society. Yet *The Hustler* is not a 'fable of the streets', and while Gordon identifies himself as a 'business-man', Eddie's victory is essentially a moral one. Eddie walks out of the pool hall alone at the end, while in Polonsky's ending for *Body and Soul* 'the neighbourhood swallows Charley up'. The emphasis is on personal growth and change, but Eddie, in his final attack on Gordon, extends his moral criticism to Gordon's materialist values.[12]

As Michael Wood has pointed out, the simple metaphor of 'winning' and 'losing' is rather overloaded with meanings, but the richness of the film is arguably enhanced by the degree of ambiguity in the central relationships. Eddie Felton has not been corrupted in becoming a success; if anything success on Gordon's terms prompts his own discovery of a greater self-confidence and sensitivity. He tells his erstwhile manager that '*We* really stuck the knife in her . . . ' and '*we* twisted it, didn't *we*, Bert' (my italics). Eddie's moral revulsion – at Gordon, and at his own complicity in Sarah's fate – is somehow broadened to cover the notion of success itself. Rossen, who still saw him-self as a radical in the early 1960s, despite the trauma of his committee testimony, was probably thinking less of the American mythology of success, in commenting on the theme of the film, than of the categories of *Body and Soul* and the social drama of the 1930s. Polonsky, with whom Rossen had argued about the ending of the 1947 film, had played on different notions of success in his script for that film; in an alternative, and unused, ending Charley had added to the line 'Everybody dies', in his final rejection of Roberts, the comment that 'You gotta win to be a winner.'[13]

The Hustler, particularly in its central scenes between Eddie and Sarah, mixes the mood of the contemporary European art film, and its emerging theme of alienation, with a documentary realism that reflects the nature of the source material, as well as Rossen's own experience in directing *All the King's Men*. To Polonsky, Rossen's talent was 'force applied everywhere without let-up', but Rossen had demonstrated an interest in more poetic approaches, for example in his script for *A Walk in the Sun*.[14] For *The Hustler*, and for his final film, *Lilith*, Rossen chose as his cinematographer the veteran Eugen Shuftan, who had worked mainly in Europe since his beginnings in Germany in the 1920s.

Rossen was already ill when he began work on *Lilith* (1964), and the resulting film was more experimental, and less obviously social, than any of his previous films. Rossen produced and directed, and (with Robert Alan Arthur) wrote a script that was close to the original novel by J.R. Salamanca. The result was a film that is distinct from Rossen's previous work, and which was poorly received in America. The emphasis is less on narrative than on mood, and an exploration through pictures and silences of the nature of madness and the thin line between the 'adjusted' and the 'maladjusted'.

Novel and film can be given a social interpretation. Vincent, recently released from the army, successfully applies for a job as a trainee occupational therapist in a private schizophrenic asylum; he wants to help people, but this public role is opposed by his private love for and obsession with Lilith (Jean Seberg), a beautiful patient. Yet Rossen felt that this reading of the film was undermined by bad casting, and in particular by Warren Beatty's playing of Vincent as seriously disturbed even at the beginning.[15]

While some have stressed the role of Shuftan's cinematography, the film can also be seen as having thematic links with the character of Sarah in *The Hustler*. There are individual scenes which are not in the novel, and which relate to the director's previous work and concerns. First, Vincent is seen watching newsreel pictures of war on television, his words, 'He dies . . . she dies . . . everybody dies', echoing the line Polonsky gives to Roberts, and finally Charley, in *Body and Soul*. Second, the clinic is seen as a haven from an ugly 'real' world; when Vincent drops in on his former girl friend, she seems unhappy alongside her crude, 'salesman' husband. But it is the expressive black and white photography of water, webs and reflections which symbolises the conflict within Vincent as the caring professional becomes increasingly silent and lost, and finally turns to the asylum's authorities for help.[16]

At his death in 1966 Rossen was working on the script for a film to be called 'Cocoa Beach', to be based on the lives of transients living in a community near to Cape Canaveral, the rocket-launching site on the east coast of Florida. Begun in 1962 as part of a two-film deal with Columbia Pictures, the 'original' script dealt with the experiences of an 'all American Boy turned sour', set against a documentary account of a new boom town which seemed to offer 'easy money'. The central character was to be a former all-star basketball player who came to Cocoa Beach after it had been revealed that he had thrown games. In Rossen's files on the project was a 1962 *Look* article by Lou Brown subtitled 'The candid confession of a young man to whom money meant too much'. As with *The Hustler* Rossen seemed intent on combining his recurring interest in the struggle for personal identity in a particular social context – and in this case with the imperial commitment to the space race – with a new interest in the forms of European cinema. In discussing his plans for 'Cocoa Beach' Rossen mentioned both *8½* and *La Dolce Vita*, but these hopes were unfulfilled with his death, in February 1966.[17]

ELIA KAZAN

Like the later film *America America*, the origins of *Wild River* (1960) came in the mid-1950s, when Kazan sent a copy of a novel by William Bradford Huie to his writer on *East of Eden*, Paul Osborn, commenting that he found the book to be 'personal and true and good'. Kazan's growing interest in autobiographical perspectives on America can be traced to this time, and perhaps to the trauma of his encounter with the House Committee. Huie's book, published at the end of the war, had dealt with the 1930s through the experiences of a Southerner who was caught between the world of his family – a 'tobacco-chewing feudalism' – and that of New Deal progressivism. Kazan worked on several drafts and others were written by Calder Willingham and Ben Maddow, but eventually it was Paul Osborn, in 1959, who was able to structure the material to the producer-director's satisfaction.

Kazan filmed in the Tennessee valley in late 1959 and early 1960, and the film became another of his studies of Southern culture, following *Panic in the Streets*, *Baby Doll* and *A Face in the Crowd*. Kazan was keen that the film show the benefits of the New Deal, and in particular of the Tennessee Valley Authority. With this object *Wild River* begins with an extract from Pare Lorentz's documentary *The River*, produced by the Farm Security Administration in 1938. In the extract a distressed man talks haltingly to camera of how most of his family had been swept away by the river in flood. The story of *Wild River* is of a TVA official – an eastern intellectual – who comes to Alabama in order to persuade an old lady to leave her island, where her family has lived since the 1790s; a new dam can then be opened which will regulate the rivers and bring electricity and change to the Southern way of life, but which will submerge the old lady's island.

Kazan's interest in the notion that something good is lost in the course of progress dated back to his decision to go to MGM after the war to make *Sea of Grass*. But the later film deals not only with the conflict between public and private authority, between national 'progress' and local interests, but with change and development at the level of the key individuals involved. Kazan goes to some length to sympathise with Ella Garth's reluctance to leave her land, and to at least understand the local resistance to the TVA hiring blacks and whites on equal rates. Only the local notables, who try to warn off the interfering Northerner, are beyond the pale; a scene in which local interests resist change is a stock one in liberal films about the South, at least since *They Won't Forget*. For the Kazan of 1960 everyone had their reasons, and much of the drama of the film stems from the relationship between Carol Garth and Chuck Glover. Kazan uses the drive of Lee Remick and the uncertainty of Montgomery Clift, and plays out their scenes with the wider social conflicts as a backdrop.[18]

Despite the setting of *Splendour in the Grass* (1961) in the period of the Great Crash of 1929, the film has been seen as a 'seedbed for the social issues which dominated the 1960s'. Kazan worked on the script with William Inge, and faithfully served the playwright's careful study of the effect of social pressures on the youthful romance of Deanie Loomis (Natalie Wood) and Bud Stamper (Warren Beatty, in his first screen role). Deanie's frustration leads to her temporary 'madness', and the most effectively directed scene is the closing one, in which Deanie visits the farm where Bud has settled down and comes to terms with the lost opportunities of the past. Bud always wanted to go to agricultural college but was pressed by his oil tycoon father into going to Yale; while Bud may regret the missed chance of marrying Deanie, he comes near to establishing a life that reflects his own identity. His rural life owes something to the idea of 'dropping out', and to the strong emphasis of student manifestos of the early sixties – notably the Port Huron statement – on young people 'finding a meaning of life that is personally authentic'.[19]

It was in 1955 that Elia Kazan had returned to Turkey for the first time in thirty years, and thought seriously of making a film about his uncle's journey to America from Anatolia in 1896. Kazan's Uncle Joe, Avraam Elia Kazanjoglou, was one of thousands of Greeks who emigrated from Greece and Anatolia to the United States at the turn of the century. Unlike mainland Greeks, whose chief motive was economic advancement, Anatolian Greeks were also influenced – as were the Armenians – by Turkish oppression, and they were more likely to view their journey as a permanent one. Kazan's experience of psychoanalysis in 1959 apparently made him more able to work on such a personal theme, and the same year he recorded on tape his father's memories of the old country. When his father died the next year Kazan used the recordings, together with his own recollections of his uncle, to write a first draft of what was to be his first original screenplay.[20]

The *America America* project faced substantial problems of finance, production and marketing. Initially Warners, followed by all the other majors, rejected Kazan's script, and only when Ray Stark's financing collapsed while the crew was already in Istanbul were Warners prevailed upon to back the project – partly on the basis of the director's previous successes at the studio, notably *East of Eden*, and *Splendour in the Grass* which had opened in New York in 1961. Filming in Istanbul was cut short because of interference by local censors, and the great bulk of the film was finally shot in and around Athens, and on a chartered liner, in the last four months of 1962. Following a prolonged period of editing in New York, Kazan viewed a complete work print for the first time in October 1963. As work continued to prepare the film for a December launch, Kazan described it to an anxious Jack Warner as a 'modern epic without any horse-shit and pretentiousness'; but to the Warners marketing executives he admitted that 'I'm not kidding myself that it's easy to sell'. *America America* (1963) opened on schedule, but after the New York run it failed to attract substantial audiences on general release. Kazan recounts that 'no-one wanted to see it', and that it lost Warners $1.5 million.

In March 1964 Kazan wrote that he 'wished to God *America America* – the picture I am most proud I ever did in all my life – had somehow come through commercially'.[21]

Critically the film fared better, at least from several influential reviewers. *Newsweek* called it 'the best American film of the year', and Hollis Alpert in the *Saturday Review* also praised the film, while suggesting that its hero's image of America was unclear. Other criticism was more mixed: Stanley Kauffman called it Kazan's 'most vivid work since *On the Waterfront*', but one that was betrayed by a 'basic artistic flabbiness', while Ernest Callenbach saw Kazan as indulging his 'idiot hero', and found disconcerting shifts in tone in the film's numerous episodes. Joan Didion called the film 'massively repetitive, insistently obvious, almost interminable, and, perhaps in spite of itself, immensely, miraculously moving'.[22]

At just short of three hours in running time, *America America* closely follows the plot and dialogue of Kazan's short novel, published in 1962. The film opens in Anatolia, and sketches the political background to the Turkish persecution of the Greeks and Armenians, and the family background of the novel's key character, the 20-year-old Stavros Topouzoglou. The central section first traces Stavros's journey to Constantinople, and then deals with his adventures there and increasingly desperate and humiliating efforts to raise the 110 Turkish pounds needed for the passage to America. Finally, novel and film deal with events on board the *Kaiser Wilhelm* and with Stavros's arrival in New York.

America America displays the same period care – in terms of art direction and costumes – as *Splendour in the Grass*. Based on Kazan's family stories, the film stays close to the look and social context of the local culture. Haskell Wexler, given his first major feature film assignment by Kazan, made a strong contribution to the documentary feel of the film with extreme long-shots of the Anatolian mountains, close-shots of faces, hand-held footage of the port and back streets of Constantinople and, most memorably, of the waiting immigrants at Ellis Island – a scene that was shot in an old Greek customs-house using refugees from Bulgaria and Rumania, bussed in from camps in northern Greece. In this scene, and in the preceding sequences on board ship, *America America* is a testament to the fears and the hopes, and the rituals, that were part of the turn-of-the-century immigrant experience.[23]

Kazan uses frequent shifts in tone, pace and visual perspective, while essentially relying on one theme at the core of the
film – Stavros's burning desire to reach America – to hold
the audience. For example, the extended observation of the
Topouzoglou family preparing for Stavros's departure is
followed by a long-shot, held for some time, of Stavros dis-
appearing into the distance, as his parents watch stoically in the
foreground. After this brief, understated scene, reminiscent of
John Ford, there is a further change of pace, as there is a cut
to Stavros crossing the river by raft, and a new musical theme
introduces the semi-comic encounter with Abdul the thief.
Manos Hadjidakis's elaborate score provides separate musical
themes for the main locations of the story, and the effect is both
to pace and unify the film and to emphasise, to Americans, the
'otherness' of the immigrant culture. The style reflected an
American incorporation of some of the forms of the French
'New Wave', in particular the use of abrupt cuts to subsequent
events, some of them making ironic comment on the narrative,
as well as speeding it up.

While the film seems faithful to the look, sound and feeling
of life in Anatolia, Kazan also emphasises the strangeness – to
Western ears and eyes – of the local cultures. The dancing in the
film, for example, invokes local traditions – as with the case of
the two old men in the Sinnikogou household – but at times it
also transcends the dominant style of documentary realism,
reflecting, in the early scene in the Turkish raki house, and later,
on board ship, the intensity, the 'madness' of the quest that is at
the centre of the film. The visual and verbal references to
memories and dreams, together with Kazan's personal narration, and the role of Stavros's parents as a chorus, all suggest
that the action also has a status as myth or fable. A number
of scenes suggest the timelessness of Greek mythology, including Stavros' first meeting with Hohannes on the hillside, the
pitching of the bodies of the anarchists into the sea – as the
women in black look on – and Stavros's flight from the scene of
Abdul's murder, a speck on a vast expanse of mountainside. In
addition the form of the drama, with Stavros (Stathis Giallelis)
encountering a series of characters – Vartan, Abdul, Garabet,
Thomna, Mr and Mrs Kebabian, and Hohannes – who try and
test him, aid or tempt him, suggests the allegorical journeys of
Spenser and Bunyan.

America America in part reflects the period in which it was made – the Kennedy years of the early 1960s. While reform and protest were in the air, there was an optimism and idealism that would fade as the war in Vietnam loomed larger. The civil rights movement still pressed for integration, and John F. Kennedy's global rhetoric about America had a fresh appeal. Kazan's book (for which he secured an endorsement from Robert Kennedy) and the film prefigured the assertion of ethnic identity and the 1970s obsession with the tracing of cultural 'roots'.

The film thus pays tribute to an ideal – to what America meant to the immigrants. Even before shooting began Kazan, while disassociating his project from 'the Irving Berlin type of patriotism', expressed the hope that his film might revive in Americans the idea that 'our country once meant everything to people in less fortunate lands'.[24] Just as in *The Grapes of Wrath* the pioneers are undaunted by stories that the promised land is a fraud. Yet while Kazan affirms the myth of America he also asserts ethnic identity as something more authentic, purer and more virtuous. The nearest equivalents to the Joads in Kazan's film are Stavros's long-suffering parents, still waiting for their journey to begin. Kazan's sympathies lie not only with the 'people waiting', but with Hohannes, who retains his gentleness, smiles too much, and does not have the strength to reach America, and with Vartan and Garabet, who stand and fight – and die – for their people.

As for Stavros, the hero of the film, his role is as ambiguous as his smile. (The dramatic power of the scenes in Constantinople comes from the tension between the American values of change and movement – represented by Stavros – and the warm, innocent, generous patriarchy of the old country, of Aleko and Thomna Sinnikoglou.) As the character who embodies the theme of the film, Stavros's arrival in New York is a triumph; his honour still intact within him, and washed clean in the new land, he will – as Kazan tells us as the film ends – bring all the family across, except for his father. Yet Stavros the human being, rather than Stavros the icon – the American Immigrant – has killed, lied and whored to get across. He has lost his innocence – including his innocence about America – and in the same process he has discovered the path to American success. He will not stay long shining shoes.

Kazan has written that one of his hopes in the film was to show

how Stavros, as he neared America, 'became an American – in other words someone who would do anything to reach his goal'. Given that he has also revealed how in writing the script he came increasingly to be writing about himself, it is easy to recall Lillian Hellman's comment about the special vulnerability of the 'children of timid immigrants' in the years of the 'investigations'; she argued that such Americans, having achieved success, were 'determined to keep it at any cost'. To Hellman, Kazan's notorious 'friendly' testimony to the House Committee on Un-American Activities was the price he paid to retain this success. In one sense *America America* is an affirmation of an American myth; in another it is an immigrant's attempt to understand his father's generation – and to come to terms with his own inheritance.[25]

Kazan began to write the novel *The Arrangement*, in the years following the sudden death in 1963 of Molly Kazan, his wife of thirty years. Only when the book was an unexpected commercial success was Kazan presented with the opportunity to write, produce and direct the film for Warners. In the film Kazan dramatises the revolt, or 'madness', of a 'successful' American executive; the revolt is against his own lifestyle, and the 'arrangement', or series of arrangements, that constitute his success. To his wife, the revolt is a romantic and irresponsible delusion, and a rationalisation of a familiar male wish for a new and younger woman. To Eddie the desire is for a 'second chance' that involves the reconsideration of his roots, and of the legacy of his parents. Notions of 'dropping out' and of rejecting materialism were in the air in the late 1960s, and may seem ridiculous twenty years after. But the notion is still one of some power – the more so because Kazan's film dealt not with youth revolt, or some romantic outlaws from the past, but with a man of middle age and from the affluent middle class.

The Arrangement (1969) begins with the 'good life' that Eddie Anderson (Kirk Douglas), a successful advertising executive, is to reject. On the radio, as the perfect couple prepare for the day at their Los Angeles house, is one of Eddie's most successful ads, of which his wife is as proud as he is. All is well with the American dream: there is a 'perfect blue sky' over Cape Kennedy, the Dow Jones is strong, and the radio audience is told to 'Live your good life through, with Zephyr cigarettes'. Yet Anderson's attempted suicide later that morning prompts his reconsideration of the relationship that led to the breakdown.

Plate 11: Vartan Damadian (Frank Wolff) and Stavros Topouzoglou (Stathis Giallelis) in the Turkish coffee house in *America America* (Athena/Warner Bros, 1964). Reproduced courtesy of BFI Stills, Posters and Designs.

Plate 12: Stavros (Stathis Giallelis) and Hohannes Gardashian (Gregory Rozakis) sighting America in *America America* (Athena/Warner Bros, 1964). Reproduced courtesy of BFI Stills, Posters and Designs.

The previous events are recalled: Anderson, as the star of the advertising firm, is attracted by Gwen (Faye Dunaway), a young woman who refuses to be impressed by his work on the Zephyr campaign. Gwen, less convincingly, tells Anderson that 'It must kill you to think what you might have been'. The middle aged rebel tells his wife that the plot of 'our true romance' is of a 'hero who hasn't got the courage to leave his wife, even though he knows it would save his life'. Anatolian music signals that the resolution of Eddie Anderson's crisis will be played out in New York, where his father is dying, and where Gwen has moved after Eddie had refused to leave his wife Florence (Deborah Kerr).

In New York Anderson indulges his father's own desire to begin again, while Gwen offers him a new 'arrangement' acceptable to her. Taking his father to the family house on the sound, Eddie – the script now refers to him as Evangelos – rejects what he sees as his immigrant legacy, of 'merchant blood', and this strengthens his own desire for a clean break from the past. As he and Gwen are in a row boat, way out in the sound, his father is kidnapped and taken away, leaving Evangelos to retreat 'into himself'. Despite a final conversation with Florence, which ends with her declaring her husband insane, and a rather cramped exposition of further plot details, the end of the film links the funeral of Evangelos' father with the tentative beginning of the new and simpler life with Gwen. In his own terms he has learnt to be selfish.

With *The Arrangement* (1969), Kazan brought together his interest in autobiography and the social ethos of the time. Kazan's script makes reference to the immigrant experience depicted in *America America*, while also drawing on aspects of his own mid-life crisis, and his feelings about Molly Kazan. In his later autobiography Kazan pictured Molly, of the New Haven Thatchers and the *Social Register*, as his trusted professional confidant for thirty years – 'my talisman of success and my measure of merit'. He revealed his compulsive unfaithfulness to Molly, whose sudden death had provoked his writing of *The Arrangement*. While Kazan claimed not to have based Florence on his first wife, he clearly drew on his own experiences, as well as, apparently, on the life of his friend Clifford Odets, who had died in 1964. In terms of the wider social context of *The Arrangement*, ideas of rejecting materialist values

and of spiritual renewal were very much in the air in the later
1960s.[26]

The Arrangement was a critical and commercial failure. At
times Kazan has bemoaned the inflated $6.8m cost, and the
Hollywood production values, and wished that he had made the
film more simply and cheaply in New York. He also regretted
the absence from the film of Marlon Brando who was originally
interested in renewing his professional relationship with Kazan,
but who withdrew, apparently to concentrate on political tasks,
following the assassination of Martin Luther King. Kazan had
problems in compressing the events of the rambling novel into
a script for a two hour film. In particular, several scenes
which emphasised central themes in the book, and which were
included at the conclusion of the final script, were either cut at
the last minute or filmed but not used. The father's own wish
for a second chance, detailed in a long deathbed scene, was
excluded, and a final scene, which made clearer the resolution
of the drama – the new life that came out of the struggle – was
not used, Kazan preferring to end the film with the old man's
funeral. The original script also emphasised the extent to which
Eddie was prepared to sacrifice his rights to the money and
property of the marriage, while the cut final scene visualised the
new life and – in something of the manner of the end of
Splendour in the Grass – questioned it.[27]

While Pauline Kael criticised Kazan for attempting to make a
non-commercial film in a commercial manner, a judgement that
Kazan would appear to have sympathy with, the critical response
might also have reflected the director's movement away from an
earlier style that was more realist (with fewer memory and
fantasy shots), and more theatrical (in the sense of allowing
central acting performances to define much of a film's meaning).
Kazan mixes the emphasis on Eddie Anderson's anguished
journey with scenes of satire (in the picture of advertising, and
the later 'I smell money' confrontation between Eddie and
Florence and her professional advisers). In *America America*
and *Wild River* Kazan had played the central emotional relationships at great length, but in the later film he attempted a much
faster and more cryptic style.

The English writer Robin Wood has criticised much of
Kazan's work for what he sees as the director's over-simple
attitude to his material, and for the repetitiveness of the 'Big
Themes'

which often dominate both characters and situations. While praising the energy and commitment of *America America* and the restraint and ambiguity of *Wild River*, he criticises Kazan's direction of *The Arrangement*, finding the director to be insufficiently distanced from his leading character; discussing the character of Eddie Anderson, Wood argues that 'from the moment we find him a boring egomaniac, the whole centre of the film crumbles'. Andrew Sarris, as part of a reassessment of a director whose work he had previously filed under 'Less than Meets the Eye' in his 1968 survey, was impressed by the autobiographical insights and the intensity of the director's involvement. Sarris saw the film as the director's 'testament to the tenacity of an entire generation of materially successful pilgrims in search of moral justification'.[28]

To Pauline Kael the film was a 'noisy glorification of anguish over selling out, with such an exaggerated evaluation of the loss to the world of the hero's wasted creativity that one does not know which way to look'.[29] Yet the film remains true to its hero's initial decision to change his life, and there is no compromise; while the emphasis is overwhelmingly on Eddie, Florence and Gwen also have their say, as they struggle towards self-awareness or a new identity. At great cost Eddie finds his simpler, less materialistic, more authentic life, while the same can be said for Gwen, and even Florence, a less self-critical character, reaches a point where she declares Eddie to be insane, giving up the struggle to save their relationship. From Florence's point of view Eddie is insane to leave the security and the 'good life' represented by their 'arrangement'.

In its own way, despite the mixing of styles, the film tests one of the ideas of the time – the belief that a more authentic personal identity could be constructed by rejecting materialism. Eddie learns to be selfish. Both *America America* and *The Arrangement* are unusually direct dramas concerning a central theme in 1960s political thought – the search for personal identity and change. (A postcard pinned up in Gwen's apartment in New York warns: 'Escape, while there's still time.') There is also in both films a strong emphasis on the facts of life – the connection between money and power. Kazan himself wrote in 1968 of the middle class student revolt as being opposed to 'our materialism, our respectability, our personal hypocrisies, our dollar orientation'.[30] Kazan's response to the studio excess of *The Arrangement* was to work on a project on Puerto Rican street life with Budd Schulberg – for which financing collapsed – and to direct *The Visitors* (1971). The first attempt to show how the traumas of Vietnam 'came home' to America, the film was shot on super 16mm for $135,000, and was based on a script by Kazan's son Chris.

ABRAHAM POLONSKY

Polonsky had been 'making a good living fixing up rotten movies' when a producer at Univeral, Frank Rosenberg, engaged him to rewrite parts of a Howard Rodman screenplay; Polonsky's shared script credit on the completed film, *Madigan*, directed by Don Siegal and released in 1968, was his first film credit since 1951. In the film there is a contrast between two policemen, a morally correct Police Commissioner Russell (Henry Fonda) and an aging street cop, Madigan (Richard Widmark), as they go about their work in New York, and deal with a particular case. Polonsky later commented on the characters as compromised, and as more or less aware of the corruption around them. Madigan in particular is portrayed as standing perilously between an uncomprehending police bureaucracy and the criminal world where he has spent most of his working life. When Commissioner Russell confronts Chief Inspector Charles Kane, an old friend, with taped evidence of him making a deal with a criminal boss, there is nothing more to say, despite – or because of – their long friendship: 'the rest is conversation', Kane tells Russell.[31]

Soon after, Universal producer Philip Waxman sent Polonsky the book *Willie Boy* by Harry Lawton, proposing that he write and direct a film for television. Universal executive Jennings Lang, a friend of Polonsky, proposed instead that a feature film be made, and when Martin Ritt dropped out of the project Polonsky prepared to direct his first film since *Force of Evil* twenty years before. Lawton's book was a 'socio-political' study of the actual case of a Paiute Indian who in 1909 was chased by eleven posses, and finally killed. Based on research, and conversations with Lawton, Polonsky wrote a spare script which drew on the essence of the facts of the case, while incorporating a number of the director's philosophical interests and some newer ideas about film.[32]

In *Tell Them Willie Boy is Here* (1969) Willie Boy (Robert Blake) returns to the Morongo Reservation Fiesta, and his request to marry an Indian girl, Lola (Katharine Ross), is refused by the girl's father. When the father, carrying a rifle, disturbs the couple in their night-time retreat in the woods, Willie Boy shoots and kills him in self-defence. As the couple escape it is explained that tribal custom accepts 'marriage by capture' as legitimate, and that Lola's mother had encouraged her to go with Willie. At first this incident only marginally impinges on the lives of the other couple in the story – Dr Elizabeth Arnold, the superintendent of the federal reservation (Susan Clark), and deputy sheriff Cooper (Robert Redford). Arnold, a 'helper' to what she calls 'my Indians', has a protective interest in Lola, who she sees as a future teacher, while the deputy sheriff is drawn into what becomes the central subject of the story, the pursuit of Willie Boy. Reluctantly, Cooper (Coop) leads a posse after the two runaways, and the climax of the film is the final confrontation of the sheriff and Willie Boy, in the mountains.

The relationship between the two white characters is unsatisfactory; neither is able to own up to what he or she wants. Arnold was born with 'Boston money' and her education has given her little sensitivity, either to her own needs, or to the racism of the local people. When Coop pushes on her door at night he tells her, prior to their love-making, 'you know it don't matter what you say'. 'Conversation', again in Polonsky's work, is contrasted with the key dynamics of human behaviour. Cooper is under-educated by contrast, and is dimly aware of the role that history and society have marked out for him. One member of the posse, Ray Calvert, remembers fondly the days when he and Coop's father killed Indians and collected scalps, and although Coop is unenthusiastic about the task of the posse – and leaves it at one point – he can see no alternative. Like Gary Cooper in *High Noon*, he does what he has to do; but to Polonsky he is, like Leo Morse in *Force of Evil*, a 'small man' who is unconscious of the path mapped out for him by larger social forces.

Visually, the director, with cinematographer Conrad Hall, strove to desaturate the colour of the film, reducing the blue skies in particular to grey or white. Polonsky sacrificed the Western traditions of placing the characters within a particular locale and of viewing the chase in graphic, spatial terms. Instead,

over the objections of a studio concerned with the appearance
of the film on television, the bleached skies remained, and long
lenses separate the individuals from the desert scrub and mountains where the drama is played out. The posse and the outlaws
seem to be circling each other, and the relationship, and the
cutting, is as much dialectical as spatial; pursued and pursuers
are the opposites in the playing out of a Western myth. In
particular the scenes of the two couples together are intercut,
suggesting the differences as well as underlying parallels in
behaviour.

Arnold is the paternalistic Boston educated 'liberal' of her age,
while Coop cannot throw off the imprint of the Western 'lawman'. Lola is also uncertain, caught between her own culture –
and Willie Boy – and her hopes of assimilation. Only Willie Boy
is given a consciousness of his place in history. Lola, becoming
aware of the advance of the posse, tells her partner that
'they're white, Willie, they'll shoot for ever'; Willie Boy replies:
'How long is that, less than you think.'

If visually the film suggests myth, in another sense Polonsky
indicates the way in which societies create their own myths.
When Calvert is accidentally shot, as Willie fires at the horses in
the posse, one of the men says that the 'whole place is full of
Indians'. The press are in the local town for a visit of President
Taft, and when news reaches town of the occurrence there is
much talk of 'a couple of hundred Indians' and of a 'dangerous
manhunt for a renegade Indian'. Polonsky intends some
reference to the myths of the American west – 'Our Paradise
Lost is the Indian's genocide' – while also alluding to what he
saw as a Cold War mythology that underlay the blacklist, and
his own exile.[33]

Coop cannot develop a new consciousness but he becomes
aware of, and unhappy with, his own role. When someone
suggests that the whole affair makes no sense he replies that
'Maybe that's the sense it makes.' Yet Coop stalks Willie Boy, and
confronts him on the boulders of Rubee mountain. They both
have rifles, but when Willie raises his as if to fire, the sheriff
shoots and kills. Only afterwards does Cooper discover that
Willie's rifle was unloaded. As Coop explains to Arnold, 'I gave
him his chance. He didn't take it.' The lawman has failed to
detach himself from the forces bearing down on him, while
Willie is – the film implies – victorious in death.

The film draws on the social conflicts and the romantic rhetoric of late 1960s America. For liberals and radicals, and for many of the educated young, there was a general disaffection with the war in Vietnam, and a strong emotional commitment to minority causes. For younger black leaders, in the wake of the assassination of Martin Luther King, there was a rejection of compromise, while the shooting of Robert Kennedy also encouraged a sense of defeat on the part of the new left. Polonsky's film drew on this contemporary liberal identification with the rebel, doomed or otherwise, but Pauline Kael was unsympathetic, seeing the film as reflecting a contemporary 'American self-hatred'.[34]

Polonsky's final film as director was *Romance of a Horse Thief* (1971). The director remembers it as a 'lucky project', the result of an unexpected offer when another director pulled out. Polonsky worked on the screenplay – by David Opatoshu – and semi-improvised a story, shot in Yugoslavia, concerning a Jewish community in a Polish border town in 1904. The film portrays a battle of wits between the local people and an occupying force of Russian cossacks. The mood is comic rather than tragic, but one reviewer found that the 'rollicking folk tale' was nevertheless a 'gallant affirmation of our ability to endure and prevail in the struggle for freedom', and another compared the sense of liberation to the 'tragic romanticism' of *Tell Them Willie Boy is Here*. There are comic scenes as the local people get the better of the cossacks and finally escape collectively to America. Polonsky remembers drawing on his grandmother's tales of the old country in his loving portrait of the community, and in this regard Stuart Byron saw the film as 'in a certain sense the anti-*America America*'. To Byron there is no 'burning desire' to get to America in the Polonsky film, and the 'emigrant emotion and experience is seen as an almost accidental occurrence resulting from social and historical demands'. While the emphasis in Kazan's film is on individual will – albeit in a clear social and economic context – the Polonsky film stresses the community and the impact on them of the wider historical changes – the cossack Captain (Yul Brynner) argues that 'Everything changes, whether we want it to or not.'[35]

Notes

PREFACE

1 Larry Ceplair and Steven Englund, *The Inquisition in Hollywood; Politics in the Film Community, 1930–1960*, Berkeley: 1983; Nancy Lynn Schwartz, *The Hollywood Writers' Wars*, New York: 1982; Victor S. Navasky, *Naming Names*, New York: 1980.
2 Jim Cook and Alan Lovell, *Coming to Terms with Hollywood*, London: 1981.
3 See, for example, the comments by Jules Dassin on Kazan, *Film Comment*, 23, 6, 1987, 44; for a comparison of the work of Kazan and Polonsky see Terence Butler, 'Polonsky and Kazan: HUAC and the Violation of Personality', *Sight & Sound*, 57, 4, 1988, 262–7.
4 Elia Kazan, soundtrack of 'Kazan, An Outsider' (Argos Films, 1982).
5 Brian Neve, 'The Screenwriter and the Social Problem Film, 1936–38; The Case of Robert Rossen at Warner Bros.', *Film & History*, XIV, 1, 1984, 2–13; Neve, 'The Immigrant Experience on Film: Kazan's *America America*', *Film & History*, XVII, 3, 1987, 62–8.

1 OUT OF THE THIRTIES

1 Lary May, 'Making the American Way: Modern Theatres, Audiences and the Film Industry, 1929–1945', *Prospects*, May 1987, 108–11; Robert S. Lynd and Helen Merrill Lynd, *Middletown in Transition: A Study in Cultural Conflicts*, London: 1937, 261; Lawrence W. Levine, 'Hollywood's Washington: Film Images of National Politics During the Great Depression', *Prospects*, 10, 1985, 191.
2 Larry S. Ceplair, 'The Politics of Compromise in Hollywood, A Case Study', *Cineaste*, VIII, 4, 1978, 7; John Cellon Holmes, 'A Decade of Coming Attractions', in Arthur F. McClure, ed., *The Movies: An American Idiom, Readings in the Social History of the American Motion Picture*, Cranbury, NJ: 1971, 115.
3 Robert Sklar, *Movie-Made America: A Cultural History of American*

Movies, London: 1978, 189; Gregory D. Black, 'Hollywood Censored, The Production Code Administration and the Hollywood Film Industry, 1930–1940', *Film History*, 3, 3, 1989, 185, 187; Stephen Vaughn, 'Morality and Entertainment: The Origins of the Motion Picture Production Code', *Journal of American History*, 77, 1, 1990, 64.

4 Lawrence W. Levine, 'American Culture and the Great Depression', *Yale Review*, 74, 2, 1985, 208.

5 Ian C. Jarvie, 'Stars and Ethnicity: Hollywood and the United States, 1932–51', in Lester D. Friedman, ed., *Unspeakable Images, Ethnicity and the American Cinema*, Urbana: 1991, 104–5; May, 'Making the American Way', 110ff; Ethan Mordden, *The Hollywood Studios: House Style in the Golden Age of the Movies*, New York: 1988, 268; Leo Rosten, *Hollywood: The Movie Colony and the Movie Makers*, New York: 1941, 160; Jeffrey Richards, *The Age of the Dream Palace: Cinema and Society in Britain, 1930–1939*, London: 1984, 24–30.

6 Levine, 'Hollywood's Washington', 178–80; Andrew Bergman, *We're in the Money, Depression America and its Films*, New York: 1971, 120; Donald Bogle, *Toms, Coons, Mulattoes, Mammies & Bucks*, New York: 1974, 47; Thomas Cripps, *Slow Fade to Black*, New York: 1977, 295; Andrea S. Walsh, *Women's Film and Female Experience, 1940–1950*, New York: 1984, 50, 91; Stanley Cavell, *Pursuits of Happiness: The Hollywood Comedy of Remarriage*, Cambridge, Mass.: 1981, 16–18; Jan-Christopher Horak, 'On the Road to Hollywood: German-Speaking Filmmakers in Exile, 1933–1950', in Helmut F. Pfanner, ed., *Exile across Cultures*, Bonn: 1986, 240; Wilder, quoted, *Los Angeles Daily News*, August 23, 1988, 15.

7 Ian Hamilton, *Writers in Hollywood, 1915–1951*, London: 1990, 162–3; Donald Ogden Stewart, *By a Stroke of Luck*, London: 1975, 217; Philip Sterling, 'A Channel for Democratic Thought', in *Films*, 1, 2, Spring 1940, reprinted with issues 1–4, New York: 1968, 16; Candace Mirza, 'The Collective Spirit of Revolt: A Historical Reading of *Holiday*', *Wide Angle*, 12, 3, 1990, 105.

8 Robert Stebbins, March 1939, quoted by Myron Osborn Lounsbury, *The Origins of American Film Criticism, 1909–1939*, New York: 1973, 459; Sterling, 'A Channel for Democratic Thought', 16; see also, on left perspectives on Hollywood in the late thirties, Peter Stead, *Film and the Working Class: The Feature Film in British and American Society*, London: 1989, 94; Peter Roffman and Jim Purdy, *The Hollywood Social Problem Film*, Bloomington: 1981, 138; Margaret Thorp, *America at the Movies*, London: 1946, 171.

9 Warren I. Susman, 'The Thirties', in Stanley Coben and Lorman Ratner, eds, *The Development of an American Culture*, Englewood Cliffs: 1970, 202, 208; Albert LaValley, 'The Emerging Screenwriter', *Quarterly Review of Film Studies*, I, 1, 1976, 26–7.

10 Jay Williams, *Stage Left*, New York: 1974, 56; Harold Clurman, *The Fervent Years: The Story of the Group Theatre and the Thirties*, London: 1946, 136; Arthur Miller, *Collected Plays*, London: 1967, 16; Robert

Brustein, 'The Legacy of the Group Theater', *The New Republic*, July 25, 1981, 28.

11 Morgan Yale Himelstein, *Drama was a Weapon: The Left-wing Theatre in New York, 1929–1941*, New Brunswick, NJ: 1963, 24; Mark W. Weisstuch, 'The Theatre Union, 1933–1937: A History', Ph.D. thesis, City University of New York: 1982, 2–4.

12 Judd L. Teller, *Strangers and Natives*, New York: 1968, 3–4, 20, 140–5.

13 Maurice Isserman, *Which Side Were You On?: The American Communist Party During the Second World War*, Middletown: 1982, 7–10; Neal Gabler, *An Empire of Their Own*, London: 1988, 322–3; Christine Noll Brinckmann, 'The Politics of *Force of Evil*: An Analysis of Abraham Polonsky's Preblacklist Film', *Prospects: The Annual of American Cultural Studies*, 6, 1981, 359; Polonsky, in Barbara Zheutlin and David Talbot, eds, *Creative Differences: Profiles of Hollywood Dissidents*, Boston: 1978, 56; Polonsky, interview with BN, August 20, 1988; Rossen file, Film Studies Center, MOMA.

14 Malcolm Goldstein, *The Political Stage*, New York: 1974, 9–10; Clurman, *The Fervent Years*, 100; Gary Carr, *The Left Side of Paradise*, 50–6; Weisstuch, 'The Theatre Union', 542; John Howard Lawson, *Theory and Technique of Playwriting and Screenwriting*, New York: 1985, 168, 348–50.

15 Michel Ciment, ed., *Kazan on Kazan*, London: 1973, 12, 21; Gabriel A. Almond, *The Appeals of Communism*, Princeton: 1954, 201–4; Susman, 'The Thirties', 207; Elia Kazan, *A Life*, New York: 1988, 450; Herbert Kline, ed., *New Theatre and Film*, New York: 1985, 363–7; Nicholas Ray, interview in *Take One*, January 1977, 9; Geoff Andrew, *The Films of Nicholas Ray*, London: 1991, 7; for reference to Ray and the Communist Party, see Bernard Eisenschitz, *Roman Americain: les vries de Nicholas Ray*, Paris: 1990, 54.

16 Kazan, *A Life*, 112; Alfred Kazin, *Starting Out in the Thirties*, New York: 1980, 81–2; Clurman, *The Fervent Years*, 117, 150; Clurman, Introduction, in *Six Plays of Clifford Odets*, New York: 1979, xi.

17 David Zane Mairowitz, *Radical Soap Opera*, London: 1974, 75; James K. Lyon, *Bertolt Brecht in America*, London: 1982, 11, 55; Mordecai Gorelik, *New Theatres for Old*, London: 1947, 243; John Lahr, 'Waiting for Success', *New Society*, May 24, 1984, 316; Jim Cook and Alan Lovell, *Coming to Terms with Hollywood*, London: 1981, 4; Clifford Odets, *The Time is Ripe*, New York: 1988, 164–5.

18 Bernard F. Dick, *Radical Innocence: A Critical Study of the Hollywood Ten*, Lexington: 1989, 83; Williams, *Stage Left*, 178; Martin Ritt, interview with Joan Cohen, unpublished; Kline, *New Theatre and Film*, 24–6.

19 Stuart Cosgrove, 'Federal Theatre', in Stephen Baskerville and Ralph Willett, eds, *Nothing Else to Fear: New Perspectives on America in the Thirties*, Manchester: 1985, 252; Arnold Goldman, *Theatre Quarterly*, III, 9, January–March 1973, 70, 72; John O'Connor and Lorraine Brown, eds, *The Federal Theatre Project*, London: 1980, 77.

20 Barbara Leaming, *Orson Welles*, Harmondsworth: 1987, 104; Welles' remarks, in 'Conversations with Orson Welles', *Cahiers du Cinéma in English*, 5, 1966, 39.
21 'Robert Rossen's Last Interview', in Joseph McBride ed., *Persistence of Vision*, Madison: 1968, 207–19; see also Robert Casty, *The Films of Robert Rossen*, New York: 1969; 'Corner Pocket', in the Robert Rossen collection, Theatre Arts, UCLA.
22 Nick Roddick, *A New Deal in Entertainment: Warner Brothers in the 1930s*, London: 1983, 155–6; Thomas Schatz, *The Genius of the System: Hollywood Filmmaking in the Studio Era*, New York: 1988, 207.
23 Richard Griffith, 'The American Film: 1929–1948', in Paul Rotha, ed., *The Film Till Now*, London: 1949, 457; Gabler, *An Empire of their Own*, 197; Edward Buscombe, 'Walsh and Warner Brothers', in Phil Hardy, ed., *Raoul Walsh*, Colchester: 1974, 53.
24 Screen Directors Guild statement quoted by Charles J. Maland, *American Visions: The Films of Chaplin, Ford, Capra, and Welles, 1936–1941*, New York: 1977, 22; Dieterle, quoted, *Velvet Light Trap*, 15, 1975, 28; Edward Buscombe, 'Walsh and Warner Brothers', 60.
25 Rossen testimony, *Hearing before the Committee on Un-American Activities*, House of Representatives, 83rd Congress, Ist Session, May 7, 1953, 1458; Lester Cole, *Hollywood Red: The Autobiography of Lester Cole*, Palo Alto: 1981, 166.
26 Rosten, *Hollywood*, 326; Richard Griffith, 'The American Film: 1929–1948', 455; on writers at Warners see Charles Higham, *Warner Brothers*, New York: 1975, 108, Tom Dardis, *Some Time in the Sun*, New York: 1976, 109–10, and Larry Swindell, *Body and Soul: The Story of John Garfield*, New York: 1975, 153; Rossen, quoted in Bernard Eisenschitz, *Humphrey Bogart*, Paris: 1967, 44; salary information from Warner Bros archive, Princeton University Library; also on salaries see Rosten, *Hollywood*, 324, and Richard Fine, *Hollywood and the Profession of Authorship, 1928–1940*, Ann Arbor: 1985, 108–112.
27 Richard Norton Smith, *Thomas E. Dewey and His Times*, New York: 1982, 176–206; *Liberty*, December 5, 1936; Warner Bros script materials are from the United Artists collection at the Wisconsin Center for Film and Theatre Research at Madison, Wisconsin; Mary Beth Haralovich, 'The Proletarian Woman's Film of the 1930s: Contending with Censorship and Entertainment', *Screen*, 31, 2, 1990, 174–5, 183–7; see also Charles W. Eckert, 'The Anatomy of a Proletarian Film: Warners' *Marked Woman*', *Film Quarterly*, XXVII, Winter 1973–4, 10–24; *DW*, April 14, 1937, 7; Hickman Powell, *Ninety Times*, London: 1939, 284–5.
28 Edelman to Wallis, July 23, 1936; J.L. Warner to Wallis, February 22, 1937, both in the *Marked Woman* files, Warner Bros archive, USC; Ward Greene, *Death in the Deep South*, New York: 1936; Robert L. Zangrando, 'The NAACP and a Federal Anti-Lynching Bill, 1934–1940', in Bernard Sternsher, ed., *The Negro in Depression and War*, Chicago: 1969, 181–92.
29 Sasha Small, *Scottsboro, Act Three*, New York: January 1934, 3.

30 'In the Deep South', undated screenplay by Aben Kandel and Robert Rossen, Warners archives, Wisconsin Center for Film and Theatre Research, Madison, Wisconsin; Breen to Jack Warner, January 30, 1937, Production Code Administration (PCA) file, *They Won't Forget*, Motion Picture Association of America, Margaret Herrick Library, Academy of Motion Picture Arts and Sciences; *NYT*, July 11, 1937, X, 4; *Motion Picture Herald*, May 8, 1937, 16; Thorp, *America at the Movies*, 19; *New Republic*, July 28, 1937, 185– 7; *NYT*, July 15, 1937, 16; *McCalls*, October 1937; *New Masses*, July 20, 1937, 28; *Monthly Film Bulletin*, September 30, 1937, 201.

31 Smith, *Thomas E. Dewey*, 221–3; *NYT*, August 11, 1938, 13; Peter Biskind, 'The Politics of Power in 'On the Waterfront', *Film Quarterly*, Fall 1975, 228.

32 'Dust Be My Destiny', Treatment Outline by Robert Rossen, undated, Madison, Wisconsin; Mark Hellinger, memorandum on 'Dust Be My Destiny', July 15, 1938, *Dust Be My Destiny* files, Warner Bros archive, USC; Inter-Office Communication, Edelman to Wallis, enclosing 'New Outline', 3 August, 1938, Warners archive, USC; *NYT*, October 7, 1939, 11.

33 Rossen collaborated on treatments entitled 'Baby Doctor', 'Story about Public Health Service', and 'Freedom of the Press', in this period, WB/USC; 'The World Moves On', Mark Hellinger, no date, WB/Wisconsin.

2 POPULISM, ROMANTICISM AND FRANK CAPRA

1 Leon Samson, 'Americanism as Surrogate Socialism', in John H.M. Laslett and Seymour Martin Lipset, eds, *Failure of a Dream? Essays in the History of American Socialism*, Garden City, NY: 1974, 427, 435; Jerome Karabel, 'The Failure of American Socialism Reconsidered', *Socialist Register*, 1979, 204–27.

2 Donald MacRae, 'Populism as Ideology', in G. Ionescu and E. Gellner, eds, *Populism*, London: 1969, 155–9; Christopher Lasch, *The Agony of the American Left*, Harmondsworth: 1973, 18.

3 Richard Hofstadter, *The Age of Reform*, New York: 1955, 4–5, 16, 18, 20, 308.

4 Lawrence Goodwyn, *Democratic Promise: The Populist Moment in America*, New York: 1976, xvii; Sara M. Evans and Harry C. Boyte, *Free Spaces, The Sources of Democratic Change in America*, New York: 1986, 154, 156, 181; James N. Gregory, *American Exodus: The Dust Bowl Migration and Okie Culture in California*, New York: 1989, 150.

5 E. Laclau, *Politics and Ideology in Marxist Theory*, London: 1977, 143; Duncan Webster, *Looka Yonder! The Imaginary America of Populist Culture*, London: 1988, 15, 33.

6 V.F. Calverton, quoted in Richard H. Pells, *Radical Visions and American Dreams: Culture and Social Thought in the Depression Years*, New York: 1973, 88.

7 Seymour Martin Lipset, *Political Man*, London: 1960, 167ff; see also Daniel Bell, ed., *The Radical Right*, New York: 1964.

8 Michael Paul Rogin, *The Intellectuals and McCarthy: The Radical Specter*, Cambridge, Massachusetts: 1967, ch. 8.

9 Godfrey Hodgson, *In Our Time: America from World War II to Nixon*, London: 1976, 421.

10 Carl Boggs, 'The New Populism and the Limits of Structural Reforms', *Theory and Society*, 1983, 343ff.

11 Garth Jowett, *Film: The Democratic Art*, Boston: 1976; Raymond Durgnat and Scott Simmon, *King Vidor, American*, Berkeley: 1988, 26.

12 Durgnat and Simmon, *King Vidor, American*, 149; Neal Gabler, *An Empire of Their Own: How the Jews Invented Hollywood*, London: 1989, 119; Nick Roddick, *A New Deal in Entertainment*, London: 1983, 84.

13 Philip French, *Westerns*, London: revised edn 1977, 43; Edward Buscombe ed., *The BFI Companion to the Western*, London: 1988, 203; Tag Gallagher, *John Ford, The Man and His Films*, Berkeley: 1986, 144.

14 Steve Neale, 'Propaganda', *Screen*, 18, 3, Autumn 1977, 23–4; John E. O'Connor, 'A Reaffirmation of American Ideals: *Drums Along the Mohawk* (1939)', in John E. O'Connor and Martin A. Jackson, eds, *American History/American Film: Interpreting the Hollywood Image*, New York: 1979, 98.

15 Russell Campbell, 'The Ideology of the Social Consciousness Movie: Three Films of Darryl F. Zanuck', *Quarterly Review of Film Studies*, 3, Winter 1978, 52, 64.

16 Gregory D. Black, 'Hollywood Censored: The Production Code Administration and the Hollywood Film Industry, 1930–1940', *Film History*, 3, 3, 1989, 185; Vivian C. Sobchack, 'The Grapes of Wrath (1940): Thematic Emphasis through Visual Style', *American Quarterly*, XXXI, 5, Winter 1979, 596–615.

17 Gallagher, *John Ford, The Man and His Films*, 176; Pare Lorentz, *Lorentz on Film: Movies 1927 to 1941*, New York: 1975, 183–6.

18 Robert Warshow, *The Immediate Experience*, New York: 1975, 150; Will Wright, *Sixguns and Society*, Berkeley: 1975, 85–8.

19 John Harvey, 'Out of the Light: An Analysis of Narrative in *Out of the Past*', *Journal of American Studies*, 18, 1, April 1984, 79, 86.

20 Glenn Alan Phelps, 'The 'Populist' films of Frank Capra', *Journal of American Studies*, 13, 3, December 1979; Morris Dickstein, 'It's a Wonderful Life, But', *American Film*, May 1980, 42–7; Charles Wolfe, 'Critical Survey', in C. Wolfe, ed., *Frank Capra: A Guide to References and Resources*, Boston, Mass: 1987, 21–33.

21 Frank Capra, *The Name Above the Title: An Autobiography*, New York: 1971, 3–6, 240; Edward Buscombe, 'Notes on Columbia Pictures Corporation 1926–41', *Screen*, 16, 3, Autumn 1975, 55–6.

22 Richard Griffith, 'The Film Since Then', in Paul Rotha and Richard Griffith, *The Film Till Now*, 1967 ed., 449–50; Jeffrey Richards, *Visions of Yesterday*, London: 1973, 222–53.

23 Raymond Durgnat, 'Correspondence', *Velvet Light Trap*, 9, Summer

1973, 58–9; Capra, *The Name Above the Title*, 346; Dickstein, 'It's a Wonderful Life, But', 45–6; Lary May, 'Popular Culture from the Top Down', *Reviews in American History*, September 1986, 440.

24 Peter Ellis, review of *Mr Deeds Goes to Town*. *New Masses*, 19, April 28, 1936, 29; Reagan's speech, quoted, *NYT*, October 18, 1981, 38.

25 Robert Vaughn, *Only Victims: A Study of Show Business Blacklisting*, New York: 1972, 157; Larry Ceplair and Steven Englund, *The Inquisition in Hollywood*, Berkeley: 1983, 382–3; see the numerous references to Buchman in Bob Thomas, *King Cohn: The Life and Times of Harry Cohn*, New York: 1967, especially 143–7.

26 Raymond Carney, *American Vision: The Films of Frank Capra*, Cambridge: 1986, 6, 300, 485; James D. Hart, *The Concise Oxford Companion to American Literature*, New York: 1986, 344.

27 'John Ford's *Young Mr. Lincoln*', reprinted in Bill Nichols, ed., *Movies and Methods: An Anthology*, Berkeley: 1976, 493–529.

28 Abraham Polonsky, 'How the Blacklist Worked in Hollywood', *Film Culture*, 50–1, Summer/Fall 1970, 44; Herbert Biberman, 'Frank Capra's Characters', *New Masses*, July 8, 1941, reprinted in Charles Wolfe, ed., *Meet John Doe*, New Brunswick: 1989, 231–5.

29 Margaret Canovan, *Populism*, London: 1981, 234; Carney, *American Vision*, 400

30 Frederick Lewis Allen, *Since Yesterday: The 1930s in America*, New York: 1972, 141.

31 Leonard Quart, 'Frank Capra and the Popular Front', *Cineaste*, VIII, 1, Summer 1977, 6.

32 Patrick Gerster, 'The Ideological Project of "Mr Deeds Goes to Town"', *Film Criticism*, Winter 1981, 41–3.

33 Charles Wolfe, '*Mr Smith Goes to Washington*: Democratic Forums and Representational Forms', in Peter Lehman, ed., *Close Viewings: An Anthology of New Film Criticism*, Tallahassee: 1990, 306.

34 Wolfe, *Frank Capra*, 151; Herbert Marcuse, *One Dimensional Man: The Ideology of Industrial Society*, London: 1964, 59; Capra, *The Name Above the Title*, 328.

35 Wolfe, in Lehman ed., *Close Viewings*, 312.

36 Capra, *The Name Above the Title*, 328.

37 Nick Browne, 'System of Production/System of Representation: Industry Context and Ideological Form in Capra's *Meet John Doe*', in Wolfe, ed., *Meet John Doe*, 279.

38 Richard Glatzer and John Raeburn, eds, *Frank Capra: The Man and His Films*, Michigan: 1975, 34 Carney, *American Vision*, 452, 470–2

39 Capra, *The Name Above the Title*, 297.

40 Andrew Sarris, *The American Cinema*, New York: 1968, 87; Richard Corliss, *Talking Pictures: Screenwriters of Hollywood*, Newton Abbot: 1975, xxii; Herbert Biberman, from *New Masses*, July 8, 1941, reprinted in Wolfe, ed., *Meet John Doe*, 232.

41 Robert Sklar, 'God and Man in Bedford Falls: Frank Capra's *It's A Wonderful Life*', in Sam B. Girgus, ed., *The American Self: Myth, Ideology and Popular Culture*, Albuquerque: 1981; Robert B. Ray, *A Certain Tendency of the Hollywood Cinema, 1930–1980*, Princeton, NJ: 1985, 213.

42 Gallagher, *John Ford: The Man and His Films*, 340; Capra, *The Name Above the Title*, 397–8, 451; Anne Edwards, *Katharine Hepburn, A Biography*, London: 1987, 254.
43 Thomas, *King Cohn*, 348.
44 Lillian Ross, 'Onward and Upward with the Arts', *New Yorker*, February 21, 1948, 48; Albert J. LaValley, ed., *Mildred Pierce*, Madison: 1980, 28; Ceplair and Englund, *The Inquisition in Hollywood*, 51.
45 Carney, *American Vision*, 474.

3 LIBERALS, RADICALS AND THE WARTIME AGENDA

1 Garth Jowett, *The Democratic Art, A Social History of American Film*, Boston: 1976, 276–8; Ernest Borneman, 'The United States versus Hollywood: The Case Study of an Anti-trust Suit', in Tino Balio, ed., *The American Film Industry*, Madison: 1985, 449.
2 Eric J. Sandeen, 'Anti-Nazi Sentiment in Film: *Confessions of a Nazi Spy* and the German-American Bund', *American Studies*, 20, 2, 1979, 69, 73; Clayton R. Koppes and Gregory D. Black, *Hollywood Goes to War: How Politics, Profits & Propaganda Shaped World War II Movies*, New York: 1987, 21–2, 27–30. Matthew H. Bernstein, 'Defiant Co-operation: Walter Wanger and Independent Production in Hollywood', Ph.D., Wisconsin-Madison: 1988, 119; John Rossi, 'Hitchcock's *Foreign Correspondent*', *Film & History*, Xll, 2, May 1982, 25–35. François Truffaut, *Hitchcock*, London: 1978, 157.
3 Charles J. Maland, *Chaplin and American Culture*, Princeton, NJ: 1989, 176–8. Richard Maltby, *Harmless Entertainment*, Metuchen, NJ: 1983, 119; Bernstein, 'Defiant Co-operation', 192; Koppes and Black, *Hollywood Goes to War*, 45; Hearings, Committee on Interstate Commerce, 'Propaganda in Motion Pictures', Washington DC: 1942. For a critical view of Koppes and Black, see Jed Dannenbaum, 'Thumbs Down: History and Hollywood in the Forties', *Radical History Review*, 44, April 1989, 178–80. The Koppes and Black study is clearly definitive on OWI influence on wartime films, although the point made by Raymond Durgnat in his review seems to me to be a good one: 'Its cursory comparison of propaganda with "the truth" can give an exaggerated sense of morally base manipulation', *Times Higher Education Supplement*, June 10, 1988, 21.
4 Dorothy Jones, 'Communism and the Movies: A Study of Film Content', in John Cogley, *Report on Blacklisting: I. – Movies*, New York: 1956, 227; Gary Carr, *The Left Side of Paradise: The Screenwriting of John Howard Lawson*, Ann Arbor: 1984, 81.
5 Edward G. Robinson, with Leonard Spiegelgass, *All My Yesterdays: An Autobiography*, New York: 1973, 218; Kenneth S. Lynn, *The Dream of Success*, Boston: 1955, 90–2; Jack London, *The Sea Wolf*, New York: 1960, 45; Rossen, 'Temporary', September 17, 1940, 'Final',

October 22, 1940 with changes to January 6, 1941, *The Sea Wolf* files, WB/Wisconsin; Larry Swindell, *Body and Soul: The Story of John Garfield*, New York: 1975, 153.

6 Nick Roddick, *A New Deal in Entertainment*, 221–3; see also Tom Flinn and John Davis, 'Warners' War of the Wolf', in Gerald Peary and Roger Shatzkin, eds, *The Classic American Novel and the Movies*, New York: 1977, 192–205; they link the film to the *film noir* tradition. Wallis, as with *Marked Woman*, was strongly involved with the 'look' of the film; he asked Curtiz to 'be sure that Polito keeps the whole picture in this interesting, low key', *Inter-Office Communication*, November 6, 1940, *The Sea Wolf* files, WB/USC.

7 Irwin Shaw, 'The gentle people', in files on *Out of the Fog*, WB/Wisconsin.

8 Bernard F. Dick, *Radical Innocence: A Critical Study of the Hollywood Ten*, Lexington: 1989, 36–7.

9 Larry Ceplair and Steven Englund, *The Inquisition in Hollywood: Politics in the Film Community, 1930–1960*, Berkeley: 1983, 132; Howard Koch, *As Time Goes By, Memoirs of a Writer*, New York: 1979, 86; Koch, *Film Comment*, December 1987, 46.

10 Quoted, Gary Null, *Black Hollywood*, Secaucus: 1975, 121; Walter White to Lt. Col. Warner, May 27, 1942, BMP, filed with Records of Lowell Mellett, 1931–43, 208/264, Washington National Records Center (WNRC).

11 Kenneth L. Geist, *Pictures Will Talk*, New York: 1978, 106–7; Richard Corliss, *Talking Pictures: Screenwriters of Hollywood*, Newton Abbot: 1975, 338–41; Ring Lardner Jr, Interview, 'Notes on the Blacklist', *Film Comment*, 24, 5, October 1988, 56–8; Dick, *Radical Innocence*, 169–70

12 Interview, BN with Cy Endfield, December 19, 1989.

13 Frank Brady, *Citizen Welles*, London, 1990, 195, 199–200; Charles Maland, *American Visions: The Films of Chaplin, Ford, Capra and Welles, 1936–41*, New York: 1977, 332–4; Barbara Leaming, *Orson Welles*, Harmondsworth: 1987, 239–41, 250; Pauline Kael, 'Raising Kane', in Kael *et al.*, *The Citizen Kane Book*, St Albans: 1974, 7–9; Welles, interviewed by Huw Weldon, *Monitor*, BBC Television, March 13, 1960, shown as part of *The Complete Citizen Kane*, BBC-2, TX October 13, 1991; André Bazin, *What is Cinema?*, Berkeley, 1967, 33–7.

14 *Daily Worker*, June 10, 1941, 7; John Howard Lawson, *Film: The Creative Process*, New York: 1964, 139; Robert Stam, 'Bakhtin, Polyphony, and Ethnic/Racial Representation', in Lester D. Friedman, ed., *Unspeakable Images: Ethnicity and the American Cinema*, Urbana: 1991, 273–4; Welles, *Free World*, May 1944, 396.

15 Note by K.R.M. Short, and *Government Information Manual for the Motion Picture Industry*, *Historical Journal of Film, Radio and Television*, 3, 2, October 1983, 171–80.

16 Clayton R. Koppes and Gregory D. Black, 'What to Show the World: The Office of War Information and Hollywood, 1942–1945', *Journal of American History*, LXIV, 1977–78, 103.

17 Lee Server, *Screenwriter: Words Become Pictures*, Pittsdown: 1987, 37; Pat McGilligan, *Backstory*, Berkeley: 1986, 73; review of script of 'Torpedoed', June 20, 1942, script review of September 1, 1942, comment on *Action in the North Atlantic*, May 19, 1943, filed in 'Motion Picture Reviews and Analyses', (208/567), Washington National Records Center, Suitland, Maryland (WNRC).

18 Michael Renov, *Hollywood's Wartime Women: Representation and Ideology*, Ann Arbor: 1988, 218.

19 *Focus on Film*, 5, November/December 1970, 54; Koppes and Black, *Hollywood Goes to War*, 94; Donald Ogden Stewart, *By a Stroke of Luck*, London: 1975, 262.

20 M. Joyce Baker, *Images of Women in Film: The War Years, 1941–1945*, Ann Arbor: 1980, 114.

21 Paper on Functions, Procedure and Results, Hollywood Office, BMP, Domestic Branch, OWI, January 23, 1943, 5, WNRC.

22 Platt, *Daily Worker*, June 2, 1943, 7; Warners press release, undated, OWI files, WNRC; David Culbert, ed., *Mission to Moscow*, Madison: 1980, 11–41.

23 Leo Rosten, *Hollywood: The Movie Colony, The Movie-Makers*, New York: 1941, 326; on writers becoming producers, *Variety*, October 6, 1943, 1, also William Dozier, 'Trends and Perspectives', *Writers Congress: The Proceedings of the Conference held in October 1943 under the sponsorship of the Hollywood Writers' Mobilisation and the University of California*, Berkeley: 1944, 37; John Gassner and Dudley Nichols, *Twenty Best Film Plays*, New York: 1943, xxix.

24 *NYT*, April 10, 1943, 12; *DW*, April 12, 1943, 7; Ceplair and Englund, *The Inquisition in Hollywood*, 447–8

25 Nancy Lynn Schwartz, *The Hollywood Writers' Wars*, New York: 1982, 192–4; *DW* (Platt) on *The Moon is Down*, April 1, 1943, 7; Paul Trivers, 'Hollywood Writers Move Up', *New Masses*, 48, September 14, 1943, 20.

26 Memos, Rossen to Warner, February 14, 1942, Warner to Blanke, October 15, 1942, and Warner to Milestone, October 17, 1942, all in WB/USC.

27 OWI review, August 8, 1942; review of release print, March 18, 1943, and Poynter to Warner, March 11, 1943, all in OWI (BMP) files, WNRC.

28 Jones, 'Communism and the Movies', in Cogley, 211–12; Koppes and Black, *Hollywood Goes to War*, 250–77.

29 Dore Schary and Sinclair Lewis, *Storm in the West*, London: 1963; Peter Roffman and Jim Purdy, *The Hollywood Social Problem Film: Madness, Despair and Politics from the Depression to the Fifties*, Bloomington: 1981, 219; David E. Meerse, 'To Reassure a Nation: Hollywood Presents World War II', *Film & History*, VI, 4, 1976, 84; Bernstein, 'Defiant Co-operation', 176; Koppes and Black, 'What to Show the World', 100–1; on *The Grapes of Wrath*, *Variety*, August 25, 1943, 1; Irving Howe and Lewis Coser, *The American Communist Party*, Boston: 1957, 410; *DW*, May 3, 1943, 1; Koppes and Black, *Hollywood Goes to War*, on 'An American Romance', 146–54; *DW*, November 28, 1944, 11, December 13, 1944, 11.

30 Darryl F. Zanuck, 35, in *Writers Congress*; on calls for films on juvenile delinquency, *Variety*, July 21, 1943, 6, *NYT*, October 31, 1943, X, 3; Joel E. Siegel, *Val Lewton: The Reality of Terror*, London: 1972, 142–4; Rossen treatment 'Marked Children', October 19, 1943, and correspondence, WB/USC; Rossen, 'New Characters for the Screen', *New Masses*, 50, January 18, 1944, 18–19 and in Richard Koszarski, ed., *Hollywood Directors, 1941–1976*, Oxford: 1977, 48–54.

31 Douglas Gomery, ed., *High Sierra*, Madison: 1979, 26; WNRC, April 1, 1943.

32 WB/USC files on 'Brooklyn USA', including Breen letter to J. Warner, January 27, 1943; John Bright, in *Film Comment*, December 1977, and Lee Server, *Screenwriter*, 68ff; Poynter on 'Brooklyn USA', January 2, 1943, OWI, WNRC.

33 On the casting of radical writers for war films see Lester Cole, *Hollywood Red: The Autobiography of Lester Cole*, Palo Alto: 1981, 202, and Ceplair and Englund, *The Inquisition in Hollywood*, 180–1; Jones, 'Communism and the Movies', in Cogley, 211–12; Bernard F. Dick, *The American World War Film*, Lexington: 1985, 207.

34 Jeanine Basinger, *The World War II Combat Film: Anatomy of a Genre*, New York: 1986, 37; John Howard Lawson, *Film: The Creative Process*, 141; Carr, *The Left Side of Paradise*, 84; Theodore Kornweibel, Jr, 'Humphrey Bogart's *Sahara*: Propaganda, Cinema and the American Character in World War II', *American Studies*, 22, 1981, 9.

35 James Agee, 'So Proudly We Fail', *Nation*, October 30, 1943, and Dorothy B. Jones, 'Tomorrow the Movies, IV. Is Hollywood Growing Up?', *Nation*, February 3, 1945, both reprinted in Gerald Mast, *The Movies in Our Midst: Documents in the Cultural History of Film in America*, Chicago: 1982, 467–75; Frank T. Thompson, *William A. Wellman*, Metuchen: 1983, 215; Joseph R. Millichap, *Lewis Milestone*, Boston: 1981, 130.

36 Thomas Cripps, 'Racial Ambiguities in American Propaganda Movies', in K.R.M. Short, ed., *Film & Radio Propaganda in World War II*, London: 1983, 131; Walter White, *A Man Called White*, London: 1949, 201–2, and in *Writers Congress*, 18; Trumbo, 'Minorities and the Screen', *Writers Congress*, 495–501; Clayton R. Koppes and Gregory D. Black, 'Blacks, Loyalty, and the Motion-Picture Propaganda in World War II', *Journal of American History*, 73, 2, 1986, 400.

37 Warner to Mellett, October 8, 1942, WNRC; 'Negro Picture', Hellman, May 7, 1942, in Box X, Stuart Heisler Collection, UCLA Special Collections; Carl Rollyson, *Lillian Hellman: Her Legend and Her Legacy*, New York: 1988, 193; 'The Launching of the Booker T. Washington', Sherman, n.d., WB archives, USC, also Cripps, 143, in Short, *Film & Radio Propaganda in World War II*; Thomas Cripps and David Culbert, 'The Negro Soldier (1944): Film Propaganda in Black and White', *American Quarterly*, Winter 1979, XXXI, 631.

38 K.R.M. Short, 'Hollywood Fights Anti-Semitism, 1940–1945', in

Short, *Film & Radio Propaganda in World War II*, 158–60; Ilan Avisan, *Screening the Holocaust: Cinema's Images of the Unimaginable*, Bloomington: 1988, 96; OWI Review, 'Lebensraum', June 23, 1943, OWI/WNRC; materials on *It Happened in Springfield*, Box 1469, WB/USC, and Cripps in Short, ed., *Film & Radio Propaganda in World War II*, 136–40.

39 Koch to J. Warner, August 3, 1945, Box 9, WB/USC; Alvah Bessie, *Inquisition in Eden*, Berlin: 1967, 147; *Hitler Lives*, National Film Archive, London.

40 Leonard J. Leff and Jerold Simmons, '*Wilson*: Hollywood Propaganda for World Peace', *Historical Journal of Film, Radio and Television*, 3, 1, 1983, 15; John B. Wiseman, 'Darryl F. Zanuck and the Failure of *One World*, 1943–1945', *Historical Journal of Film, Radio and Television*, 7, 3, 1987, 279–87.

41 Parker Tyler, *Magic and Myth of Movies*, London, 1971, 166; Thomas Schatz, *The Genius of the System: Hollywood Film-making in the Studio Era*, New York: 1988, 354; Albert J. LaValley, ed., *Mildred Pierce*, Madison: 1980, 20; Lloyd Shearer, 'Crime Certainly Pays on the Screen', *NYT*, August 8, 1945, in Gene Brown, ed., *New York Times Encyclopedia of Film*, New York: 1984.

42 Edward Dmytryk, 'The Director's Point of View', *Writers Congress*, 46; Malcolm Cowley, 'The End of the New Deal', *New Republic*, May 31, 1943, 729–32.

4 POST-WAR HOLLYWOOD

1 Adrian Scott, 'The American Film Industry', discussion with Roger Manvell, BBC, November 5, 1946, BFI Library, London; Tino Balio, ed., *The American Film Industry*, Madison, Wisconsin: 1985, 401–2; Thomas Cripps, '*Casablanca, Tennessee Johnson* and *The Negro Soldier* – Hollywood Liberals and World War II', in K.R.M. Short, ed., *Feature Films as History*: London: 1981, 151–2.

2 Dorothy B. Jones, 'Communism in the Movies', in John Cogley, *Report on Blacklisting: I – Movies*, New York: 1956, 219, 232, 284.

3 Dorothy B. Jones, 'Tomorrow the Movies: IV. Is Hollywood Growing Up?', *Nation*, February 3, 1945, 123–5; John Howard Lawson, 'Organising the Screen Writers Guild', *Cineaste*, VIII, 2, Fall 1977, 11; Raymond Chandler, 'Writers in Hollywood', *Atlantic Quarterly*, November 1945, 51.

4 David Caute, *The Great Fear*, London: 1978, 25–9; Mary Sperling McAuliffe, *Crisis on the Left*, Amherst: 1978, 4–7.

5 Frank Capra, 'Breaking Hollywood's Pattern of Sameness', *NYT*, May 5, 1946, in *NYT Encyclopedia of Film* (E); Fredric Marlowe, 'The Penguin Film Review, 3, August 1947, 72–5; Fred Stanley, 'New Hollywood Units', *NYT*, March 17, 1946 (E); Balio, ed., *The American Film Industry*, 416–17; Thomas F. Brady, 'Closed Confab', *NYT*, February 27, 1949A (E).

6 Balio, ed., *The American Film Industry*, 405; Leonard J. Leff and

Jerold L. Simmons, *The Dame in the Kimono*, London: 1990, 128; A. Scot Berg, *Goldwyn*, London: 1989, 416–17; PCA file, *Gentleman's Agreement*, Academy.

7 Ian Jarvie, 'The Postwar Economic Foreign Policy of the American Film Industry: Europe 1945–1950', *Film History*, 4, 1990, 280, 283; Paul Swann, *The Hollywood Feature Film in Postwar Britain*, London: 1987, 89; *NYT*, February 27, 1949A (E).

8 Cogley, *Report on Blacklisting: I, – Movies*, 60–73; Gordon Kahn, *Hollywood on Trial*, New York: 1948, 11; Lary May, 'Movie Star Politics: the Screen Actors Guild, Cultural Conversion, and the Hollywood Red Scare', in Lary May, ed., *Recasting America*, Chicago: 1989, 125–53.

9 Nancy Lynn Schwartz, *The Hollywood Writers' Wars*, New York: 1982, 239, 250; *Variety*, November 26, 1947, 3; Ronald Brownstein, *The Power and the Glory: The Hollywood-Washington Connection*, New York: 1990, 115. The Hollywood Ten were Alvah Bessie, Herbert Biberman, Lester Cole, Edward Dmytryk, Ring Lardner Jr, John Howard Lawson, Albert Maltz, Samuel Ornitz, Adrian Scott and Dalton Trumbo. An eleventh man, Bertolt Brecht, also testified; he denied being a communist, and immediately left the country for Europe. Making up the nineteen 'unfriendly' witnesses who agreed not to cooperate with the committee were Richard Collins, Gordon Kahn, Howard Koch, Lewis Milestone, Larry Parks, Irving Pichel, Robert Rossen and Waldo Salt. (Howard Suber, 'The Anti-Communist Blacklist in the Hollywood Motion Picture Industry', UCLA, Ph.D., 1968, 24, 26, 285; on Brecht's testimony, James K. Lyon, *Bertolt Brecht in America*, London: 1982, 327–34.)

10 Schary, Goldwyn and Wanger are reported to have objected to the firing of the Ten, Suber, 'The Anti-Communist Blacklist', 32; Darryl Fox, '*Crossfire* and HUAC: Surviving the Slings and Arrows of the Committee', *Film History*, 3, 1, 1989, 36; poll evidence in Kahn, *Hollywood on Trial*, 177; Philip Dunne, *Take Two: A Life in Movies and Politics*, New York: 1980, 199–200; Polonsky, interview with BN, August 20, 1988.

11 May, 'Movie Star Politics', 127, 145; Thom Andersen, 'Red Hollywood', in Suzanne Ferguson and Barbara Groseclose, eds, *Literature and the Visual Arts in Contemporary Society*, Columbus: 1985, 178–9; Darryl F. Zanuck, 'Free Speech on the Silver Screen', *Free World*, March 1945, 61; Richard Maltby, '*Film Noir*: The Politics of the Maladjusted Text', *Journal of American Studies*, 18, 1, 1984, 64; State Department concern, June 1947, referred to in Ralph H. Gundlach, 'The Movies: Stereotypes or Realities?', *Journal of Social Issues*, 3, 3, 1947, 26; *Variety*, November 5, 1947, 1.

12 Thomas Cripps, 'Wartime Liberalism Survives: *Pinky* as a Case', IAMHIST Conference, Gottingen, 1985; William H. Chafe, *The Unfinished Journey: America Since World War II*, New York: 1986, 89–91; Carol Traynor Williams, *The Dream Beside Me*, Rutherford: 1980, 203; James Naremore, 'The Trial, The FBI vs Orson Welles', *Film Comment*, 27, 1, January-February 1991, 25.

13 Ralph Ellison, 'The Shadow and the Act', *The Reporter*, 1, 17, December 6, 1949, 17–19; Regina K. Fadiman, *Faulkner's 'Intruder in the Dust': Novel into Film*, Knoxville: 1978, 27–8, 38.

14 Carey McWilliams, 'With Whom is the Alliance Allied', *Thought Control in the USA; the Collected Proceedings of the Conference on the Subject of Thought Control in the US*, Beverly Hills: 1947, 309; Walter Goodman, *The Committee*, London: 1968, 187, 202.

15 Dalton Trumbo, letter to Sam Sillen, December 5, 1953, in *Additional Dialogue: Letters of Dalton Trumbo, 1942–1962*, New York: 1972, 289; Abraham Polonsky on social radicals in *Film Culture*, 50/51, Summer/Fall 1970, 43–4; Polonsky interview in *Screen*, 11, 3, Summer 1970, 58; John Howard Lawson, *Film in the Battle of Ideas*, New York: 1953, 14, 27.

16 Abraham Polonsky, interviewed in Eric Sherman and Martin Rubin, *The Director's Event: Interviews with Five American Film-Makers*, New York: 1970, 10; Hortense Powdermaker, *Hollywood, the Dream Factory*, London: 1951, 39–40, 327–32; articles by Thomas F. Brady and Lewis Milestone, *New Republic*, January 31, 1949, 12–17; Eric Hodgins, 'A Round Table on the Movies', *Life*, 26, June 27, 1949, 90–110; *Motion Picture Herald*, September 4, 1948, 7.

17 Keith Kelly and Clay Steinman, '"Crossfire": A Dialectical Attack', in *Film Reader 3*, February 1978, 110; Lester D. Friedman, 'A Very Narrow Path: The Politics of Edward Dmytryk', *Literature/Film Quarterly*, 12, 4, 1984, 216–17; First draft continuity, *Cornered*, March 26, 1945; 'Miscellaneous Notes on *Cornered*', John Wexley, March 28, 1945; RKO collection, Theater Arts Library, UCLA; Bernard F. Dick, *Radical Innocence: A Critical Study of the Hollywood Ten*, Lexington: 1989, 145; Larry Ceplair and Steven Englund, *The Inquisition in Hollywood: Politics in the Film Community 1930–1960*, Berkeley: 1983, 314–16; Richard English, 'What makes a Hollywood Communist?', *The Saturday Evening Post*, May 19, 1951, 30–31, 147–50.

18 Dick, *Radical Innocence*, 122; Scott letter, n.d., *Crossfire* files, RKO collection, Theater Arts, UCLA, also in Ceplair and Englund, *The Inquisition in Hollywood*, 451–4; Dore Schary, *Heyday, An Autobiography*, Boston: 1979, 104, 106, 156.

19 Siegfried Kracauer, 'Those Movies with a Message', *Harper's Magazine*, June 1948, 569; Kelly and Steinman, '"Crossfire": A Dialectical Attack', 111, 114; Colin McArthur, '*Crossfire* and the Anglo-American Tradition', *Film Forum*, 1, 2, Autumn 1977, 23–4; Adrian Scott, 'Some of My Worse Friends', typescript, RKO collection, Theater Arts Library, UCLA, also in *Screen Writer*, October 1947, 1–6.

20 Losey had directed the Los Angeles production of Brecht's play *Galileo*, which opened in July 1947; Beaton story, RKO collection, Box 1290, Theater Arts Library, UCLA; Michel Ciment, *Conversations with Losey*, London: 1985, 81; Tom Milne, *Losey on Losey*, Garden City, NY: 1968, 61–2, 68–72; Ben Barzman to BN, Interview, August 31, 1988.

21 Letter, Odlum to Rathvon, June 29, 1948, revisions by Rathvon,
    July 9, 1948, both in the Losey Special Collection, British Film
    Institute library (BFI); *NYT*, September 5, 1948, *Ebony*, December
    1948, 60, *NYT*, May 30, 1948, in Losey collection, BFI; Schary,
    Heyday, 157.
22 *Daily Worker*, January 13, 1949, and *Ebony*, March 1949, in Losey
    collection, BFI library, London; Douglas Gomery, *The Hollywood
    Studio System*, London: 1986, 132.
23 William Rafferty, 'A Reappraisal of the Semi-Documentary in
    Hollywood, 1945–1948', *Velvet Light Trap*, 20, 1983, 22–6;
    Gomery, *The Hollywood Studio System*, 95–7; Russell Campbell, 'The
    Ideology of the Social Consciousness Movie: Three Films of Darryl
    F. Zanuck', *Quarterly Review of Film Studies*, 3, 1978, 49–71; Zanuck
    to Nichols, November 1, 1948, *Pinky* files, Twentieth Century-Fox
    collection, USC.
24 Thomas H. Pauly, *An American Odyssey*, Philadelphia: 1983, 90;
    James Agee, *Agee on Film*, Boston, 1958, 141–43; Memorandum
    from Mr Zanuck to Elia Kazan, June 18, 1947, *Gentleman's Agreement*
    files, Twentieth Century-Fox collection, Archives of Performing
    Arts, USC.
25 Zanuck, conference notes, *Pinky*, November 17, 1948, *Pinky* files,
    Twentieth Century-Fox collection, Theater Arts Library, UCLA;
    Dunne to Zanuck, April 19, 1948, *Pinky* files, Twentieth Century-
    Fox collection, Archives of the Performing Arts, USC; June 11,
    1948 script, UCLA; comments by Dunne, to Zanuck, October 25,
    1948, USC; Dunne, *Take Two, A Life in Movies and Politics*, 60–2;
    Philip Dunne, in Pat McGilligan, ed., *Backstory: Interviews with
    Screenwriters of Hollywood's Golden Age*, Berkeley: 1986, 160–1;
    Zanuck to Nichols, November 1, 1948, *Pinky* file, USC; Elia Kazan,
    A Life, London: 1988, 332–3; Thomas H. Pauly, 'Black Images and
    White Culture During the Decade before the Civil Rights
    Movement', *American Studies*, 31, 2, 1990, 107.
26 Conference notes, *No Way Out*, February 1, 1949, Box 700, UCLA
    Theater Arts; Zanuck memorandum, *Call Northside 777* file, March
    5, 1947, USC; Conference with Mr Zanuck, *House on 92nd Street*,
    January 9, 1945, USC.
27 'Conference notes with Mr Zanuck', on 'The Perfect Case', May 21,
    1946, *Boomerang* file, USC; Kazan, *A Life*, 316–18; Memoranda
    from Zanuck, February 3, 1947, and March 5, 1947, *Call Northside
    777* file, USC; Daniel J. Leab, '*The Iron Curtain*: Hollywood's First
    Cold War movie', *Historical Journal of Film Radio and Television*, 8, 2,
    1988, 158, 176–7.
28 Koch to Col. J.L. Warner, August 3, 1945, *Hitler Lives* file, Warner
    Bros collection, USC; strike materials and correspondence, includ-
    ing Gene Price and Jack Kistner, 'The Story of the Hollywood Film
    Strike in Cartoons', ud., and Western Union telegram to Jack and
    H. Warner, October 8, 1945, in strike files, Warner Bros archive, USC.
29 Alvah Bessie, *Inquisition in Eden*, Berlin: 1967, 157–8; Howard
    Koch, *As Time Goes By, Memoirs of a Writer*, New York: 1979, 134;

Thomas Schatz, *The Genius of the System: Hollywood Film-making in the Studio Era*, New York: 1988, 413; E. Buscombe, 'Walsh and Warner Brothers', in Phil Hardy, ed., *Raoul Walsh*, Colchester: 1974, 60; Andersen, 'Red Hollywood', in Ferguson and Groseclose, eds, *Literature and the Visual Arts in Contemporary Society*, 184.

30 Testimony of J. Warner, *Hearings Before the Committee on Un-American Activities, House of Representatives, In the Matter of Un-American Propaganda, Vol. 1.* Washington DC, October 20, 1947, WB/USC; Howard Suber, 'Hollywood's Political Blacklist', in Donald E. Staples, ed., *The American Cinema*, Washington DC: 1973, 296.

31 References to *The Story of G.I. Joe* and *The Stranger* script materials in the Huston collection, Margaret Herrick Library/Academy; James Naremore, ed., introduction, *The Treasure of the Sierra Madre*, Madison: 1979, 13; Agee, *Agee on Film*, 290–93, 325, 398–401; Ceplair and Englund, *The Inquisition in Hollywood*, 289; Huston to Margaret Case, February 10, 1948, John Huston collection, Academy; John Huston, *An Open Book*, New York: 1980, 171.

32 Huston to Margaret Case, February 10, 1948, John Huston collection, Academy; Ericsson on *Key Largo*, in *Sequence*, 7, Spring 1949, 34–5; Breen to Warner, November 13, 1947, and Stephen S. Jackson to Warner, November 28, 1947, *Key Largo* file, Production Code Administration collection, Motion Picture Association of America, Inc., Academy; Wald letter to Steve Trilling, and Richard Brooks 'statement', in Rudy Behlmer, *Inside Warner Bros.*, London: 1985, 292–5.

33 Huston, *An Open Book*, 170; Patrick McGilligan, *Cagney, The Actor as Auteur*, London: 1975, 188–9; Lawson, *Film in the Battle of Ideas*, 23–4.

5 POST-WAR: NEW DIRECTORS AND STRUCTURES

1 Editorial, *Screen Writer*, 1, 1, June 1945, 36–7; Lester Koenig, *Screen Writer*, August 1945, 27–9; editorial, *Hollywood Quarterly*, 1, 1, October 1945; Paul Trivers, 'Town Meeting Comes to Hollywood', *Screen Writer*, 1, 5, October 1945, 11; Emmet Lavery, letter to Bosley Crowther, in *Screen Writer*, 1, 9, February 1946, 35; Sherwood, *NYT*, December 1, 1946 (E).

2 Richard Koszarski, ed., *Hollywood Directors, 1941–1976*, New York: 1977, 85, 116.

3 David Bordwell *et al.*, *The Classical Hollywood Cinema*, London: 1985, 331; Axel Madsen, *William Wyler*, London: 1974, 280.

4 Abraham Polonsky, '*The Best Years of Our Lives*: A Review', *Hollywood Quarterly*, 2, 3, April 1947, 257–60; Robert Warshow, *The Immediate Experience*, New York: 1975, 159; Martin A. Jackson, 'The Uncertain Peace: *The Best Years of Our Lives*', in John E. O'Connor and Martin A. Jackson, eds, *American History/American Film*, New York:

1979, 147–165; Charles J. Maland, *Chaplin and American Culture: The Evolution of a Star Image*, Princeton: 1989, 233.

5 Tino Balio, *United Artists: The Company Built by the Stars*, Madison: 1976, 229; Malvin Wald, 'Carl Foreman', in Robert E. Morsberger *et al.*, *Dictionary of Literary Biography, Vol. 26: American Screenwriters*, Detroit: 1984, 104–9; Foreman, transcripts of four lectures on *High Noon*, Louis B. Mayer library, American Film Institute consulted in Carl Foreman collection, BFI, London; Donald Spoto, *Stanley Kramer: Film Maker*, Hollywood: 1990, 35; Peter Roffman and Jim Purdy, *The Hollywood Social Problem Film: Madness, Despair and Politics from the Depression to the Fifties*, Bloomington: 1981, 246.

6 On *We Were Strangers*, Robert Sklar, *Cineaste*, XV, 3, 1987, 56–7 and Gavin Lambert, *Sequence*, 9, Autumn 1949, 127; Andrew Sinclair, *Spiegel: The Man Behind the Pictures*, London: 1987, 46–9. 'Fagan', in letter, Art Arthur to John Huston, June 22, 1949, Huston collection (HUAC folder), Academy.

7 Thom Andersen, 'Red Hollywood', in Suzanne Ferguson and Barbara Groseclose, eds, *Literature and the Visual Arts in Contemporary Society*, Columbia: 1985, 184–6; Abraham Polonsky, 'Introduction', in Howard Gelman, *The Films of John Garfield*, Secaucus, NJ: 1975, 8; Jim Cook and Alan Lovell, *Coming to Terms with Hollywood*, London: 1981, 2.

8 Matthew H. Bernstein, 'Defiant Co-operation: *Walter Wanger and Independent Production in Hollywood, 1934–1949*', Ph.D., University of Wisconsin, Madison: 1987, 153–4, 313–5, 210, 157–8.

9 Jules Dassin, interview, *Cineaste*, IX, 1, Fall 1978, 23; Siegfried Kracauer, 'Those Movies with a Message', *Harper's Magazine*, June 1948, 569; Wald, 'Afterword', in Albert Maltz and Malvin Wald, *The Naked City*, Carbondale: 1979, 136–45; Dassin, in *Accio*, Transcription, Panel on Blacklisting at Barcelona Film Festival, 1989, 42; James Agee, *Agee on Film*, Boston: 1964, 301.

10 Abraham Polonsky, in Nancy Lynn Schwartz, *The Hollywood Writers' Wars*, New York: 1982, 224–5; Albert Maltz, 'What shall we ask of writers?', *New Masses*, February 12, 1946, 19–22.

11 Jack Salzman, *Albert Maltz*, Boston: 1978, 115; on *Broken Arrow*, *Los Angeles Times*, June 29, 1991, F1, F16; microfiche on *Broken Arrow*, BFI library; Barry Gifford, *The Devil Thumbs a Ride*, New York: 1988, 151; Lee Server, *Screenwriter: Words Become Pictures*, Pittsdown: 1987, 40–2; Colin McArthur, *Underworld USA*, London: 1972, 98.

12 Michel Ciment, ed., *Conversations with Losey*, London: 1985, 90–3, 61, 96, 100; 'Paramount: Oscar for profits', *Fortune*, 35, June 1947, 221; cuttings, Losey collection, BFI; Breen to Luigi Luraschi, Director of Censorship, Paramount, October 4, 1949, in PCA file, *The Lawless*, Academy; *Ebony*, *B'Nai B'rith Messenger* (June 16, 1950), *New Republic* (July 17, 1950), in Losey collection, BFI; Foster Hirsch, *Joseph Losey*, Boston: 1980, 19.

13 PCA file, *The Prowler*, Academy; cuttings, Losey collection, BFI; Ciment, *Conversations with Losey*, 109, 110; James Leahy, *The Cinema of Joseph Losey*, London: 1967, 52–3.

14 Interview, Abraham Polonsky with BN, August 20, 1988; Allen Eyles, 'Films of ENTERPRISE, A Studio History', *Focus on Film*, 35, April 1980, 14.

15 Interview, Abraham Polonsky with BN, August 20, 1988; Abraham Polonsky, *Body and Soul*, Final Shooting script, January 13 1947, in Box 6, Robert Rossen collection, Theater Arts library, UCLA; Robert Parrish, *Growing Up in Hollywood*, St Albans: 1980, 189–97.

16 Allen Eyles, 'Films of ENTERPRISE, A Studio History', 21; BN, interview with Polonsky, August 20, 1988; Christine Noll Brinckmann, 'The Politics of *Force of Evil*: An Analysis of Abraham Polonsky's Preblacklist Film', *Prospects: The Annual of American Cultural Studies*, 6, 1981, 360. Also Jack Shadoian, *Dreams and Dead Ends*, Cambridge, Mass.: 1977, 134–48; Alberta Marlow on *Force of Evil*, *Sequence*, 8, Summer 1949, in BFI microfiche on *Force of Evil*; Guy Brenton, 'Two Adaptations', *Sequence*, 12, Autumn 1950, 33–6.

17 Stephen S. Jackson, April 5, 1948, PCA file, *Force of Evil*, Academy; Abraham Polonsky, *Film Culture*, Summer/Fall 1970, 43–4.

18 John Houseman, *Front and Center*, New York: 1979, 178–9.

19 *Hearings before the Committee on Un-American Activities*, Washington, 1951, 1953: Rossen testimony, June 25, 1951, 678–9; May 7, 1953, 1,489.

20 Janet Staiger, 'Individualism Versus Collectivism', *Screen*, 24, 4–5, 1983, 72; Rossen, 'Love Lies Bleeding', September 21, 1945, 93, Kirk Douglas collection, Wisconsin Center for Film and Theatre Research.

21 Harold J. Salemson, ed., *Conference on the Subject of Thought Control in the US*, July 9–13, 1947, 309; Bob Thomas, *King Cohn*, New York: 1962, 262; Polonsky on Rossen, in 'correspondence with William Pechter, 1962', Andrew Sarris, ed., *Hollywood Voices*, Indianapolis: 1971, 142; Tavernier, introduction to showing of *Johnny O'Clock*, BBC-2, TX February 6, 1988.

22 Alvah Bessie, *Inquisition in Eden*, Berlin: 1967, 179–83; Rossen testimony, June 25, 1951, 675.

23 *New York Telegraph*, March 25, 1947, Rossen collection, Theater Arts, UCLA, Box 8.

24 *Film Index*, 11, 1971, 115; Parrish, *Growing Up in Hollywood*, 200–6; T. Harry Williams, *Huey Long*, Toronto: 1970, xi; William Walling, 'In Which Humpty Dumpty Becomes King', in Gerald Peary and Roger Shatzkin, eds, *The Modern American Novel and the Movies*, New York: 1978, 170; *Hollywood Reporter*, November 4, 1949, cited in the PCA file on *All the King's Men*, Academy; Tom Milne, *Monthly Film Bulletin*, 625, February 1986, 56–7.

25 Walling, 'In Which Humpty Dumpty Becomes King', 177; Thomas, *King Cohn*, 264; Joel W. Finler, *The Hollywood Story*, London: 1988, 76; on left reactions to *All the King's Men*, Edward Dmytryk, *It's a Hell of a Life But Not a Bad Living*, New York: 1978, 126, and Ring Lardner Jr, cited in Schwartz, *The Hollywood Writers' Wars*, 170; Victor S. Navasky, *Naming Names*, New York: 1980, 303; Richard Collins testimony, April 12, 1951, *Hearings*, Washington,

1951, 240; Alan Casty, *The Films of Robert Rossen*, New York: 1969, 29.

6 *FILM NOIR* AND SOCIETY

1 Colin McArthur, '*Crossfire* and the Anglo-American Critical Tradition', *Film Forum*, 1, 2, 1977, p 24–5; J.A. Place and L.S. Peterson, 'Some Visual Motifs of *Film Noir*', in Bill Nichols, ed., *Movies and Methods*, Berkeley: 1976, 326; Richard Maltby, '*Film Noir*: The Politics of the Maladjusted Text', *Journal of American Studies*, 18, 1, April 1984, 56–7.

2 Spencer Selby, *Dark City: The Film Noir*, Chicago: 1984, 204–10; Joel W. Finler, *The Hollywood Story*, London: 1988, 280.

3 Jon Tuska, *Dark Cinema: American Film Noir in Cultural Perspective*, Westport: 1984, 151–2; Warren Susman, 'Did Success Spoil the United States?: Dual Representations in Postwar America', in Lary May, ed., *Recasting America: Culture and Politics in the Age of the Cold War*, Chicago: 1989, 29; Frank Krutnik, *In a Lonely Street: Film Noir, Genre and Masculinity*, London: 1991, xii, xiii.

4 Tuska, *Dark Cinema*, 151.

5 Charles Flynn and Todd McCarthy, eds, *Kings of the Bs: Working within the System*, New York: 1975, 403; George Lipsitz, *Class and Culture in Cold War America*, New York: 1981, 179; David Thomson, 'A Cottage at Palos Verdes', *Film Comment*, 26, 3, May-June, 1990, 16–21.

6 Carlos Clarens, *Crime Movies: From Griffith to the Godfather and Beyond*, London: 1980, 195; Mike Davis, *City of Quartz*, London: 1990, 37–44; Thom Andersen, 'Red Hollywood', in Suzanne Ferguson and Barbara Groseclose, eds, *Literature and the Visual Arts in Contemporary Society*, Columbus: 1985, 183–9; James Agee, *Agee on Film*, New York: 1964, 119; on *film noir* and the Breen Office see Leonard J. Leff and Jerold L. Simmons, *The Dame in the Kimono: Hollywood Censorship and the Production Code from the 1920s to the 1960s*, London: 1990, 131–34, Laurence Jarvik, 'Reforming the Breen Office: Censorship and Film Noir', unpublished paper, 1991.

7 Robert G. Porfirio, 'No Way Out: Existential Motifs in the Film Noir', *Sight & Sound*, 45, 4, 1976, 213–14.

8 See E. Ann Kaplan, ed., *Women in Film Noir*, London: 1980, in particular Sylvia Harvey, 'Woman's place: the absent family of film noir', 22–34; Deborah Thomas, 'Film Noir: How Hollywood Deals with the Deviant Male', *CineAction*, 12/13, August 1988, 18–28; M. Wolfenstein and Nathan Leites, *Movies: A Psychological Study*, Glencoe: 1950, 20.

9 David Bordwell *et al.*, *The Classical Hollywood Cinema*, 77; Paul Kerr, 'Out of the Past? Notes on the B *film noir*', in Kerr, ed., *The Hollywood Film Industry*, London: 1986, 236, 239–40; J.P. Telotte, *Voices in the Dark: The Narrative Patterns of Film Noir*, Urbana: 1989, 221

10 Malvin Wald, 'Afterword' to the screenplay, in Matthew J. Bruccoli, ed., *The Naked City*, Carbondale: 1979, 143.

11 Edward Dmytryk and Richard Fleischer, interviewed for *The RKO Story*, BBC-2, TX July 31, 1987; Abraham Polonsky, in Barry Norman, *Talking Pictures: The Story of Hollywood*, London: 1987, 160; Michael Walker, 'Hawks and Film Noir: *The Big Sleep*', in *CineAction*, 13/14, Summer 1988, 30. On the technical departments and RKO style, see Beverly Heisner, *Hollywood Art: Art Direction in the Days of the Great Studios*, Jefferson: 1990, 218, 253–4; but see the friction between Mordecai Gorelik, previously associated with the Group Theatre, and the RKO art department in the forties, in Gorelik, 'Hollywood's Art Machinery', *Hollywood Quarterly*, January 1947, reprinted in Jim Cook and Alan Lovell, *Coming to Terms with Hollywood*, London: 1981, 64–9.

12 Paul Schrader, 'Notes on *Film Noir*', in David Denby, ed., *Awake in the Dark: An Anthology of American Film Criticism, 1915 to the Present*, New York: 1977, 285–6; Hal Wallis and Charles Higham, *Star Maker: The Autobiography of Hal Wallis*, New York: 1981, 129–30.

13 Lipsitz, *Class and Culture in Cold War America*, 177; Whittaker Chambers, *Witness*, London: 1953, 356; Irving Pichel, 'Areas of Silence', *Hollywood Quarterly*, III, 1, Fall 1947, 51–5.

14 Dana Polan, *Power and Paranoia: History, Narrative and the American Cinema, 1940–1950*, New York: 1986, 201; Ring Lardner Jr, 'First Steps in Arithmetic', *Screen Writer*, 3, 3, August 1947, 17; *New Yorker*, February 21, 1948, 46; on Maltz, Polonsky, interview with BN, August 20, 1988.

15 Thomson, 'A Cottage at Palos Verdes', 21.

16 Susman, 'Did Success Spoil the United States?', in May, *Recasting America*, 25–30; Philip Kemp, 'From the Nightmare Factory: HUAC and the Politics of Noir', *Sight & Sound*, 44, 4, Autumn 1986, 266–70; William H. Chafe, *The Unfinished Journey: America Since World War II*, New York: 1986, 82.

17 Clyde Kluckhohn, C. Wright Mills and David Riesman *et al.*, in Chester E. Eisinger, ed., *The 1940s: Profile of a Nation in Crisis*, New York: 1969, 158, 166, 183–4.

18 Maltby, '*Film Noir*: The Politics of the Maladjusted Text', 56–7; Carol Traynor Williams, *The Dream Beside Me: The Movies and Children of the Forties*, Rutherford: 1980, 29–30, 233; Geoffrey O'Brien, *Hardboiled America*, New York: 1981, 14–15.

19 *Motion Picture Herald*, March 29, 1949, quoted in *Sequence*, 8, Summer 1949, 51; Michael W. Miles, *The Odyssey of the American Right*, New York: 1980, 222–7; Susman, 'Did Success Spoil the United States?', in May, *Recasting America*, 31–3.

20 Leff and Simmons, *The Dame in the Kimono*, 134–5; Breen 'personal note' to William Gordon of RKO, June 12, 1946, quoted by Laurence Jarvik, 'Reforming the Breen Office: Censorship and Film Noir', unpublished paper, 1991, 14.

21 Lipsitz, *Class and Culture in Cold War America*, 179–81.

22 Linda Williams, 'Feminist Film Theory: *Mildred Pierce* and the

Second World War', in E. Deidre Pribram, ed., *Female Spectators: Looking at Film and Television*, London: 1988, 13–16.

23 Elliot E. Cohen, 'Letter to the Movie-Makers: The Film Drama as a Social Force', *Commentary*, August 1947, 110–18; Louis E. Raths and Frank N. Trager, 'Public Opinion and *Crossfire*', *Journal of Educational Sociology*, 21, 1948, 363.

24 Alexander Shelley Carter, 'Film as a Teaching Tool for Examining Social and Political Issues: Robert Siodmak's *The Spiral Staircase*', MEd. thesis, La Trobe University, Melbourne: 1984, 60–7.

25 Telotte, *Voices in the Dark*, 115.

26 Victor S. Navasky, *Naming Names*, New York: 1980, 276; Maurice Yacowar, 'Cyrano de H.U.A.C.', *Journal of Popular Film*, I, January 1976, 68–75.

27 W.R. Burnett, 'The Asphalt Jungle', MGM collection, Archives of the Performing Arts, USC; 'Ben Maddow: The Invisible Man', in Pat McGilligan, ed., *Backstory 2: Interviews with Screenwriters of the 1940s and 1950s*, Berkeley: 1991, 175–6.

28 Thomas Schatz, *Hollywood Genres: Formulas, Filmmaking, and the Studio System*, New York: 1981, 116–20.

29 Barbara Leaming, *Orson Welles*, Harmondsworth: 1987, 340–1.

30 Navasky, *Naming Names*, 262–3.

31 Robert Murphy, *Realism and Tinsel*, London: 1989, 163–4.

32 Alain Silver and Elizabeth Ward, *Film Noir: An Encyclopedic Reference Guide*, London: 1988, 334–5.

33 On Latimer see O'Brien, *Hardboiled America*, 84–5, and Krutnik, *In a Lonely Street*, 183, 186.

34 Polan, *Power and Paranoia*, 201; Susman, 'Did Success Spoil the United States?', in May, *Recasting America*, 30; Polonsky, quoted in Norman, *Talking Pictures*, 160.

35 'Robert Wise at RKO', *Focus on Film*, 12, Winter 1972, 48; Gavin Lambert, *Sequence*, 7, Spring 1949 (BFI microfiche).

36 Kemp on *Where Danger Lives*, 'From the Nightmare Factory', 266–7; Andersen, 'Red Hollywood', 187.

7 INTO THE FIFTIES

1 Richard H. Pells, *The Liberal Mind in a Conservative Age: American Intellectuals in the 1940s & 1950s*, New York: 1985, 272; Howard Suber, 'The Anti-Communist Blacklist in the Hollywood Motion Picture Industry', Ph.D., University of California, Los Angeles: 1969, 38, 45, 52, 68–9; Counterattack, The Newsletter of Facts to Combat Communism, *Red Channels: The Report on Communist Influence in Radio and Television*, New York: 1950.

2 Victor S. Navasky, *Naming Names*, New York: 1980, 199–222; Elia Kazan, *A Life*, London: 1988, 464–5, 470; *New York Times*, April 12, 1952, 7; Kazan, interview with BN, September 16, 1980; Pells, *The Liberal Mind in a Conservative Age*, 129; Arthur Schlesinger Jr, *The Vital Center: The Politics of Freedom*, Boston: 1949.

3 I.F. Stone, *The Haunted Fifties*, London: 1964, 47; Larry Ceplair and Steven Englund, *The Inquisition in Hollywood: Politics in the Film Community, 1930–1960*, Berkeley, 1983, 431; Jeffrey C. Goldfarb, *The Cynical Society: The Culture of Politics and the Politics of Culture*, Chicago: 1991, 88; Thomas H. Pauly, *An American Odyssey: Elia Kazan and American Culture*, Philadelphia: 1983, 160; Kazan's list of credits, in Eric Bentley, *Thirty Years of Treason: Excerpts from Hearings before the House Committee on Un-American Activities, 1938–1968*, New York: 1971, 492–5; Arthur Miller, *Timebends, A Life*, London: 1987, 334–5.

4 Howard Suber, 'Politics and Popular Culture: Hollywood at Bay, 1933–1953', *American Jewish History*, 68, 1979, 517; Clancy Sigal, 'Hollywood During the Great Fear', *Present Tense*, 9, 1982, 45–8; see Thom Andersen, 'Red Hollywood', in Suzanne Ferguson and Barbara Groseclose, *Literature and the Visual Arts in Contemporary Society*, Columbus: 1985, especially 161ff; Gregory Black's review of Navasky, *Philosophy of the Social Sciences*, 13, 1, 1983, 126; Lillian Hellman, *Scoundrel Time*, Boston: 1976, 39; Erik Erikson, 'Autobiographic Notes on the Identity Crisis', in *Daedalus*, 99, 4, Fall 1970, 747; Budd Schulberg, in Navasky, *Naming Names*, 246.

5 Edward Dmytryk, 'A Very Narrow Path: The Politics of Edward Dmytryk', *Literature/Film Quarterly*, 12, 4, 1984, 218; Dmytryk testimony in Eric Bentley, ed., *Thirty Years of Treason*, 379; Dmytryk, *It's a Hell of a Life But Not a Bad Living*, New York: 1978, 145.

6 Endfield interview, December 19, 1989; Polonsky, interview with BN, August 20, 1988.

7 John Francis Kredl, *Nicholas Ray*, Boston: 1977, 44; Jarrico in *Film Comment*, December 1987, 45; Louis Marks, 'Hood Winked', *The Listener*, January 18, 1990.

8 The section on Cy Endfield was based on an interview, December 19, 1989, supplemented by information provided in a letter from Endfield to the author, September 6, 1991; Robert Stillman, 'No Complaints', NYT, April 23, 1950 (E); Andersen, 'Red Hollywood', 187; *Film Dope*, 14, March 1978, 33–4.

9 Richard Hofstadter, *The Paranoid Style in American Politics*, New York: 1964, 43; Arthur Miller, interview in *Theatre Journal*, 32, 2, May 1980, 197; Dorothy B. Jones, 'Communism in the Movies', in John Cogley, *Report on Blacklisting*: I, – *Movies*, New York: 1956, Bernard Vorhaus, interview with BN, October 15, 1987; Neil Sinyard and Adrian Turner, *Journey Down Sunset Boulevard: The Films of Billy Wilder*, Ryde: 1979, 126.

10 Wald to Fuchs, November 21, 1949, and Wald to Irv Kupcinet, November 11, 1949, in *Storm Warning*, files, WB/USC.

11 James W. Palmer, 'In a Lonely Place: Paranoia in the Dream Factory', *Film/Literature Quarterly*, 13, 3, 1985, 203–4; Peter Biskind, *Seeing is Believing: How Hollywood Taught Us to Stop Worrying and Love the Fifties*, New York: 1983, 37. Ray's efforts to create his own production company in the fifties were unsuccessful. For discussion of personal and liberal motifs in his studio films, see Geoff Andrew,

The Films of Nicholas Ray, London: 1991. Also, on *Rebel Without a Cause* (Warners, 1955), see Peter Biskind, 'Rebel Without a Cause: Nicholas Ray in the Fifties', *Film Quarterly*, Fall 1974, 32–8.

12 Kramer, interview, *Word into Image*, American Film Foundation, 1981, TX HTV, October 21, 1986; transcripts of AFI (Louis B Mayer Library) lectures on *High Noon*, Carl Foreman collection, BFI; Zinnemann, *Arena*, BBC-2, TX March 9, 1990; see interpretations of *High Noon* in Philip French, *Westerns*, London: revised edn, 1977, 13; John H. Lenihan, *Showdown: Confronting Modern America in the Western Film*, Urbana: 1980, 117–21; Richard Combs, *Monthly Film Bulletin*, 53, 629, June 1986, 186–88.

13 'Philip Yordan: The Chameleon', 330–81, and 'Ben Maddow: the invisible man', in Pat McGilligan, ed., *Backstory 2: Interviews with Screenwriters of the 1940s and 1950s*, Berkeley: 1991; Taradash, in *Accio*, 1989, 30, 32; Al LaValley, 'Invasion of the Body Snatchers: Politics, Psychology, Sociology', in LaValley, ed., *Invasion of the Body Snatchers*, New Brunswick: 1989, 3–17.

14 Stephen E. Ambrose, *Nixon: Volume 1 – The Education of a Politician, 1913–1962*, New York: 1987, 159; Daniel Leab, '"The Iron Curtain" (1948): Hollywood's first Cold War movie', *Historical Journal of Film, Radio and Television*, 8, 2, 1988, 176–7; Russell E. Shain, 'Cold War Films, 1948–1962: An Annotated Filmography', *Journal of Popular Film*, 3, 4, 1974, 334–50; Lawrence L. Murray, 'Monsters, Spies and Subversives: The Film Industry Responds to the Cold War, 1945–1955', *Jump Cut*, 9, October–December, 1975, 14.

15 On John Lee Mahin, Pat McGilligan, ed., *Backstory*, 242, 261; Michael Paul Rogin, *The Intellectuals and McCarthy: The Radical Specter*, Cambridge, Mass.: 1967, 242; Michael Rogin, *Ronald Reagan, the Movie: and other Episodes in Political Demonology*, Berkeley: 1987, 262

16 Jim Kitses, 'Elia Kazan: A Structural Analysis', *Cinema*, 7, 3, Winter 1972–3, 25; Pauly, *An American Odyssey*, 112; Polonsky on Kazan's 'bad conscience', quoted in the entry by Lloyd Michaels on Kazan, in Christopher Lyon, ed., *The Macmillan Dictionary: Films and Filmmakers*, Vol. II, London: 1984, 288.

17 Warner testimony on Kazan and mob (see p 252, note 30); Warners archive, USC, Kazan to Warner, October 19, 1950, *A Streetcar Named Desire* files, WB/USC; Kazan, 'Pressure Problem', *NYT*, October 21, 1951, II, 5; Hollis Alpert on *A Streetcar Named Desire*, *Saturday Review of Literature*, September 1, 1951, 28; Laurence Jarvik, 'I Don't Want Realism, I Want Magic: Elia Kazan and *A Streetcar Named Desire*', unpublished paper, 1–21; Manny Farber, 'Movies Aren't Movies Any More', *Commentary*, June 1952, reprinted as 'The Gimp', in Farber, *Negative Space*, London: 1971, 71–83; Navasky, *Naming Names*, 87–8; Miller, *Timebends*, 308; Kazan, *A Life*, 413–4

18 Fred Zinnemann to Jack Chertok, Inter-office communication, MGM, August 8, 1941, Zinnemann special collection, BFI; Cole, quoted in Peter Biskind, 'Ripping off Zapata – Revolution Hollywood Style', *Cineaste*, VII, 2, 1976, 14; Paul Vanderwood, 'An

American Cold Warrior: *Viva Zapata!*', in John E. O'Connor and Martin A. Jackson, *American History/American Film*, New York: 1979, 189; Kazan treatment, October 17, 1949, Fox collection, USC.

19 Zanuck on *Deadline USA*, recalled by Richard Brooks, *Movie*, 12, Spring 1965, 4; Zanuck on *Viva Zapata!*, *The Grapes of Wrath* etc. at conference, December 26, 1950, Fox collection, USC; John Howard Lawson, *Film in the Battle of Ideas*, New York: 1953, 42; John Womack Jr, *Zapata and the Mexican Revolution*, Harmondsworth: 1972, 565; *Tribune*, May 2, 1952, in microfiche on *Viva Zapata!*, BFI library; Dan Georgakis, 'Still Good After All these Years', *Cineaste*, VII, 2, 1976, 16.

20 Kazan on *Viva Zapata!* as an anti-communist film, in Bentley, ed., *Thirty Years of Treason*, 484–95; Kazan's letters in the *Saturday Review*, April 5, 1952, May 24, 1952; Pauly, *An American Odyssey*, 151; Morsberger, 'Steinbeck's Zapata: Rebel Versus Revolutionary', in Robert E. Morsberger, ed., *Viva Zapata!: The Original Screenplay*, New York: 1975, xii.

21 Biskind, 'Ripping Off Zapata', 11; Charles Silver, programme notes on *Viva Zapata!*, Kazan file, Museum of Modern Art Film Studies Center; Pells, *The Liberal Mind in a Conservative Age*, 272.

22 Memo to Philip Dunne, May 7, 1953, cited in Aubrey Solomon, *Twentieth Century–Fox: A Corporate and Financial History*, Metuchen: 1988, 71; Zanuck, March 12, 1953, in Solomon, *Twentieth Century–Fox*, 86; Mel Gussow, *Darryl F. Zanuck*, London: 1971, 179.

23 'Agreement', Kazan and Warners, on *East of Eden*, January 23, 1953, Warners archive, Princeton University Library; Schulberg in Navasky, *Naming Names*, 307–10; on Spiegel, Andrew Sinclair, *Spiegel*, London: 1987, 70; Schulberg, 'Why Write it When You Can't Sell it to the Pictures?', *The Saturday Review*, September 3, 1955, 6; Corridan, quoted in Brian Neve, 'The 1950s: the case of *On the Waterfront*', in Philip Davies and Brian Neve, eds, *Cinema, Politics and Society in America*, Manchester: 1981, 101; see also Kenneth Hey, 'Ambivalence as a Theme in *On the Waterfront* (1954): An Interdisciplinary Approach to Film Study', *American Quarterly*, XXXI, 5, 1979, 666–95.

24 On neo-realism, Miller, *Timebends*, 195; Leo Braudy, *The World in a Frame: What We See in Films*, Garden City, NY: 1977, 241; Peter Biskind, 'The Politics of Power in "On the Waterfront"', *Film Quarterly*, Fall 1975, 29; see also Lindsay Anderson, 'The Last Sequence of *On the Waterfront*', *Sight & Sound*, 24, 3, 1955, and the reply by Robert Hughes, *Sight & Sound*, 24, 4, 1955.

25 Kazan to Jack Warner and Finlay McDermott, letter postmarked November 15, 1955, *Baby Doll* materials, WB/USC; Thomas Schatz, *The Genius of the System: Hollywood Film-making in the Studio Era*, New York: 1988, 439.

26 Kazan, private notes, January 4, 1958, in Michel Ciment, ed., *Elia Kazan: An American Odyssey*, London, 1988, 112; Kazan, *A Life*, 568.

27 Deborah Silverton Rosenfelt, 'Commentary', in Michael Wilson and

Rosenfelt, *Salt of the Earth*, New York: 1978, 103, 108, 117; on Jarrico and Wilson, Nancy Lynn Schwartz, *The Hollywood Writers' Wars*, New York: 1982, 152, and Ceplair and Englund, *The Inquisition in Hollywood*, 78, 233, 262, 299, and (on *Tom, Dick and Harry*), 302; Dalton Trumbo, *Additional Dialogue*, New York: 1972, 328; Michael Wilson, 'Hollywood's Hero', *Hollywood Review*, 1, 5, April–May 1954, 1–4.

28 Wilson, 'Hollywood's Hero', 1, 4.

29 Bernard F. Dick, *Radical Innocence: A Critical Study of the Hollywood Ten*, Lexington: 1989, 70–81; George Lipsitz, 'Herbert Biberman and the Art of Subjectivity', *Telos*, 32, 1977, 181–2; Paul Buhle, *Marxism in the USA: From 1870 to the Present Day*, London: 1987, 189; Deborah Silverton Rosenfelt, 'Commentary', 102; William Z. Foster, *The Twilight of World Capitalism*, New York: 1949, 146.

30 Pauline Kael, 'Morality Plays Right and Left', in Kael, *I Lost it at the Movies*, Boston: 1965, 331–46; on Hurwitz, see Rosenfelt, 'Commentary', 134.

31 Barbara Zheutlin and David Talbot, eds, *Creative Differences: Profiles of Hollywood Dissidents*, Boston: 1978, 85–7; Conference notes, *I Can Get it For You Wholesale*, Fox collection, Theater Arts, UCLA; interview with Abraham Polonsky, BN, August 20, 1988.

32 Robert Horowitz, 'History Comes to Life and *You Are There*', in John E. O'Connor, ed., *American History/American Television: Interpreting the Video Past*, New York: 1983 84; John Schultheiss, in *The Films of Abraham Polonsky*, pamphlet prepared for the Abraham Polonsky Film Retrospective, USC School of Cinema/Television, n.d.; Polonsky, *Film Culture*, 50/51, 47.

33 Polonsky, in Zheutlin and Talbot, *Creative Differences*, 83; *Masses and Mainstream*, 9, August 1956, 44–5; Abraham Polonsky, *A Season of Fear*, New York: 1956, 133.

34 Adrian Scott, 'Blacklist: The Liberal's Straightjacket and its effect on Content', *Hollywood Review*, 2, 2, September–October 1955, 5–6.

35 Stevens on a 'sellout', referred to in Axel Madsen, *William Wyler: The Authorised Biography*, London: 1974, 288; on Dreiser, Nora Sayre, *Running Time*, New York: 1982, 130; Stevens on *A Place in the Sun*, script for 'Movietime USA', for release October 19, 1951, George Stevens collection, Margaret Herrick Library, Academy; on Wilson, Ceplair and Englund, *The Inquisition in Hollywood*, 78, 299, and an interview in *Take One*, September 1978, 34; Patricia Bosworth, *Montgomery Clift*, 1979, 181–2; Lambert, review, BFI microfiche, *A Place in the Sun*; George Barbarow, 'Dreiser's Place on the Screen', *Hudson Review*, 1952, 5, 290.

36 Gerald Gardner, *The Censorship Papers*, New York: 1987, 166–8; Richard S. Randall, 'Censorship: From "The Miracle" to "Deep Throat"', in Tino Balio, *The American Film Industry*, Madison: 1985, 510–12.

37 Fred Zinnemann, '*From Here to Eternity*', *Sight & Sound*, 57, 1988, 20; Herman Wouk, *The Caine Mutiny*, London: 1972, 504; Joel W. Finler, *The Hollywood Story*, London: 1988, 76.

38 Richard Combs, ed., *Robert Aldrich*, 52–3; Aldrich, 156, in Alain Silver and Elizabeth Ward, *Robert Aldrich: a guide to references and resources*, Boston, Mass.: 1979; Edwin T. Arnold and Eugene L. Miller, *The Films and Career of Robert Aldrich*, Knoxville: 1986, 37, 42.

39 William Manchester, *The Glory and the Dream: a narrative history of America, 1932–1972*, London: 1975, 773; Godfrey Hodgson, *In Our Time: America from World War II to Nixon*, London: 1976, 68; Navasky, *Naming Names*, 242.

40 Thomas M. Pryor, 'Movies' Decline Held Permanent', *NYT* (E), April 7, 1958; Braudy, *The World in a Frame*, 157; Biskind, *Seeing is Believing*, 20, on *Twelve Angry Men*.

8 THE SIXTIES

1 Joel W. Finler, *The Hollywood Story*, London: 1988, 280; Bordwell *et al.*, *The Classical Hollywood Cinema*, 320ff; Michael Wood, *America in the Movies*, New York: 1975, 14.

2 Martin F. Norden, '*Sunrise at Campobello* and 1960 Presidential Politics', *Film & History*, xvi, 1, Feb 1986, 8.

3 See Michael Ryan and Douglas Kellner, *Camera Politica, The Politics and Ideology of Contemporary Hollywood Film*, Bloomington: 1988, 3. On Dalton Trumbo's role in the making of *Spartacus*, see several articles on the film in *Cineaste*, XVIII, 3, 1991, 18–37.

4 Herbert J. Gans, 'The rise of the problem-film: An Analysis of Changes in Hollywood films and the American audience', *Social Problems*, 11, 1964, 328; Lawrence Suid, 'The Pentagon and Hollywood: *Dr Strangelove* (1964)', in John E. O'Connor and Martin A. Jackson, *American History/American Film*, New York: 1979, 225.

5 Nicholas Ray, interviewed in Michael Goodwin and Naomi Wise, 'Nicholas Ray. Rebel!', in *Take One*, 1976, 19; Joseph McBride, *Orson Welles*: London: 1972, 146.

6 Ryan and Kellner, *Camera Politica*, 3–6.

7 Stokely Carmichael and Charles V. Hamilton, *Black Power: the Politics of Liberation in America*, Harmondsworth: 1969, 58.

8 Donald Bogle, *Toms, Coons, Mulattoes, Mammies and Bucks*, New York: 1974, 317.

9 Richard Slotkin, 'Gunfighters and Green Berets: *The Magnificent Seven* and the Myth of Counter-Insurgency', *Radical History Review*, 44, April 1989, 67; Gans, 'The Rise of the Problem Film', 330. The later films of Aldrich, Ritt and Lumet reflected something of the concerns of the thirties generation. In Aldrich's last film, *The California Girls* (*All the Marbles*) (1981) there is reference to Clifford Odets, and an ending in the spirit of *Body and Soul*. Lumet has dealt with the experiences of radicals of different generations in *Daniel* (1983) and *Running on Empty* (1988), while 'naming names' is a sub-theme of his police corruption dramas, notably *Prince of the City* (1981). According to writer Arthur Laurents a political scene dealing with the blacklist was cut from *The Way We Were* (1973)

(McGilligan, *Backstory 2*, 152). Martin Ritt dealt with the blacklist era directly in *The Front* (1976), written by Walter Bernstein, but previously his *The Molly Maguires* (1968) – also written by Bernstein – had reflected something of his feelings about informing, and in particular about the testimony of his former friend and mentor Elia Kazan. (See Ritt, interviewed by Rex Reed, *Valentines and Vitriol*, New York: 1977, 102; and by Lyn Goldfarb and Anatoli Ilyashov, *Cineaste*, XVIII, 4, 1991, 21.) Abraham Polonsky dealt with the case of a communist called before the committee in a script that he wrote for the film *Guilty by Suspicion* (1990); but Polonsky's work was unused, and in the released film the victim is a director with no particular interest in politics. Producer-director Irwin Winkler preferred to make the film about what he has called an 'innocent', rather than a radical, during that period. Perhaps the most complex treatment of the question on film is in *Fellow Traveller* (1990), directed by Philip Saville and written by Michael Eaton. On *Fellow Traveller*, see Brian Neve, in *Sight & Sound*, 59, 2, 1990, 117–19; on *Guilty by Suspicion*, see Larry Ceplair, *Cineaste*, XVIII, 3, 1991, 46–7.

10   *Cahiers du Cinéma in English*, no 7, January 1967, 22; Rossen file, MOMA; Alan Casty, *The Films of Robert Rossen*, New York: 1969, 40.

11   Walter Tevis, *The Hustler*, London: 1960; *Cahiers du Cinéma in English*, no 7, January 1967, 22.

12   Rossen, *Scene*, 23, March 1963, BFI microfiche on Rossen; *Film & Filming*, August 1962; original screenplay, January 13, 1947, Rossen collection, Theater Arts Library, UCLA.

13   Wood, *America in the Movies*, 90; Norman Podhoretz, *Breaking Ranks, A Political Memoir*, New York: 1979, 241; Polonsky, Final Shooting script, January 13, 1947, Box 6, Rossen collection, Theater Arts Library, UCLA.

14   Polonsky in Andrew Sarris, ed., *Hollywood Voices*, Indianapolis: 1971, 142.

15   *Cahiers*, 23; Rossen, *Arts in Society*, Winter 1966–7, in Jay Leyda, *Film Makers Speak*, New York: 1977, 407.

16   Daniel Millar, 'The Method of Rossen's Late Films', *Journal of American Studies*, 6, 3, December 1972, 316.

17   Box 2, Robert Rossen Collection, Theater Arts Library, UCLA; *Evening Standard*, February 15, 1963, Rossen microfiche, BFI.

18   On *Wild River*, Kazan letter to Osborn, undated, and Kazan to Osborn, undated, Paul Osborn collection, Wisconsin Centre for Film and Theatre Research; William Bradford Huie, *Mud on the Stars*, London: 1944, 146.

19   Kenneth Hey, 'Another Look: *Splendour in the Grass*', *Film & History*, xi, 1, February 1981, 12; Port Huron statement, quoted in Paul Jacobs and Saul Landau, *The New Radicals*, Harmondsworth: 1967, 159.

20   Charles C. Moskos, Jr, *Greek Americans: Struggle and Success*, Englewood Cliffs: 1980, 10; Theodore Saloutos, 'The Greeks', in Stephan Thernstrom, ed., *Harvard Encyclopedia of American Ethnic Groups*, Cambridge, Mass.: 1980, 430–40. Kazan, unpublished

article on *America America* sent to Jack Warner, November 20, 1963, in Warner Bros archives, USC.

21 Kazan to Jack Warner, October 28, 1963, in Warner Bros archives, USC; Kazan to William Blowitz, Richard Lederer, October 14, 1963, and Kazan to Richard Lederer, March 25, 1964, Warner Bros archives, Princeton University Library.

22 *Newsweek*, December 23, 1963, 52; *Saturday Review*, December 28, 1963, 29; Stanley Kauffman, *A World in Film: Criticism and Comment*, New York: 1966, 155–6; Ernest Callenbach, *Film Quarterly*, 17, 4, Summer 1964, 55–6; Joan Didion, *Vogue*, February 1, 1964 (cutting, Kazan file, Film Studies Center, Museum of Modern Art, New York).

23 Dennis Schaefer and Larry Salvato, *Masters of Light: Conversations with Contemporary Cinematographers*, Berkeley: 1984, 256; on these rites of passage, see David Brownstone et al., *Island of Hope, Island of Tears*, New York: 1986, 105–235.

24 Kazan to Richard Lederer, undated, from Istanbul; in the Warner Bros archives, Princeton University Library.

25 Kazan, National Film Theatre programme note, translated from Claudine Tavernier, 'Kazan vieux comme le monde', *Cinema*, no. 143, February 1970; Michel Ciment, ed., *Kazan on Kazan*, London: 1973, 145–6; Lillian Hellman, *Scoundrel Time*, Boston, Mass.: 1976, 39.

26 Kazan on Odets, *Evening Standard*, March 29, 1967, BFI microfiche on *The Arrangement*; see for example, Charles A. Reich, *The Greening of America*, New York: 1970.

27 Revised Final Script, June 21, 1968, with changes up to November 1, 1968, Kirk Douglas Papers, Box 47 folder 2, Wisconsin Center for Film and Theatre Research; Kirk Douglas, *The Ragman's Son, An Autobiography*, London: 1988, 405.

28 Robin Wood, 'The Kazan Problem', *Movie*, No. 19, Winter 1971–2, 29–31; Andrew Sarris, *Village Voice*, November 27, 1969, 55; *Show*, February 1970, summarised in Lloyd Michaels, *Elia Kazan: A Guide to References and Resources*, Boston, Mass.: 1985, 109–10.

29 Pauline Kael, *Deeper into Movies*, Boston: 1973, 48–53.

30 Elia Kazan, 'Political Passion Play, Act II', *New York*, September 23, 1968, 27; on money and power in Kazan's work, see Lloyd Michaels, 'Critical Survey', in Michaels, *Elia Kazan*.

31 Eric Sherman and Martin Rubin, *The Director's Event: Interviews with Five American Film-Makers*, New York: 1970, 24; 'Abraham Polonsky, 1910—', pamphlet for Abraham Polonsky Film Retrospective, School of Cinema/Television, USC, undated.

32 Interview, Polonsky with BN, August 20, 1988.

33 Jim Cook and Kingsley Canham, interview with Abraham Polonsky, *Screen*, 11, 3, Summer 1970, 71; Polonsky, interview with BN, August 20, 1988.

34 Pauline Kael, *New Yorker*, December 27, 1969 (BFI microfiche, *Tell Them Willie Boy is Here*).

35 Kevin Thomas, *Los Angeles Times*, September 15, 1971, and Stuart Byron, *Village Voice*, September 9, 1971, in *Film Facts*, XIV, 16, 1971, 401–4; Terry Curtis Fox, *Focus*, 7, Spring 1972, 16–19; Polonsky, 'Making Movies', *Sight & Sound*, 40, Spring 1971, 101.

Select bibliography

Agee, James, *Agee on Film*, Boston, Beacon Press, 1964.

Almond, Gabriel A., *The Appeals of Communism*, NJ, Princeton, Princeton University Press, 1954.

Andrew, Geoff, *The Films of Nicholas Ray*, London, Letts, 1991.

Balio, Tino, ed., *The American Film Industry*, University of Wisconsin Press, Madison, 1985.

Basinger, Jeanine, *The World War II Combat Film: Anatomy of a Genre*, New York, Cambridge University Press, 1986

Baskerville, Stephen and Willett, Ralph, eds, *Nothing Else to Fear: New Perspectives on America in the Thirties*, Manchester, Manchester University Press, 1985.

Behlmer, Rudy, *Inside Warner Bros*, London, Weidenfeld & Nicolson, 1985.

Bentley, Eric, ed., *Thirty Years of Treason: Excerpts from Hearings before the House Committee on Un-American Activities, 1938–1968*, London, Thames and Hudson, 1972.

Bergman, Andrew, *We're in the Money, Depression America and its Films*, New York, Harper Colophon Books, 1971.

Bernstein, Matthew H., 'Defiant Cooperation: Walter Wanger and Independent Production in Hollywood, 1934–1949', Ph.D., University of Wisconsin, Madison, 1987.

Bessie, Alvah, *Inquisition in Eden*, Berlin, Seven Seas Publishers, 1967.

Biskind, Peter, *Seeing is Believing: How Hollywood Taught Us to Stop Worrying and Love the Fifties*, New York, Pantheon Books, 1983.

Bogle, Donald, *Toms, Coons, Mulattoes, Mammies and Bucks*, New York, Bantam, 1974.

Bordwell, David, Staiger, Janet and Thompson, Kristin, *The Classical Hollywood Cinema: Film Style and Mode of Production to 1960*, London, Routledge & Kegan Paul, 1985.

Brady, Frank, *Citizen Welles*, London, Hodder & Stoughton, 1990.

Braudy, Leo, *The World in a Frame: What We See in Films*, Garden City, New York, Anchor Books, 1977.

Brownstein, Ronald, *The Power and the Glory: The Hollywood–Washington Connection*, New York, Pantheon Books, 1990.

Capra, Frank, *The Name Above the Title: An Autobiography*, New York, Macmillan, 1971.

Carney, Raymond, *American Vision: The Films of Frank Capra*, Cambridge, Cambridge University Press, 1986.

Carr, Gary, *The Left Side of Paradise: The Screenwriting of John Howard Lawson*, Ann Arbor, Mich., UMI Research Press, 1984.

Casty, Alan, *The Films of Robert Rossen*, New York, The Museum of Modern Art, 1969.

Caute, David, *The Great Fear*, London, Secker & Warburg, 1978.

Cavell, Stanley, *Pursuits of Happiness: The Hollywood Comedy of Remarriage*, Cambridge, Mass., Harvard University Press, 1981.

Ceplair, Larry and Englund, Steven, *The Inquisition in Hollywood: Politics in the Film Community, 1930–1960*, Berkeley, University of California Press, 1983.

Ciment, Michel, ed., *Kazan on Kazan*, London, Secker & Warburg, 1973.

——, ed., *Conversations with Losey*, London, Methuen, 1985.

Clarens, Carlos, *Crime Movies: From Griffith to the Godfather and Beyond*, London, Secker & Warburg, 1980.

Clurman, Harold, *The Fervent Years; the Story of the Group Theatre and the Thirties*, London, Dennis Dobson, 1946.

Cogley, John, *Report on Blacklisting: I, – Movies*, New York, The Fund for the Republic, 1956.

Cook, Jim and Lovell, Alan, *Coming to Terms with Hollywood*, British Film Institute, London, 1981.

Corliss, Richard, *Talking Pictures: Screenwriters of Hollywood*, Newton Abbot, David & Charles, 1975.

Cripps, Thomas, *Slow Fade to Black: The Negro in American Film, 1900–1942*, London, Oxford University Press, 1977.

Deming, Barbara, *Running Away from Myself: a Dream Portrait of America Drawn From the Films of the Forties*, New York, Grossman Publishers, 1969.

Dick, Bernard F., *Radical Innocence: A Critical Study of the Hollywood Ten*, Lexington, University Press of Kentucky, 1989.

Dmytryk, Edward, *It's a Hell of a Life But Not a Bad Living*, New York, Times Books, 1978.

Dunne, Philip, *Take Two: A Life in Movies and Politics*, New York, McGraw-Hill, 1980.

Durgnat, Raymond and Simmon, Scott, *King Vidor, American*, Berkeley, University of California Press, 1988.

Eisinger, Chester E., *The 1940s: Profile of a Nation in Crisis*, New York, Doubleday, 1969.

Evans, Sara M. and Boyte, Harry C., *Free Spaces: The Sources of Democratic Change in America*, New York, Harper & Row, 1986.

Ferguson, Suzanne and Groseclose, Barbara, eds, *Literature and the Visual Arts in Contemporary Society*, Columbus, Ohio State University Press, 1985.

Fine, Richard, *Hollywood and the Profession of Authorship, 1928–1940*, Ann Arbor, UMI Research Press, 1985.

Friedman, Lester D., ed., *Unspeakable Images: Ethnicity and the American Cinema*, Urbana, University of Illinois Press, 1991.

Gabler, Neal, *An Empire of Their Own: How the Jews Invented Hollywood*, London, W.H. Allen, 1989.

Gelman, Howard, *The Films of John Garfield*, Secaucus, NJ, The Citadel Press, 1975.

Girgus, Sam B., ed., *The American Self: Myth, Ideology and Popular Culture*, Albuquerque, University of New Mexico Press, 1981.

Goldstein, Malcolm, *The Political Stage: American Drama and Theater in the Great Depression*, New York, Oxford University Press, 1974.

Gomery, Douglas, *The Hollywood Studio System*, London, Macmillan, 1986.

Goodman, Walter, *The Committee*, London, Secker & Warburg, 1968.

Goodwyn, Lawrence, *Democratic Promise: The Populist Moment in America*, New York, Oxford University Press, 1976.

Gorelik, Mordecai, *New Theatres for Old*, London, Dobson, 1947.

Hamilton, Ian, *Writers in Hollywood, 1915–1951*, London, Heinemann, 1990.

Himelstein, Morgan Yale, *Drama Was a Weapon: the Left-wing Theatre in New York, 1929–1941*, New Brunswick, NJ, Rutgers University Press, 1963.

Hodgson, Godfrey, *In Our Time: America from World War II to Nixon*, London, 1976.

Hofstadter, Richard, *The Age of Reform*, New York, Vintage Books, 1955.

——, *The Paranoid Style in American Politics*, New York, Vintage Books, 1967.

Huston, John, *An Open Book*, New York, Ballantine Books, 1980.

Ionescu, Ghita and Gellner, Ernest, eds, *Populism: Its Meanings and National Characteristics*, London, Weidenfeld & Nicolson, 1969.

Isserman, Maurice, *Which Side Were You On?: The American Communist Party During the Second World War*, Middletown, Wesleyan University Press, 1982.

Jowett, Garth, *Film: The Democratic Art: A Social History of American Film*, Boston, Little, Brown and Company, 1976.

Kahn, Gordon, *Hollywood on Trial: The Story of the Ten Who Were Indicted*, New York, Arno Press, 1972.

Kaplan, E. Ann, ed., *Women in Film Noir*, London, British Film Institute, 1980.

Kazan, Elia, *A Life*, London, André Deutsch, 1988.

Kazin, Alfred, *Starting Out in the Thirties*, New York, Vintage Books, 1980.

Kerr, Paul, ed., *The Hollywood Film Industry*, London, Routledge & Kegan Paul, 1986.

Kline, Herbert, ed., *New Theatre and Film, 1934 to 1937*, San Diego, Harcourt Brace Jovanovich, 1985.

Koppes, Clayton R. and Black, Gregory D., *Hollywood Goes to War: How Politics, Profits and Propaganda Shaped World War II Movies*, New York, The Free Press, 1987.

Koszarski, Richard, ed., *Hollywood Directors, 1941–1976*, Oxford, Oxford University Press, 1977.

Krutnik, Frank, *In a Lonely Street:* Film Noir, *Genre, Masculinity*, London, Routledge, 1991.

Lasch, Christopher, *The Agony of the American Left*, Harmondsworth, Penguin Books, 1973.

Laslett, John H.M. and Lipset, Seymour Martin, *Failure of a Dream?: Essays in the History of American Socialism*, Garden City, New York, Anchor Press, 1974.

Lawson, John Howard, *Film in the Battle of Ideas*, New York, Masses and Mainstream, 1953.

——, *Film: The Creative Process: The Search for An Audio-Visual Language and Structure*, New York, Hill and Wang, 1964.

——, *Theory and Technique of Playwriting and Screenwriting*, New York, Garland Publishing, 1985.

Leaming, Barbara, *Orson Welles*, Harmondsworth, Penguin Books, 1987.

Lehman, Peter, ed., *Close Viewings: An Anthology of New Film Criticism*, Tallahassee, The Florida State University Press, 1990.

Lewy, Guenter, *The Cause That Failed: Communism in American Political Life*, New York, Oxford University Press, 1990.

Lipsitz, George, *Class and Culture in Cold War America: 'A Rainbow at Midnight'*, New York, Praeger, 1981.

Lyon, James K., *Bertolt Brecht in America*, London, Methuen, 1982.

McArthur, Colin, *Underworld USA*, London, Secker & Warburg, 1972.

McAuliffe, Mary Sperling, *Crisis on the Left: Cold War Politics and American Liberals, 1947–1954*, Amherst, University of Massachusetts Press, 1978.

McClure, Arthur F., ed., *The Movies: An American Idiom, Readings in the Social History of the American Motion Picture*, Rutherford, Fairleigh Dickinson University Press, 1971.

McGilligan, Pat, ed., *Backstory: Interviews with Screenwriters of Hollywood's Golden Age*, Berkeley, University of California Press, 1986.

——, ed., *Backstory 2: Interviews with Screenwriters of the 1940s and 1950s*, Berkeley, University of California Press, 1991.

Madsen, Axel, *William Wyler: The Authorized Biography*, New York, Thomas Y. Crowell, 1973.

Mairowitz, David Zane, *Radical Soap Opera*, Harmondsworth, Penguin Books, 1976.

Maland, Charles, *American Visions: The Films of Chaplin, Ford, Capra and Welles, 1936–41*, New York, Arno Press, 1977.

——, *Chaplin and American Culture: The Evolution of a Star Image*, Princeton, NJ, Princeton University Press, 1989.

Maltby, Richard, *Harmless Entertainment: Hollywood and the Ideology of Consensus*, Metuchen, NJ, The Scarecrow Press, 1983.

Mast, Gerald, *The Movies in Our Midst: Documents in the Cultural History of Film in America*, Chicago, University of Chicago Press, 1982.

May, Lary, ed., *Recasting America: Culture and Politics in the Age of Cold War*, Chicago, University of Chicago Press, 1989.

Michaels, Lloyd, *Elia Kazan: A Guide To References and Resources*, Boston, Mass., G.K. Hall & Co., 1985.

Miles, Michael W., *The Odyssey of the American Right*, New York, Oxford University Press, 1980.

Navasky, Victor S., *Naming Names*, New York, Viking Press, 1980.

Nichols, Bill, ed., *Movies and Methods, An Anthology*, Berkeley, University of California Press, 1976.

Pauly, Thomas H., *An American Odyssey*, Philadelphia, Temple University Press, 1983.

Pells, Richard H., *The Liberal Mind in a Conservative Age: American Intellectuals in the 1940s and 1950s*, New York, Harper & Row, 1985.

Powdermaker, Hortense, *Hollywood, the Dream Factory*, London, Secker and Warburg, 1951.

Pribram, E. Deidre, ed., *Female Spectators: Looking at Film and Television*, London, Verso, 1988.

Quart, Leonard and Auster, Albert, *American Film and Society since 1945* (2nd edn, revised by Quart), New York, Praeger, 1991.

Ray, Robert B., *A Certain Tendency of the Hollywood Cinema, 1930–1980*, Princeton, NJ, Princeton University Press, 1985.

Richards, Jeffrey, *Visions of Yesterday*, London, Routledge and Kegan Paul, 1973.

Roddick, Nick, *A New Deal in Entertainment*, London, British Film Institute, 1983.

Roffman, Peter and Purdy, Jim, *The Hollywood Social Problem Film: Madness, Despair and Politics from the Depression to the Fifties*, Bloomington, Indiana University Press, 1981.

Rogin, Michael Paul, *The Intellectuals and McCarthy: The Radical Specter*, Cambridge, Mass., MIT Press, 1967.

——, *Ronald Reagan, the Movie: and other Episodes in Political Demonology*, Berkeley, University of California Press, 1987.

Rosten, Leo, *Hollywood: The Movie Colony, The Movie Makers*, New York, Harcourt, Brace and Company, 1941.

Rotha, Paul and Griffith, Richard, *The Film Till Now: A Survey of World Cinema*, London, Vision Press, 1949.

Ryan, Michael and Kellner, Douglas, *Camera Politica, The Politics and Ideology of Contemporary Hollywood Film*, Bloomington, Indiana University Press, 1988.

Salzman, Jack, *Albert Maltz*, Boston, Twayne, 1978.

Sarris, Andrew, *The American Cinema*, New York, E.P. Dutton, 1968.

Sayre, Nora, *Running Time: Films of the Cold War*, New York, The Dial Press, 1982.

Schary, Dore, *Heyday, An Autobiography*, Boston, Little, Brown & Co., 1979.

Schatz, Thomas, *Hollywood Genres: Formulas, Film-making and the Studio System*, New York, Random House, 1981.

——, *The Genius of the System: Hollywood Filmmaking in the Studio Era*, New York, Pantheon Books, 1988.

Schwartz, Nancy Lynn, *The Hollywood Writers' Wars*, New York, Alfred A. Knopf, 1982.

Selby, Spencer, *Dark City: the Film Noir*, London, McFarland and Co., 1984.

Server, Lee, *Screenwriter: Words Become Pictures*, Pittsdown, The Main Street Press, 1987.

Short, K.R.M., ed., *Feature Films as History*, London, Croom Helm, 1981.
——, ed., *Film and Radio Propaganda in World War II*, London, Croom Helm, 1983.
Silver, Alain and Ward, Elizabeth, *Film Noir: An Encyclopedic Reference Guide*, London, Bloomsbury, 1988.
Sklar, Robert, *Movie-Made America: A Cultural History of American Movies*, London, Chappell & Company, 1978.
Spoto, Donald, *Stanley Kramer*, Hollywood, Samuel French, 1990.
Stead, Peter, *Film and the Working Class: The Feature Film in British and American Society*, London, Routledge, 1989.
Stempel, Tom, *FrameWork: A History of Screenwriting in the American Film*, New York, Frederick Ungar, 1991.
Stewart, Donald Ogden, *By a Stroke of Luck*, London, Paddington Press, 1975.
Stone, I.F., *The Haunted Fifties*, London, Merlin Press, 1964.
Suber, Howard, 'The Anti-Communist Blacklist in the Hollywood Motion Picture Industry', University of California, Los Angeles, Ph.D., 1968.
Susman, Warren, *Culture as History: The Transformation of American Society in the 20th Century*, New York, Pantheon, 1985.
Swann, Paul, *The Hollywood Feature Film in Postwar Britain*, London, Croom Helm, 1987.
Teller, Judd L., *Strangers and Natives*, New York, Dell, 1968.
Thorp, Margaret, *America at the Movies*, London, Faber and Faber, 1946.
Tuska, Jon, *Dark Cinema: American Film Noir in Cultural Perspective*, London, Greenwood Press, 1984.
Walsh, Andrea S., *Women's Film and Female Experience, 1940–1950*, New York, Praeger, 1984.
Warshow, Robert, *The Immediate Experience*, New York, Atheneum, 1975.
Webster, Duncan, *Looka Yonda! The Imaginary America of Populist Culture*, London, Routledge, 1988.
Williams, Carol Traynor, *The Dream Beside Me: The Movies and the Children of the Forties*, Rutherford, Fairleigh Dickinson University Press, 1980.
Williams, Jay, *Stage Left*, New York, Charles Scribner's Sons, 1974.
Wolfe, Charles, ed., *Frank Capra: a Guide to References and Resources*, Boston, G.K. Hall, 1987.
Michael Wood, *America in the Movies; Or 'Santa Maria, It Had Slipped My Mind!'*, New York, Basic Books, 1975.
Wright, Will, *Sixguns and Society: a Structural Study of the Western*, Berkeley, University of California Press, 1975.
Zheutlin, Barbara and Talbot, David, eds, *Creative Differences: Profiles of Hollywood Dissidents*, Boston, South End Press, 1978.

Index of films

General index